LIFE A PEACH!

The secret life of an

international fruit trader

A TRAVEL ADVENTURE BY STEVE ASKHAM

This edition published in 2021
by DreamEngine Publishing
Email: DreamOn@DreamEngine.co.uk
www.dreamengine.co.uk
ISBN 979-8-54542-920-2

PREFACE AND ACKNOWLEDGMENTS

Writing this book has been harder than I could have imagined, but it's also been far more rewarding than I ever thought possible. All the following people have made both the journey and the destination worthwhile.

To my Editor, David Baboulene of DreamEngine, thank you! You were the first person to read my initial ramblings and our first two-hour meeting at mutual friend's wedding will live long in my memory. You were brutal, but what you did changed the way I write forever – you inspired me Davey, and for that I am eternally grateful! "A great writer must know how to murder his babies".

To my Publisher, Edward Marsh of Dream Engine, thank you for the magnificent job! Rarely have I hit it off so well on a first meet, especially when I realised you had flown to Spain to offer me a contract. You have helped me to create a legacy for my daughters and for that I will forever be in your debt.

To my long-suffering parents, I am immensely grateful to both of you. Who would have thought it? You have supported me through thick and thin (still do!) and have shaped me into the man I am. Dad, you are my inspiration; I have always admired you for your strength and your character and your utter brilliance in everything you do. Mum, you are simply the best! Love you both forever!

To my darling daughters, Katy and Alice. Dad loves you both so much. Thank you for listening to my constant ramblings about this book, thank you for your patience and thank you for believing in me. I could not be prouder of you.

To my brothers, Richard and Kevin. The best brothers any boy could have. Richard, you are a leader and a winner. I am so happy that you've found everything you've dreamed of. Thank you for always being there for me, emotionally and financially. Kevin, I am close to you still, even though we are apart. I wish you all the happiness in the world.

To my cousins, Neil Hutchinson and Scott Leather. Thank you, boys! You gave me hope and inspiration and encouragement all the way and that is priceless. Neil, thank you for your wise counsel and your enthusiasm - let's crack North America together! Scotty, I just love your pragmatism, optimism and good heart, there's a big job to come for you! Love you both!

To my proof-readers all over the world. Yes, you! The girls and the guys that were there at the start and who stuck with me all the way through, even through the rubbish that would eventually end up in the bin. You were never sycophantic, always positive in your criticism and your feedback. Without you, I would have fallen long before reaching my destination. I am so grateful to you all.

Sue Mackie, Sarah Winton, Karen Isaac, Vhari Tanner, Hayley Hickling, Ron Broersma, Elena Gago, Margit Perstolen, Alison Davies, Bev Silk Reeves. Let's have a party together soon – drinks are on me!

To my friend Ben Hickling for backing me. Not once but twice! I will be forever grateful pal. Up the Gunners!

Same to you my dear friend Spencer Curtis. By my side through good times and bad.

To my best buddy, Dave Lyons, my friend and my banker. Where would I be without you brother? You are my wisest confidante and advisor and I can't thank you enough for seeing me through. I know that you will go on to realise your dreams too and I wouldn't want to be anywhere else but by your side. Love you mate.

To my pal James O'Brien. The voice of reason. Always there for me buddy – love you Jamesy!

To my amazing friends Debora and Antonio Diaz from Bar El Fuego in Nerja. You saved my life twice. First when I was physically broken after a mission too far. Where else could I find a sanctuary where I could recover? Secondly, when my heart was ripped in two – nobody cared for me the way you did. El Fuego is the only place where I am always assured of a fabulous welcome and a friendly face. Thank you for believing in me without ever judging. Jullie twee zijn de beste!

To my dear friend Martin Davey. Thank you Bhat for backing me. I am so happy to be a part of your extraordinary journey from Hell and back. So happy for you Mart!

To my fellow Tyke, Nigel Duffy. What a pal you are Nige. Whenever I need a chill out, a rack or two of pool and a few beers or a round of golf, it's always you that I would pick. Top, top bloke! Leeds, Leeds, Leeds! Rhubarb, rhubarb!

Same goes for you Barry Fitzpatrick. A Gentleman with a great sense of humour and a gigantic heart. Thank you pal, for your patience and your generosity.

To my beautiful Danish friend Knud Byrjalsen, thank you buddy for being such an inspiration. When there was only darkness, you gave me light. When there was no hope, you gave me strength. I love you Knuddy.

To my compadre Manolo Peña. Love you brother, I will always be there for you, just as you have always been there for me!

Thank you to all my padel brothers and sisters, for just being you and for being there for me from the beginning of this story and right to the end. Let´s party now!

Paul and Vhari Tanner, Mark Peters, David Jenkins, Mikael Wallen, Charlotte Randau, Chris Brookes, Ben and Hayley Hickling, Jarno and Cecilia Paananen Burman, John and Lesley Corderoy, Peter and Kathy Hayden, Spencer and Ros Curtis, Nina Therese Haaland, Anders Sodergren, Claes Ringblad, Philippe Adam, Chris Taylor, Eddie Mues, Grant Mackie

Finally, I want to thank and acknowledge all of my amazing chums at Bar El Fuego." - The   hottest place for a cool down". Without you, I would be less than who I am.

Paco Pino, Miguel Garcia, Steve Tulley, Nikki and Vicki Herdman, Steve "The Dollar" Langford, Caroline McCudden-Hughes, Felix Fitzpatrick, Rob Edwards, Johnny and Karen Holt, Odmund and Anne Margrethe Brynhildsvoll, Robert Ian Pratt, Stephanie Maas, Dani and Francis, Freddie Diaz, Joe and Noreen Byrne, Rolfie Clements, Johnny "The Barber" Morgan, Colin Paton, Neil Francis, Sharon Aldridge, Emy Isdahl, Carlos Michaud, and the hundreds of visitors from all over the world that only know me as ´El Capitain.´

TABLE OF CONTENTS

A IS FOR AGRICULTURE

***Agriculture. Farming. Easily the most important thing that
Mankind does on our planet.***

Think about it. Nearly everything that the world's ever-expanding
human population eats is farmed food. Without it, there is no
future for humans. All food production involves agriculture in one
way or another; even some of the food that comes from the sea. To
give you an idea of the scale of global agriculture, if I said that a
trillion dollars in value of fresh produce is traded every single day
of the year, would that resonate with you? How about if I told you
that annual production of fresh fruit alone is over one billion metric
tonnes, could you picture that? Global annual production of just one
species of fruit, the humble apple, now exceeds eighty million metric
tonnes. If I convert that number into individual apples, the Earth's
human inhabitants get through approximately 625,000,000,000 of
them each and every year. That's more than 1.7 billion *every day*.

Citrus, mangos, bananas, pineapples, soft fruits and berries? All
of them in equally massive numbers and this is just fruit production.

There would be no world, good or bad, without people that grow
food – in livestock, fish farming, vegetable and salad production,

potatoes, rice, wheat, fruit. There would be no banks or bankers, no industry, no construction or manufacturing, no trade, no commerce, no travel nor vehicles to travel in. Just stop for a moment and examine an average day's food that you may consume. Cereals, bread, eggs, rice, milk, juices, meat and fish, dairy, fruit and vegetables, and all the derivatives of all of these. For the vast majority of the Earth's human population, every single thing will have come from a farm somewhere and it will definitely have involved care and nutrition in the sea or the soil, carried out by incomparably passionate people who take care of our lands and our soils. Brave, intelligent, risk-taking, loss-suffering, belligerent, cussed, saviours-of-the-human-race-people. Our farmers.

Imagine facing every day, every month and every year amongst Nature's extremes of weather and climate change; soil erosion, compaction or disappearance; the sudden loss of crop or herd with no recompense; rising costs in all areas of the production and logistics chains, labour and energy; pollution, pests and diseases; the gamble and risks of investing in a business, in deciding to plant or not. The list is a long one and there are so many challenges, and whilst this never-ending battle goes on the farmers must guard our soil and our land. They must use and interact with Nature and the environment innovatively, properly and responsibly. They must maintain good soils, care for, protect and provide for their livestock or their crops, pay for vets, for agronomists and advisors. They must provide good and fair working conditions for their employees and, in a lot of cases, they must examine and understand all aspects of the logistical supply chain involved in getting their produce to market so that they have the best possible chance of making a price that means they can continue to invest in sustainable food production. Sustainability is a word that, in my opinion, is overused these days. In the case of agriculture and good use of the land and the environment, however, I believe that it is the correct word. My underlying message in this book is not about my life of travel and adventures in the fruit world. My message is fundamentally about the importance of acknowledging and recognising our farms and farmers and allowing them to achieve prices necessary to ensure that they and future generations can continue to make a fair profit so that they can continue to be the very best custodians of our greatest and most important resources.

Over the course of the following chapters, I will hopefully be able to give you some insights into global agriculture and fresh food production; some knowledge of how the produce is grown, packed, shipped, stored and sold. I will examine and explain all parts of the fresh produce supply chain and I will justify the vital roles that each part of the supply chain performs. I will also identify the parts of the supply chain that do not perform fairly and that need attention.

It is predicted that the Earth's population will be upwards of nine billion people by 2050. Scientists predict that we will not be able to produce sufficient food for this population from the current areas of cultivated land in the world. Even with the careful introduction of Genetically Modified (GM) crops, alongside ongoing and continuous research into new varieties or species that produce bigger yields or are more resistant to weeds, pests and diseases; even if clever entrepreneurs soon turn to the production of edible insects as a major food source (something that I believe will be an extremely valuable aid to the challenge of feeding us in the long term), we are in deep trouble.

Agriculture is the biggest and, possibly, the oldest industry. Without food, nobody exists. My story, my message and my passion for everything that I fundamentally believe in is about Nature and the environment, the farmers and the land that feeds us.

Canterbury, Kent, UK. Around 1980.

My father was a college lecturer in mining engineering, but he had three sons to feed, so he worked as a consultant engineer for our neighbour, who was an importer of fruit spraying machines, a dealer for a Dutch fruit grading line manufacturer and a supplier of fruit trees, windbreak trees, picking buckets and anything associated with apple and pear growing, harvesting, grading and packing.

I had more or less grown up with his two daughters and I was close to this Dutch family from the age of ten. Now 17 and jobless, my dad persuaded him that he needed an apprentice. A lad that would go to college to learn some engineering skills, some welding ability and above all, a skill to sew together the heavy-duty felt belts on chains that formed the basic principle of the early diverging belt grading machines, used to size pears. My job was to be an agricultural engineer. To travel to fruit farms in the English countryside to service sprayers, replace belts on grading lines, to drill holes in packhouse floors and to bolt machinery in place. I drove a battleship grey Morris Marina van and I had an old seat from a Citroen 2CV in the back so that I could drive my pals around in my own version of HMS Invincible. I never thought that this introduction to the world of fresh fruit would ever lead to my life of adventures in the international fresh produce world, that I would stay in the industry for the next forty years, that I would criss-cross the planet throughout my whole career as a sales /

account manager, a procurement executive, a business director and a farm assessor and auditor.

This is my story of a life in the oldest and easily the most important business on Earth. A tale of my travels and stories in a lifetime of fresh produce, the way it grows, the land, the people that inhabit this world and their roles in bringing you your food from the four corners of the earth to your table.

A IS FOR APPLE

"Not all those who wander are lost." J.R.R. Tolkien

I was twenty-three and had already moved a couple of times in my early fruit career. I was employed by a company in Kent that was importing fruit from around the world to supply to UK retailers. My bosses sent me to Montpelier in the south of France for an important meeting concerning the new apple on the block, the Pink Lady. The meeting was attended by some pretty heavy hitters in the fruit world; the future stakeholders that would decide where to plant, how to limit supply volumes, how to market and manage what was a unique prospect at that time. There is a dinner in an expensive restaurant, maybe twelve or thirteen "players" around a circular table. On my left is a well-known Norwegian fruit trade gentleman, perhaps in his seventies then. Opposite me are two powerful French apple growers, the Australian variety owners, opposite me to the left. I feel young, unprepared, self-conscious, but I want to make an impression. I know that this meal is the crucial point in making sure that my company will get the rights to sell the product in the UK. The starters arrive, I am looking at the plate of smoked salmon in front of me, noticing the small glass bottle of vodka in front of my plate and glancing at the meal's set menu and reading "Smoked Salmon Finlandia." I am already struggling to participate in the small talk that is firing all over the table and I think, "be assertive Steveo, take the vodka, pour it on the salmon, look them in the eyes and get stuck in." So I do.

The Norwegian gentleman nudged my elbow, I barely noticed because the two Frenchies opposite had stopped talking, they put their cutlery down and they were staring at me and my plate of salmon, now awash with cold vodka. The Norwegian leans in, he says softly into my ear, "Steve, look at the glass there in front of you, look at the tray of crushed ice it's sitting in, you're supposed to sip the vodka as you eat the fish!" I could have died of embarrassment there and then but no! He picks up his miniature bottle of vodka, cracks it open, just as I have just done, he looks me in the eye and proceeds to follow me in drenching his salmon with the vodka. The two French apple growers stare at me expressionlessly… and then they do the same. I know, they know, they all know, that I had made a massive *faux pas* with my food, but they choose not to humiliate me. They choose to save me by copying my actions.

I have never forgotten this story and their act of kindness that stopped a young professional man, just starting his fruit trade career, from being hugely embarrassed. The one thing we do have in this industry is integrity. If your reputation is damaged or it is perceived that you lack integrity, you won't survive for very long. This lesson has stayed with me all my working life: Be honest. Use your knowledge and power to help others. Be kind.

On the subject of Pink Ladies, four years later I was invited to give a speech in Melbourne, Australia. I had three weeks' notice with a brief to deliver no more than a twenty-five-minute talk. The theme: The European Marketplace. This to a conference comprised of Australia's leaders in the fresh produce industry. I have worked hard on my thoughts and am not nervous as I rise to my feet at a quarter to eleven in the morning, the last speaker before coffee. I do not feel strange that I am the only speaker to stand so far and I try to make my points clearly and calmly. Europe is a massive market for Australian fruit. Your seasons are interesting to a northern hemisphere consumer base, because they are the opposite to ours. We know that you have excellent agricultural codes of practice in place and that interstate and national laws are robust in terms of disease prevention and fruit infection. Air freighted fresh fruit is a necessity when opening new seasons: cherries would be a good case in point. Why wait for sea-freighted cherries to arrive after a thirty-day journey, when you could ship smaller consignments by air, start a season and then use the economic facts of much cheaper sea-freighted arrivals, to make a promotion? Sell more, run the category. But my point was this. We Brits are the most demanding customers in the world for freshness and quality. We are ruthless in our continued examination of fresh produce supply chains. Air freighted fruit will only ever work if it is uncontested by other countries sending fruit to market by sea at much less cost. The fact is simple, I continued: You are 12,000 miles away from us and that is never going to change. Making sure that your fruit does not just leave these shores in the best possible condition is not enough. No, you must take all steps to ensure that it also arrives in the same condition. Do not ever send fruit to Europe that is not planned as a part of programmed supply. Do not ship fruit to Europe 'on spec' or, in other words, not pre-ordered and pre-sold at a guaranteed fixed and agreed price. I plough on, coming towards the end of my message. There is nothing at all to encourage me as I stand in front of perhaps three hundred delegates. In my mind the delegates are all already beginning to shift positions in order to get the best run to the tucker about to be offered, adjacent to the conference room.

No, I say. If your fruit arrives with us in anything than in a state of absolute perfection, competitively priced and with all of the required i´s dotted and t's crossed, then WE WILL SPANK IT! That is a polite explanation of a fruit trade expression meaning to very rapidly undersell the product on account of its being lesser quality than another offer. I am done. I thank the chairman of the conference and I sit. It´s coffee time and in a weird kind of "was anybody at all listening then?" state, I make my way to the refreshment area. I am there, I am collecting a scalding cup of coffee on a saucer, my hands are by now shaking, the tremors caused by my newly released nerves are sending my coffee all over the saucer and onto the carpet. Nobody is speaking to me and I feel alone in a very crowded place. I sense a man approaching me and he does, he extends his hand and I find myself at once confronted, gripped and stared at. "Bob Hawkes, Governor, Western Australia," he strides at me in a very aggressive manner. I blink, open-mouthed and drowning. He continues, "I´ve got one word to say to you mate, "NO!!" he screams. "You´re a bastard!"

I think I died.

But, no! It turns out the Guvnor Bob was most impressed with my singular message – tell it straight and tell it hard mate and that taught me a lesson on international relations with our cousins down under on how to get your message across without losing your own beliefs!

I have the utmost affection for Australia, as I do for New Zealand, but I can't resist a quick joke at this point…

How do you tell the difference between a New Zealander and An Australian?

Look a New Zealander square in the eye. Ask him, "Would you have sex with an eight-year-old?"

He'd look you square back in the eye and he'd say, "Naaaah!"

Ask an Australian: "Would you have sex with an eight-year-old?"

He'd look you square back in the eye and he'd say, "An eight-year-old what, mate?"

An early thought has occurred to me. The barbers, the hairdressers, the beauticians; you've almost certainly spent time in one or all of these places. What's the first thing they say to you aside from: "Been on holiday this year?" It is always "What do you do for a living?"

My answer is always the same: "I'm in the fruit and veg industry."

"Got your own stall in a market?" is almost always the next question. I laugh every time, as I try to explain what it is that I do, but what is surprising every time is not the predictable question, it is the fact that so few people know anything about where their fresh produce comes from! I am writing about apples in this little chapter so I'm wondering if you know where apples come from, how they are grown and harvested and, most interestingly, what happens to the apples when they are harvested?

If you look at the globe, our planet, you'll know what and where the Equator is. You'll know that if you look upwards, north of the Equator or downwards, south of the Equator, that the world gets cooler both ways, ending up at either the south or the north poles. Now imagine breaking down these two hemispheres into "bands" of climate. Simple stuff, eh? Well, in each of these bands of climate, different types of fruits can be produced, according to their requirements for heat, for cold and for water. Soil comes into it of course, but it is weather that is the determining factor as to what can be produced where. So, the Equator and the band of climate on either side is what is called Tropical - the zone that is inside the Tropic of Cancer and the Tropic of Capricorn. This area covers the whole of Asia, Africa, Central America, The Caribbean and Oceania. In this zone, tropical fruits can be produced: Bananas, pineapples, limes, papayas, jackfruit, breadfruit, mangosteens, and so on.

The next band, north or south, would be a sub-tropical zone. Less rain, lower temperatures but with temperate winters. In these zones, one in each hemisphere of course, sub-tropical fruits are produced: Citrus, mangos, avocados, lychees, figs, pomegranates, olives, and so on. Not always, but most probably, from evergreen trees, most of these fruits have very long growing periods and they require stable winter conditions for their dormancy needs. They can withstand some frosts if conditions are managed properly but they need consistent numbers of what we shall call heat units.

Further north and south of the subtropics, are the final climate bands that have the right properties and these fruits and trees are known as Deciduous. Deciduous means "falling off at maturity"; that is, trees that lose their leaves seasonally or their fruits when ripe. It is not so much the heat that is important in the production of deciduous fruit, it is the cold. Deciduous fruit trees require a minimum number of cold units per winter so they can achieve correct dormancy in order to emerge from winter properly rested and ready for new leaf and new life in spring. Deciduous fruits include apples and pears, grapes, cherries, peaches, plums, apricots and nectarines.

Don't forget that the hemispheres mirror each other. June, July and August are summer in the northern hemisphere, but winter in the south. November, December and January are summer in the southern hemisphere and winter in the north, so it's now easy to see that by looking at the climate bands that encircle the planet, there will be two seasons each year for the same crops and this fact may help to debunk the myth about fruits that are "out of season" being sold in your local stores. They will be in season, but perhaps in season on the other side of the world!

Being a fruit trader basically means therefore, to follow the sun and the seasons of the Earth. If I am buying apples for example, my growers to supply my market from September to March will be growers in the northern hemisphere. Fruit for my market from March to August, will come from the southern hemisphere. In the case of apples, however, and this is the case for many types of fruit, there are often overlaps or periods in the year when apples from both hemispheres are in the stores. Why is this? Think back to your school days, to Harvest Festival, Season of mists and mellow fruitfulness. At the end of summer, after spring has sprung and the blossoms have gone, the flowers have been pollinated and the fruits are set. They will have prospered and developed all summer and they are mature; they are ready for harvest. In the northern hemisphere, harvesting of early producing species will begin in late August, later varieties will go into September and early October but in all cases, when a particular variety is considered mature, the entire crop will be harvested in a matter of days. They will be picked and transported to a packing station and there, they will be graded for size and for quality. In many cases, they will arrive for sorting in orchard "bulk bins" of 300-400 kgs of fruit or more. Often, they will be graded for size and quality and then repacked back into the bulk bins. From there, they will go into two types of cold store. The first will be short term storage from where they can be packed and sold to client order or by packaging type. The majority of the crop, however, will go into long term or CA (Controlled Atmosphere) stores. These are effectively large, sealed rooms, in which levels of oxygen, carbon dioxide and nitrogen, as well as temperature and humidity are controlled. Using these controls, prolonged storage is possible with only a very slow loss of quality. My point is this: You may find yourself eating a fresh, juicy English apple in February, perhaps a Cox or a Royal Gala or a Braeburn, sweet, crunchy and delicious. Is it fresh you ask? Well yes, it definitely is. It will have all the properties that it had at the moment of harvest. But that harvest took place the previous year in September. The same thing in June in the northern hemisphere, your healthy and tasty fruit snack may well have come from New Zealand, harvested in March, graded and stored, then packed and shipped to destination in sea containers, transported by road in a refrigerated truck, received and stocked and then sent out daily to fulfil client orders.

There are many fruit types that involve the above process of harvest and long-term storage before sale and consumption – incidentally, the process I have described for apples is very similar to that for grain: one harvest at the right time and then storage and sales from these stores to last a season. Other common fruits and vegetables that are stored and marketed this way, include, citrus, pears, kiwifruit, and potatoes.

Not all fruits can be stored over a season though, in fact many are harvested each day and each week, according to variety and maturity and these are shipped fresh and are sold and consumed in days or in some cases, weeks after harvest. These include cherries, peaches, plums, strawberries, lettuce, mangos, avocados and bananas. It also explains why there are gaps in supply of some products, and cherries would be a prime example of this.

This is the beginning of Steveo's basic guide to global fruit and vegetable production and supply: Part 1.

A IS ALSO FOR AIR MILES!

I had been travelling the world for a decade. Australia, New Zealand, all of South America. California, Washington, Oregon, New York State, South Africa many times, Europe, all in the bag. My mum had had some troubles at this time, however. She had a deep vein thrombosis in her leg and her doctor had advised her not to fly long distances in cramped economy seats. She was upset as she knew that she probably wouldn't see her sister in Canada again. I was twenty-nine, I had close to a million British Airways miles put aside from my work adventures. I put my mum and dad on a BA 747 Heathrow to Vancouver. Return. First class. Their joy was only matched by my own. After all, I reasoned, they'd never done anything for me had they?!

Following the trip, Mum recounted a moment of hilarity in the air on the flight out of Heathrow. They've had dinner, personally cooked just for them by the on-board chef. BA first class pyjamas have been issued. Mum is resplendent in hers and she's possibly prouder of the PJ's than anything else associated with flying first class. In the night she awakens. She is curious to see the other passengers on the flight - the "poor people"- and so she rises from her bed and as quietly as she can, being careful not to waken her companions in her luxury cocoon / cabin, she makes her way to the rear of the first-class cabin – on a Boeing 747 that is an immediate left turn on boarding. You're directly behind the pilot, as opposed to business class, which is a right-turn on boarding and up a little spiral staircase, where you sit above and behind the pilot. It is dark, only the dimly lit cabin lights guide her as she reaches the galley area that joins first class with economy. She's about to move the curtain to take a peek at the masses beyond, when the shadowy shape of a very well-spoken female crew member appears as if from nowhere, blocking her passage further. The stewardess touches her arm lightly and whispers solicitously, "Don't go down there Mrs. Askham, stay here with us." My mum looks at the stewardess who shakes her head with a degree or urgency as if danger lurks around every corner down there. My mum turned back, and the stewardess breathed again. Danger had been averted for her charge. Mum had never been in a situation like this, my family on both sides come from Yorkshire coal mining stock. She'd always aspired but now she knew she belonged!

Another day, another 747. I am finishing a tough leg of a six-week journey across the important stone fruit producing countries of the southern hemisphere. (Stone fruits are from deciduous trees and have a stone inside: apricots, peaches, plums and nectarines.) I am in Argentina. I have been tasked with challenging and changing a major UK retailer's year-round offer in "Ready-to-Eat" stone fruit. I am able to convince growers all over the world to sell me their best fruit, selected from a small portfolio of only the best varieties. One peach variety, for example, will only be available for ten to fifteen days – they must be harvested as fresh and then worked. To make a full availability of fresh peaches across a summer, you'd probably need twenty to thirty different varieties that flower and produce fruit one after each other or at least overlapping each other for the whole season. This is why all stone fruit, with a couple of exceptions, is always sold as its product name, or in this case, as a brand name, perhaps 'Finest' or 'Taste the Difference'. This is unlike apples or pears or citrus, which are always sold by their variety name, Granny Smiths or Pink Ladies, for example. For my cunning plan, I propose that the fruit at the top end of the range will be sold at a premium price, agreed in advance. By giving my growers prior knowledge of the volumes I am going to need and in what sizes I want them, and by offering them a pre-agreed high price for their premium fruit, I am able to build a global offer of high-class fruit that is sold in a ripe and ready to eat format. No need to wait for the fruits to ripen in your fruit bowl! What excites me also in my cunning plan is that I can now access all of the crop. I can develop a sales plan for the smaller fruits, perhaps by creating a punnet offer for fruit in the 'Value' category or by selling scarred fruit as a Class 2 offer aimed at families with a smaller budget. With this strategy, I am able to build a global portfolio of the world's best stone fruit growers, for the first time playing a direct part in a clear year-round supply plan, in full knowledge of the whole cost chain from planting and production to retail price in the chain's shops. My plan is a massive game changer in the UK and our reward was to be the first fresh produce company ever to win an award called 'Firsts', this particular supermarket's recognition of innovation and business development. Each one of my growers around the world received a replica of this award and it remains one of my greatest sources of pride. I cannot say this without giving a huge pat on the back to my dear friend Bob Wiltshire, who was by my side all the way through possibly my greatest achievement in my fresh produce career. Thank you, Bobby!

I am a genius. It's going to work. I know this after three weeks in Chile and Argentina and two weeks before that in Australia and New Zealand, but now it's time to get to the airport in Buenos Aires to board my bird and to cross the Atlantic Ocean through the night to my final destination, Cape Town, South Africa, which will be crucial in completing my southern hemisphere template. I board the aircraft from an airbridge, I flash my boarding pass and I turn right, I go up the little spiral staircase and I am met by a stewardess. It is Malaysian Airways, she is beautiful, in traditional dress and full make-up. She knows my name. "Mr. Askham, welcome aboard. Your seat is here." She takes my hand luggage and my jacket and I settle into my plush chair in the upper cabin. I feel relieved and happy, but I am shattered. "Drink, Mr. Askham?" she asks. I order a Vodka and Tonic, one of my favourite aperitifs. She brings me the drink, it's in a cut crystal tumbler and I am in heaven. Four or five of these, some food and I am away with the fairies for the next seven hours. I awake as my seat is being slowly elevated from recline to landing position. My stewardess is there in front of me, she's still beautiful and she still looks immaculate. We are descending into Cape Town; it is 7.30 a.m. local time. My sleepy eyes meet hers. "Another Vodka Tonic, Mr. Askham?" she asks me in a profoundly serious voice. I laugh. Life is good.

A is also for Avocados. I have been to hundreds of fruit farms all over the world. The avocado is my favourite of all fruits – I never cease to be amazed when I see a crop ready for harvest. How can trees produce such a magnificent fruit as a mature, hefty, delicious avocado? Classed as a sub-tropical fruit, the avocado is a work of extraordinary beauty. Grown in a variety of conditions, from tropical parts of Colombia to the parched semi-deserts of Spain, Israel and Peru. South Africa, Brazil, Dominican Republic, Chile, Mexico and the USA too. I am writing this whilst looking at a small parcel of avocados here in my home in southern Spain. It´s April, the trees are in flower and they look a strange yellow colour. I know - because I´ve seen it a thousand times - that this is because the flowers are yellow and each tree can have around ten million tiny flowers. The avocado plant is a hermaphrodite. Botanically, it is known as a "perfect" flower: it has both female and male sexual organs in its flowers. On a Tuesday afternoon, all the flowers could be male; erect stamens standing up for attention, covered in pollen and shouting their male status proudly at any passing bee, wasp, crawling insect, desperate for pollination. By Wednesday morning, they may well have changed to be all female, fruit genitalia sending off their message – please come and impregnate me!

In this way, Nature ensures that the avocado tree has the maximum chance of pollination and therefore to produce fruit. It is also what is known as a climacteric species, which means that it goes through a *mature* phase before it becomes *ripe*. Mature means that the fruit is going to have an acceptable level of oil content and dry matter and that after harvest, it will ripen and deliver the texture and flavour that we humans desire. what it also means is that just because the avocado fruit is mature, it doesn´t have to be picked. You can leave it on the tree for up to six months and it won´t change, aside from increasing in size. Citrus is also a climacteric species, but not all deciduous tree crops are. So, when an apple or a peach grower checks his fruit for sufficient sugar content or fruit at the right pressure to pick, he must then harvest his whole crop, or it will rot on the tree and drop to the floor. I love avocado, and soon I am going to realise a dream. I'm going to plant, plant, plant and I'm going to become an avocado grower! Poacher turned Gamekeeper; some might say!

B IS FOR BAFFLED BY A BIG BERRY!

Here we go, then. Which fruit am I talking about?

1. It's a type of berry.

2. It's main variety – almost certainly in your house today – is called a Cavendish.

3. It is technically sterile and cannot reproduce naturally. It can only be cloned.

4. The American government has a dark history of political and military intervention in Central and Latin America to protect its interests in this berry!

Well, a berry has seeds and pulp (properly called 'pericarp') that develop from the ovary of a flower. The pericarp of all fruit is actually subdivided into 3 layers. The exocarp is the skin of the fruit, and in berries it's often eaten (like in grapes) but not always (like in bananas). The mesocarp is the part of the fruit we usually eat, like the white yummy part of an apple, or the bulk of a plum, though in citrus fruits the mesocarp is actually the white, sort of inner peel that we remove. Last is the endocarp, which is the closest layer that envelopes the seeds. In stone fruits, it's the stone. In many fruits, it's actually a membrane that we don't really notice, often because it's been bred to be thin, like in bananas. In citrus, the endocarp is actually the membrane that holds the juicy parts of the fruit, that is, the part you don't want to pierce unless you want to get sticky.

If most fruit have these three layers, then why are berries special? It's mostly due to the nature of their endocarps. Although not exactly quantified, berries generally have thin endocarps and fleshy (not dry) pericarps. Of course, these rules aren't rigid, as watermelons and citrus fruits are berries, and neither are thought to have especially thin skins.

So, if your favourite fruit isn't a berry, what might it be? If it has a thick, hard endocarp, it's probably a <u>drupe</u>, a fancy term for a stone fruit. This group encompasses apricots, mangoes, cherries, olives, avocados, dates and most nuts. Basically, if you wouldn't want to just bite into it, it's probably a drupe.

If your snack has a core, it's probably a <u>pome</u>. From its name you probably guessed that this bunch includes apples and pears. If you're a bit more adventurous, your favourite breakfast might include a <u>multiple fruit</u>, which is a fruit that is actually make up of a cluster of fruiting bodies. Two examples of this are figs and mulberries. These fruits turn out to be part of a greater group called <u>accessory fruits</u>, in which the fruit (or many fruiting bodies) is not derived from the ovary, but some other part of the developing plant. This is where the "not-a-berry" strawberry falls.

Finally, if you, like me, consider your favourite fruit to be a raspberry or blackberry, then you love <u>aggregate fruits</u>. These are formed by many ovaries merging to become one flower, and most are also accessory fruits. Botany is weird, isn't it?

Berry weird.

So now you know that this fruit is botanically classified as a berry, and it is a product of large flowering plants under the genus of the Musa. They come in different colours, sizes and firmness but are recognized by their curved, elongated shape, starchy flesh, and rind. The fruits grow in clusters and hang from the plant, ready to be collected. They are usually seedless and come from two species: the Musa Acuminata and the Musa Balbisiana. 90 percent of the world's exports of this fruit are the Cavendish variety and around 100 billion of them are sold throughout the world annually, which equates to every person on earth eating 130 of them a year or a rate of nearly three a week! Got it yet?

This wasn't always the case. Until the latter half of the 19th century, the dominant variety was called the Gros Michel (Big Mike!). It was widely considered tastier than the Cavendish, and more difficult to bruise. But in the 1950s, the crop was swept by a strain of Panama disease, also known as Fusarium Wilt, brought on by the spread of a noxious, soil-inhabiting fungus, a pathogen that infected the plants' roots and vascular system. Unable to transport water and nutrients, the plants wilted and died. Desperate for a solution, the world's farmers of this fruit turned to the Cavendish. The Cavendish was resistant to the disease and was an excellent fit for other market needs. It could stay green for several weeks after being harvested (ideal for shipments to Europe), it had a high yield rate and it looked good in stores. Plus, multinational fruit companies had no other disease-resistant variety available that could be ready quickly for mass exportation.

The switch worked. As the Gros Michel was ravaged by disease, the Cavendish took over the world's markets and kitchens. In fact, the entire global supply chain is now set up to suit the very specific needs of that variety.

There are thirteen types of this fruit that are grown commercially around the world, but easily the most popular variety is the Cavendish. The Cavendish is popular with fruit growers because they're predictable, but this uniformity comes at a high price and therefore we must pity this fruit. Despite its unmistakably phallic appearance, it hasn't had sex for thousands of years. The world's most erotic fruit is a sterile, seedless mutant—and therein lies a problem. It is genetically old and decrepit. It has been at an evolutionary standstill ever since humans first propagated it in the jungles of Southeast Asia at the end of the last ice age and we are still eating the descendants of the original cuttings taken by these Stone Age cultivars, and this is why it could be doomed. It lacks the genes to fight off the pests and diseases that are invading the banana plantations of Asia and beyond. Unable to reproduce sexually, instead they are propagated using identical clones, so in this way every single fruit produced, anywhere, is fundamentally a doppelganger of its parents. But this means that the genetic diversity of this fruit is very low. The extreme lack of any biodiversity and the fact that the Cavendish is planted in dense chunks in a monoculture without any natural species or plants buffering them, means that the Cavendish is extremely vulnerable to disease, fungal outbreaks and genetic mutation possibly leading to eventual commercial extinction. And this is exactly what has happened in the last couple of decades; the Cavendish has succumbed to a more virulent form of Panama disease, known in the fruit world as Tropical Race 4 or TR4, and a new virus called Black Sigatoka, both of which cause serious production losses and are difficult to control. First identified in the early 1990s in Taiwan, Malaysia and Indonesia, TR4 has since spread to many Southeast Asian countries and on into the Middle East and Africa. If TR4 makes it to Latin America and the Caribbean region, the export industry in that part of the world could be in big trouble.

Cavendish varieties have shown little if any resistance against TR4. Growers are relying on temporary solutions—trying to prevent it from entering new regions, using clean planting materials and limiting the transfer of potentially infected soil between farms, but science needs to intervene urgently. Over a thousand species of this fruit have been recorded in the wild. Although most do not have the desired agronomic characteristics — such as high yields of seedless, nonacidic fruits with long shelf life — that would make them a direct substitute for the Cavendish - an untapped genetic resource. Scientists are now searching within them for resistance genes and other desirable traits to use in engineering and breeding programs.

Now I know that you've got this. Of course, it's the BANANA.

"I spent 33 years and four months in active military service," an American veteran named Smedley Butler once wrote, "and during that period, I spent most of my time as a high-class muscle man for Big Business, for Wall Street and the bankers."

Butler had fought in the so-called Banana Wars of the early 20th century, when the American military sent their troops south into Central America to keep their business interests there intact.

It was a time when mistreated workers across Central America were getting fed up with working long hours in harsh conditions for less than a living wage. Workers started grumbling. Some went on strike. Some threw together militias and waged full-on rebellions to fight for better conditions.

For the American government, all this fighting for freedom was bad for business. Companies like the United Fruit Company had a vested interest in keeping their Central American plantations stable and so they called in the American Army to crack down on those who were disrupting the system.

Butler and other soldiers like him were thus sent to Central America to fight the Banana Wars. When a rebellion in the Dominican Republic, for example, damaged an American-owned sugar cane plantation, American troops were sent in, starting in 1916. They took over a small castle called Fort Ozama, killed the men inside and set up a military presence to protect their business interests.

Troops also moved into Haiti to quell the Cacao Rebellion in 1915, partly to protect the interests of the Haitian-American Sugar Company. The U.S. Army stayed behind even after the war was over, patrolling the streets of Haiti and making sure that no one got out of line.

And in Honduras, where the United Fruit Company and the Standard Fruit Company were worried about their banana sales, the American Army marched in on seven separate occasions throughout the early 20th century. Sometimes the army was called in to crush strikes, other times to stop revolutions — but every time, it was to keep business booming.

Hundreds of American soldiers and thousands of locals died in the Banana Wars. Strikes and revolutions were crushed and put to an end – all while the profits of a handful of companies were maintained.

"I might have given Al Capone a few hints," Butler said. "The best he could do was to operate his racket in three districts. I operated on three continents."

B IS ALSO FOR BUYER

What is the difference between a supermarket buyer and a terrorist? You can negotiate with a terrorist!

I bought my first house at eighteen and I couldn't afford to pay the mortgage. As well as my full-time job as a trainee agricultural engineer, I had a football pools round, I was selling Betterware home products, door-to-door, and I worked several shifts in the pub that was part owned by my Dutch boss. One of the pub regulars, a distinguished gentleman called Henry Bond, was the managing director of a fruit importing company, based close by. He saw something in me that bar work had brought out. I was good with people and he offered me a trainee management role with his firm. He was persuasive, I liked the sound of this new and exotic business and soon I had an offer to start. They were major fruit suppliers to Marks and Spencer (a huge, high-end UK supermarket) and from my first day, I was immediately exposed to all types of fruit from around the world, arriving in refrigerated containers or trucks, or collected from airports around the country. All required unloading, checking, sorting, labelling, ripening perhaps, or repacking in another format to a customer order. My start in the production office, on the packhouse floor, gave me my first look at what became my lifelong passion for agriculture and in particular, fresh fruit production from all around the globe. After a couple of years in production, I moved to quality control. From QC, I moved to logistics and from logistics, I moved to sales. Of vegetables! And then I got my first accounts to manage. With buyers!

My first account was with a northern based supermarket called Hillards. My first potential sale was to try to start the supply of English Iceberg lettuce. I'll never forget the buyer grilling me on the phone about the specification he demanded for each head of lettuce. He wanted a count 10 – that means ten heads of lettuce in a 60x40cm carton. He asked me what the minimum weight per lettuce was. I had no clue, so I said "eight ounces" as quick as you like. My blood froze when he menacingly stated that if my lettuces weren't at least sixteen ounces each, I wasn't getting the order. I got the order and I learned that to lie or to guess in this game was not going to get me far!

That was almost as much fun as travelling to Portugal with the Sainsbury's lettuce buyer to inspect an important crop and to negotiate the deal for that season. As we travelled, the lettuce growing area in Portugal suffered devastating storms that literally removed every single head of lettuce from the fields and dumped them in a pile of mud and crap in the streets. There was no crop, nothing to inspect and no deals to negotiate. I had three days with a Portuguese(!) lettuce buyer from Sainsbury's in Portugal and I'm convinced to this day that he enjoyed watching me squirm. No Portuguese language skill and no lettuce to talk about gave me a hideous introduction of how to spend quality time with buyers. I got revenge some years later in an inter-company football match. Hell of a player, but he didn't like getting kicked!

My boss, my guru, at that time was a guy called Rob Sayle. He was eleven years older than me and he was an excellent salesman. I was his "boy." He taught me so much and I owe him forever. We had business with a supermarket called Finefare. Rob was taking a holiday. He prepped me for the week and I was to ask the buyer, a very scary chap called Ron Palmer, for an increase in the price of the Desiree red potatoes that we supplied to them. It took me an hour to rehearse my telephone call to Mr. Palmer. Scared? I was petrified. On answering the phone, I informed Mr. Palmer that I was Steven Askham from Saphir Produce and that I was covering for Rob who was on holiday. There was a long silence and then very softly and in a gruff voice, I heard him whisper down the line to me, "Another lamb to the slaughter."

Reputations precede us and Rob had prepared me well for Ron Palmer's fear tactics. My feet drummed on the floor in a nervous ballet. (Some years later, another boss of mine observed this characteristic of mine during difficult calls and he said that he knew I would succeed every time he saw my particular tick kick in! I still do it unconsciously today.) I pressed on with scary Ron. I gave my rehearsed speech about dry conditions reducing yield, about high demand and short supply, about how we needed a small price rise in order to continue to supply his 3,000 x 25kg sacks of spuds per week. Again, the long silence (later I would learn that this silent period in negotiation technique is taught to buyers. Stay silent, let the other guy break first, win the deal). I waited. I broke. I asked, "Mr Palmer, could I have your agreement to increase the price?"

Eventually Mr. Palmer spoke. He said very slowly and very clearly, "Do you want the fucking programme or not?"

I took the programme. We did not get a price increase.

Some weeks later, I find myself on the road to Ron's office to deliver a sample 25kg bag of fresh onions. My intention is to meet the great man and to get an order for my onions. I'm extremely nervous on arrival at their head office and as I make my way upstairs to the produce department reception area, I am met by a very pretty young lady. She tells me immediately that Mr. Palmer is taking his lunch and that I can put the sack of onions next to his desk, there in the corner of the office. I stride purposefully to the desk and see his chair, a beautiful leather specimen on a chrome base with five legs, all singing and dancing, as they say. I can picture the scene now, plonking myself into the great RP's chair, still holding the onions. I lean back in the luxurious seat and it snaps at the base with me in it. To this day, I remain embarrassed. I never got the onion order...

Speaking of lettuces reminds me of the time I was the first to negotiate fixed-pricing and contracted supply of fresh produce to a retailer. It was Iceberg lettuce and the contract was with a large UK supermarket which should remain anonymous, so let's call them Tasbury's. What they had was an incredible demand for Iceberg lettuce. In the summer months, this demand could be as much as 30 full trucks of lettuce per week. If I do some basic maths, this equates to 30 lorries of 26 pallets of lettuce. Each pallet would be 100 cartons and each carton would contain an average of ten lettuces. So that is a weekly order of 780,000 heads of lettuce. Per week!

What they didn't have was continuity of price, however. To this day, most trades in fruit and vegetables are negotiated weekly and this is because we are all in the hands of Mother Nature in terms of climate and weather. Natural laws of supply and demand also apply, as does seasonality and source of the produce and logistics involved in getting it to market.

So, Tasbury's were looking for a fixed price for their Iceberg lettuce and I knew that this is because they felt that by 'protecting' their customers from price changes and by applying a retail price that they could hold for a whole season, they would retain the loyalty of their shoppers, if not gain more.

I would have been perhaps 27-years-old at this time, so we are talking about the year 1990 or so. My company at that time was one of the biggest suppliers of fresh produce to the British retail sector. Not only were we massive importers of fruit and vegetables from the four corners of the world, but we were also major growers of British produce, including lettuce! We were innovators, we were young and ambitious and so were our counterparts in the ivory towers of their head office. I was in charge of this new style deal and negotiations went well. Prior to commencement of supply, there had been many meetings with the client and many hours of thorough examination of lettuce supply trends, annual pricing graphs and much chin and head scratching as to the pros and cons of agreeing to such a radically differ type of contract.

By late spring of that year, however, we had reached agreement and I recall now that the cost price that we agreed for full supply and for the whole summer, was four pounds and fifty pence per carton, delivered to their depots across the whole country.

Let the games commence, we all thought, as we entered the new season.

It is a bright and sunny morning on the Chat Moss in Salford, Greater Manchester. The Moss is a vast area (thirty percent of the area of Salford) of over three thousand hectares. That's close to seven and a half thousand acres. It is land that was reclaimed in the nineteenth century using a large-scale network of drainage ditches. These are still required today to prevent the land getting waterlogged and they have resulted in a patchwork landscape with fields often separated by ditches rather than hedges or walls. It is also a source of significant wildlife interest, such as a wealth of farmland birds and remnants of lowland bog - a rare and declining habitat which can only be found on peat. At the time it was the biggest cultivated area for lettuce in the UK and this is where we have sowed our lettuce plantlets by the million in preparation for the commencement of the Tasbury's supply contract. I am with our farming general manager, a very straight-talking Mancunian gentleman called Andy Brooks and we are hosting a day in the fields with my opposite number from Tasbury's William Cloudstone. Even though the day is warm and dry, Andy and I are dressed for our task: Stout shoes or boots, field trousers and a hat to protect us from the sun. We carry a pocketknife each so that we are able to stop randomly and cut a sample head of lettuce. We are on the job. We know our Iceberg. We are looking at the density of the lettuce head, making sure of weightiness and maturity and an absence of bolting. We are looking for evidence of pests or diseases and we are proud of our crop. Mr. Cloudstone, who is a young man of a similar age to me, is one of Tasbury's top young executives. He is a tough negotiator, self-assured, not cocky but very aware of the power he has. We walk our fields, dusty and hot, stopping every few yards in each row and cutting a sample. It is going well; the Iceberg looks good; we have had ideal growing conditions and we are optimistic of good and continuous supply to our esteemed client. It is normal for us to receive and host client visits on farms, whatever type of produce we may be supplying. What is strange however, is that Bill has turned up to see our operation in full London executive mode. From his Church's brogues to his tailored three-piece blue pinstripe suit, matching tie and top pocket 'kerchief, his red braces flashing from under his jacket as he walks. Jacket now removed, the day is hot, his elasticated steel sleeve garters now glint in the bright sunshine, his Mont Blanc fountain pen in his top pocket, shouting at us that he means business this day. Strange attire indeed, particularly given the location, field conditions and the job in hand in walking miles and miles of lettuce fields.

Notwithstanding Mr. Cloudstone's appearance, Andy and I go about our business like the professionals that we are, finally reaching the end of a plot of lettuce and calling a halt to our inspection, all parties so far satisfied with what we have seen. An offer of something to drink and a bite to eat is proposed as we brush ourselves down and stamp the mud and dust from our shoes on the hard, dry ground on the field headland. It's a good plan and we head for the only pub on The Moss, now in clear sight and not far from us.

We stand in the large, but crowded public bar attempting to get service, to get a desperately needed drink for the three of us. The saloon is full; a mass of working people in a sunlit bar, particles of dust and debris float in the air and the voices and sounds of scores of local farmers, agricultural workers and drivers fill the room.

Andy is at the bar now and he is being served. He hasn't had time for much interaction with our buyer all morning – that's your job he would say, to look after the southern softies! It's so noisy and so crowded that we are shouting our orders from behind two lines of customers to Andy at the bar who is then semi-shouting the orders to the barman who is alternating his gaze from Andy to me and then to William in his Saville Row suit.

"So that's two pints of bitter shandy then, and what's the other fella after?" shouts the barman in his Mancunian brogue.

"Aye," says Andy, now struggling to hear what William is ordering to wash away the dust in his throat from the morning's graft out on The Moss.

At the same time as the whole bar becomes silent - everyone is straining to hear what this dude from London is ordering. In a clear and expensively educated voice, Mr. C raises his voice to be heard: "I'd like a large Tio Pepe with ice!" (*that's a dry Spanish Sherry*!)

It wasn't loud in the bar anymore. You could hear a pin drop.

To complete this story, I can tell you that four weeks into the supply deal Tasbury's pulled the plug. There was an over-supplied market and the wholesale price of Iceberg dropped below the contract price. Rather than go through this period at the agreed level, no doubt that prices would be corrected at some point, if not swinging the other way when under supply would inevitably happen, Tasbury's reneged on the agreement and they withdrew from the contract!

Some buyers are easier to deal with than others. Of all the retail chains I have dealt with, one stands out. I have found that buyer / seller relationships are complicated things, especially in the fresh produce world, where deals are done every week on a word. A verbal contract to supply at a changed price for example. Supply of fresh fruit and vegetables to supermarkets in just the UK is a multi-billion-pound industry. Tesco, for example, will sell something like thirty trucks of blueberries in a week. That value is enormous, maybe five million pounds worth of blueberries a week. So, it goes without saying that you need a buyer's trust if you're representing your company for their account, and vice versa.

"Life is either a daring adventure or nothing at all." Helen Keller

I am in Bologna, Italy. I am on a shared supplier mission to plan summer peach and nectarine supply. The other supplier is a competitor but a pal. Chris Chapman is older than me and he carries his experience well. I look up to him and he is something of a guru to me. We are dining with the buyer and his technical manager (TM). We christened the TM 'Simon the Pieman' for his habit of always choosing the most expensive items from dinner menus and for never paying! Robin, the buyer, is 28-years-old and is cocksure. His mentor is the director of food for this particular supermarket. He's going places. He is brilliant but flawed. The two are a double act in the sense of being totally professional on a day's work but demanding to be entertained when work finishes for the day. After dinner, we are in the bar and my pal, Chris, decides to play a tune on his teeth, using a biro to hammer his gnashers, which appear to be unsurprisingly cracked and grey. At this point, Robin decides that he's going to give us fifty words for female genitalia and he gets to twenty-one with a lot of help from us. Beaver is allowed, of course, but Badger is not!

The following day, I am with the clients, visiting orchards and packing stations. A busy day in the field, lots of miles walked, many meetings had, much fruit discussed. They are complete pros, as always. We get the job done. Supply programs and changes in specifications are negotiated and agreed. It's now early evening and thoughts turn to returning to our hotel, after which Simon the Pieman wants to go to a club for some fun. This is becoming the norm with these guys. I remember being in Seville with the same team earlier that year. We were planning the early season supply of peaches and nectarines from there, and after a day of supplier visits and negotiations, we end up in a local bordello known as La Casita or 'The Little House'. It is a cathouse and surprise, surprise, my pal Chris is there but about to leave. We share a quick drink and Chris departs. Simon and I are alone at the bar and the barman tells us that Chris has left his Diner's Club card and that his account is open still. Simon doesn't hesitate, dinner, cava, gin and tonics and several hours of extreme silliness follows. I think the bill was twelve hundred Euros...

My point is that it is possible to create a special relationship with certain supermarket personnel, but not all of them! I clearly recall a good day when I worked in Ireland for a large importer and grower in Dublin. It was 2006 and it was Ryder Cup year, hosted by the K Club in County Kildare. My bosses gave me the huge honour of asking me to accompany and entertain key customers on the Saturday and Sunday of the competition. Saturday was wet, very typical Irish summer weather. I had a driver and a car at my disposal; a Mercedes S Class limousine to travel in style to and from the course. We stopped early to collect my client – a UK supermarket berry technologist. We stopped at his home in Skerries in the early dawn. It was pouring with rain as he emerged, ready for the day. I couldn't believe it when he trotted down his front path to the car in his blazer, slacks and brogues. It was lashing it down and we were to spend the day on a wet, muddy golf course. I sent him back to change into waterproofs and golf shoes! A couple of hours later, we are standing on the first fairway, a few hundred yards from the first tee, approximately where the balls would land from the opening tee shots, I reasoned. We are behind the ropes and there in front of us, no more than ten feet away, stands Bill Clinton and the then wife of a certain Tiger Woods, Elin Nordegren. Crowds are gathering despite the incessant rain and we find ourselves at the rope that separates the players and their guests from the spectators, a mass of people pushing forwards, beside us and behind us. Some people are abusing Bill Clinton. We are not laughing. Mr. Clinton has his back to us and I can see his aura glowing clearly in the rain. That's power! Clearly very annoyed by the jeers and taunts from the crowd, Clinton turns, looking for his assailant. He affixes his gaze directly on me and I feel his eyes burning into my soul. "Not guilty, Mr. President," I wanted to say, but it was pointless and I am burned by the most powerful man on Earth at that time.

That night I have dinner with two guys from Tesco. We plan our day, the Sunday of the Ryder Cup. They want to know what time the gates open as they want to be early to see the players warm up. My driver calls for me very early and by 5.00 a.m. we have collected the clients and we are on our way.

At 7.00 a.m. on the dot, at the front of the queue, we are first in and we immediately make our way to the putting green. It is just getting light and right there, ten feet from us, is the man himself, the aforementioned Tiger. He's putting one-handed, sending ball after ball unerringly into the hole, ten feet away. His caddy is fishing out the balls as they disappear into the cup. After about twenty putts, Mr. Woods, stops. He stretches, he turns and he looks me straight in the eye. "Play well, Mr. Woods," I say. "We are counting on you."

He touches the peak of his cap and he says, "Thank you, Sir, I sure will do my best."

I turn to my guests; their mouths are open. "You just spoke to Tiger Woods and he spoke back!" they say in unison. I look at my watch. It is 7.15 in the morning and life is good.

Things did not always go to plan with buyers, however. I worked for one of the UK's biggest players in fresh produce. Apparently, the founder, a legend called Joe Saphir, used to get to Spitalfields fruit market very early every day. He would do his market walk and he would know what was 'trumpy' – the industry term for short in supply and therefore very likely to go up in price - and he would work the market and buy every single case. He would then add a shilling to his purchase price and sell on to his upcoming and fast-growing supermarket clients. He was known as Joe Shilling or Joe Five Percent for that reason and his company was highly successful. I was head of the stone fruit and grape department at the time, with a team of ten sales and procurement people and a couple of administrators. I was twenty-six and I had just been promoted. My boss told me that I could upgrade my company car from the Rover 820 I had been driving to a brand new 323i BMW coupe in cherry red. I loved that car, but I ruined it. Mathew Wale was the buyer for Gateway, another supermarket blast from the past. Saphir Produce, my employers, had three tables in the Prince Obolensky Suite at Twickenham. I took Matthew to see England versus South Africa and I got very drunk on whisky and water before lunch. Matthew drove me home while I laid in the back being sick in the rear footwell. The smell of whisky and vomit never left that car.

And then there was 'Him'. It was around this time, in the early years, that He met his first handler, Henry Bond, pub regular and Managing Director of Saphir Produce. His background had always really led to this point. The Cubs, Scouts, Air Training Corps, flying lessons, basic firearm skills, some martial arts abilities, multiple language skills and a love for his country brought him to the attention of somebody in the British Government, and so it came to be that his other career was launched. His was the perfect cover and in many ways, Henry Bond, the cigar chomping, expensive-suit-wearing, ex-English public schoolboy, became the perfect handler. Long-term intensive training began in some of the areas that he would use throughout the rest of his working life. Hand-to-hand combat, knife and weapons training, low and high-altitude parachute jumps and survival skills were welded onto another parallel career. Without being in the military, he became a highly trained operative, capable of sustaining long-term positions in hostile environments, whilst maintaining diplomatic relations and, of course, remaining under cover throughout his assignments. He was to become a specialist in counter espionage, military strategy, target acquisition and elimination. His handlers would change as time went by, but his dedication to his country and his ability to provide the essential services desired by his government, coupled by his excellent cover story, ensured that he continued to be active for more than three decades. He would eventually specialise in Central and South America, but no continent or country would be out of bounds for Him.

B IS FOR BLUEBERRIES

To give you some idea of the scale of the global blueberry business, here are a couple of interesting facts: The largest UK food retailer sells up to thirty full trucks of blueberries – each week! To put that into context, if you buy blues in a standard punnet of fruit of one 125 grams, then three trucks per week amounts to some half million of these punnets of fruit. Do some maths and work out how many big outlets there are in the UK and Europe and then the world. Try to figure out, based on my number for Tesco's weekly sales, how many are sold by each and then have a go at calculating global weekly sales. It's in the hundreds of millions of kilos!

Growth in worldwide blueberry production has increased exponentially in recent years to keep up with this demand. Main producing countries include the whole of Europe (Poland is a massive contributor these days and even the UK has a highly specialised blueberry farm in the acid soils of deepest Dorset), South Africa, Australia, New Zealand and Japan. But the real statistic to give you some idea of how popular these little super fruits have become is that, since 2008, North and South America combined have planted in excess of 70,000 hectares. To better visualise that area, one hectare is a perfect square of one hundred by hundred square metres, the pitch at the international rugby ground at Twickenham in West London is 0.875 or three quarters of one hectare, so new production in the Americas alone is now well over 80,000 Twickenhams!

Larache, North Morocco, early March.

I am always delighted when a producer surprises me. I have seen more than a few fruit farms, packing plants and innovative companies in my short career (Ha, ha!) but today I have seen one of the most impressive organisations I've ever seen. A blueberry farmer here who is not only involved in planting, nurturing, harvesting and packing these wonderful fruits, but also absorbed totally in the development of a new variety that is early flowering and early fruiting; a variety that requires fewer cold hours for dormancy than other varieties and a cultivar that delivers a perfect acidity / sweetness balance. Incredibly, one that also produces in abundance extremely firm violet-blue berries over a three-month season - longer if planted, as these are, in different climatic zones.

How is this possible, I ask? Well, years of research and study of different and existing varieties and a selection ultimately of two potential parents that have the combined characteristics that this grower has found. We are all, I am convinced, - as is everything that Mother Nature delivers - totally and unequivocally, made from the sum of our parts!

I can't name this producer for professional reasons, but if I were giving out medals for innovation, courage, sheer bloody mindedness for perseverance and for paying the serious costs involved in initial investment and ongoing farm and packing costs, these fellows would take the gold.

I am amazed and so proud to be here, and I feel so privileged to play a small role in assisting in their continued development.

B IS FOR BRAZIL

"Take only memories, leave only footprints." Chief Seattle

To say that Brazil is a large country would be an understatement. If you could pick up Australia, it would fit inside Brazil´s borders with space to spare, and at 8.5 million square miles in area, it sure is a diverse country. In five days, I have already covered thousands of kilometres but have not yet left one state!

Today's car journey takes me from Pernambuco into Bahia state, across Lake Sobradinho, source of all the irrigation and drinking water for thousands of square kilometres and also the largest fresh water lake in the world at over 500 kms long! This is the second time in my life that I have felt insignificant in this huge world and it just reinforces the feeling of joy I have to do this job that enables me to make and to retain such beautiful friends.

Petrolina, in the eastern state of Pernambuco, a city of a quarter of a million souls on the San Francisco River and my base for the next two weeks for a series of visits to a dozen or so mango farms in Pernambuco and in the neighbouring state of Bahia.

Some of these farms are ten-hour´s drive or more from home base and often a large part of each day´s drive is on unmade roads. You need good teeth to live and work in Brazil.

One of the things that strikes me about this marvellous country is the sheer massiveness of it. We drive out of Petrolina on a sunny morning. As the bustle of the city subsides and we pass through industrial estates heading east into the interior, the landscape changes. Gradually, civilisation disappears, as the road becomes a highway; an artery of asphalt piercing the arid landscape around me, unending and rigidly straight, I can see forever from my front passenger seat view. Brush, stark-looking, leafless bushes on either side of us and all around, stretching out forever in dark, scorched-looking earth. Occasional quick bridge passages over long-dried up rivers and a flash of golden sand here and there below us, help to break up the journey, as the highway beckons unerringly before us and we settle into a long day on the road.

We stop for a very sugary cup of coffee at a roadside shack. Coffee? This way or nothing but it's welcome and I am as happy as I've ever been as I take a stroll, smoke a roll-up and take in my surroundings in the morning heat. The sky. I suddenly realise the vastness of my position and the insignificance of myself as I turn and gaze into the distance all around me. A clear, fine blue colour, interspersed with wispy white clouds, the space around me is just huge and I feel as if I can see forever. I always feel alive in the realness of Nature and I feel in my soul the privilege to share this earth, despite my miniscule presence on it.

Excitement ahead as we reach our turn-off, but excitement turns to disappointment as I soon realise that the stony road we are now bone-shatteringly traversing at a steady thirty miles-per-hour is going to be our route into the farm for at least the next four hours. It doesn't matter, I am in great company: Diana is my Agronomist from the exporting firm back in Petrolina. She's ably assisted by Smiling Shirley and then there's our driver and general do-everything-person, Edilson, a young chemical engineering graduate and possibly one of the most likeable human beings I have ever come across. Mr-Steve-I can-do-anything-just-give-me-a-chance-I-need-to-learn-everything-about-everything-as-fast-as-possible-I-am-Edilson-please. I think Edilson was twenty-five at this time and in a way, he was a kind of Messiah to me, showing me a new light; a new way of treating and respecting our fellow humans. I will never forget him.

Shirley is another young university graduate. She has wonderful deep eyes, big round glasses and magnificent teeth. Teeth that she shares with us almost all our waking hours. I am certain that Brazilians care for their teeth more than any other part of their bodies and that's taking into account that taking care of one's body is big business in Brazil, especially, but not exclusively, in the case of the female of this species!

Permanently effervescent, fragrant, helpful and funny, Shirley is the perfect assistant and she is a wonderful travelling companion.

Diana is twenty-seven, a degree in agronomy in her bank and some years of experience in mango growing and packing for international markets behind her. A joy to work with, she is both beautiful and professional. We would spend some weeks together over the years to come; her job to escort me to the farms that supply us and to provide me with the information I need to confirm that our growers are at the top of their game.

We drive on and the stony road thankfully disappears, as we join another highway, close now to our overnight destination in a small town about two hours from the farm. It is dusk and the road is dangerous. Huge trucks hurtle towards us, heading through the night to who-knows-where. The road is as fast as a motorway but is single carriageway tarmac and the potholes are invisible and as big as garden ponds. I am glad to reach our hotel, to check in and to get some dinner and a cold beer with my Brazilian friends. I mean real friends: I have had another epiphany on this long journey; a sensation built from the days and weeks I have spent working with these amazing people: Brazilians may not always be united in politics or beliefs; there are terrible disparities in wealth and poverty and crime is a blight on this magnificent land. But, you see, this is the lesson: Brazilians are the most diverse race of people on earth; black, brown, white, coffee-coloured, ginger, blonde, brunette. Hispanic, negro, Caribbean, whatever; two hundred million people, a melting pot of humanity, united by one thing. They are proud of their nation. Irrespective of where we are, what we look like, what we do: We are Brazilian, and we are one.

We awake early the next morning and we are on the road as the sun is rising. Our highway becomes a sandy road for the next two hours and at nine in the morning, we arrive at the farm. Except there's an obstacle between us and it.

A large and black-looking lagoon stops our pickup from progressing further. Maybe two-hundred yards across, the water is still and threatening. I have always had a fear of deep, slow-moving waters and this ticks the boxes and adds one. As I alight from the truck, grateful for a stretch of the legs, I approach the edge of the lagoon and I note that the water is indeed black. I roll a smoke as I take in the scene. From the water's edge, I can see to the far bank, there is a man sheltering in the shade beneath a large tree, his motorcycle leaning up against the tree beside him. I take in the shape of a pontoon. No, it's a boat of some kind, I see. And there's a rope. The rope is stretched across the lagoon to our side and I see that it's connected to a rail and a pole ten yards to my left on the other side of what is clearly a concrete slipway.

"Ah, I see, we are going across on the boat, the ferry," I assume. In fact, it turns out that we are to board the car onto what is actually a raft and then pull ourselves over, using the rope. As I stand happily at the edge of the lagoon, smoking my cigarette and observing the man from the other side of the lagoon begin his exertions in pulling the raft across to us, I stare into the dark waters at my feet seeing everything but seeing nothing in the murk. All is still in the depths, and in my mind too, as I begin to prepare myself mentally for the business to come on the other side.

I am aware of a presence at my side and the feel of an arm half-encircling my waist, gently guiding me half a step backwards, away from the water. "Tenha cuidado senhor. Crocodilos são conhecidos por atacar humanos aquí," a previously unseen stranger whispers in my ear, indicating the water below me with his other hand. The C-Word registers in my mind and the shapes and shadows in the water unscramble and become form and there, some four feet from me on the bottom of the river and facing me directly, is the clear image of the head of a gigantic crocodile, mouth half-open and with its lidless eyes fixed on me.

I would cross this lagoon many more times in the future and I always loved driving the car up and onto the raft and helping to pull us across the dark and creepy crossing. But I never stood and smoked by the water's edge again and I would never, ever, do again what I did that day as we reached the "safety" of the far side.

As we approach the far bank and the concrete slipway comes into range, all thoughts of reptiles have left my mind. I am now in "farm audit mode" and I am tuned in to my task ahead. A large and important mango farm needs my attention and as our raft comes to ground against the concrete ramp, I am first off, leaping ashore, eager to get the truck off and onwards and up to the farm entrance. As I land in my farm boots, confident of making an easy transition from raft bound to terra firma, I slip on the algae that I have failed to notice on the slope, and I am down! Slipping back down the ramp, inevitably towards the dark waters and the horrors within, I am helpless, I can't grip with hands or feet and panic kicks in as I see the surface of the smooth waters break twenty feet in front of me. It's the croc and he's zeroed in on me as I slide slowly but inexorably downwards. He reaches the concrete ramp and there's no hesitation as the beast's head emerges from the water and I see front feet make land. I see the teeth, the massive teeth, water-dripping, saliva wetting, all skin and scales and I am a dead man. He's out of the water now, tail swishing and a piercing, scream-hiss shreds my nerves as I continue to slip, slide slither, helplessly down the green ramp and into the snapping jaws of death. There is no time to think; no time to contemplate my fate, fear is put aside as survival kicks in, even though the rational part of mind has already accepted that I am croc food…

Strong hands grab me under each shoulder, shouting and screaming is all I hear as my companions rush in, in a blur of movement to save me, others charging to the giant reptile, making a tremendous row and thrashing at the thing with sticks as the distance between us stops and the crocodile makes a one-movement fluid turn and splashes back into the black lagoon and away.

A change of underwear, some dry clothes, a smoke and a coffee and I am alive and ready to go. It was a great audit that day. For some reason, I had an alert mind and a clear focus!

B IS FOR BEIRUT

Landing in a rice paddy is not quite the same as setting a whirlybird down on the sandy hills of Beirut, and you can't use the same methods. One of the two standard procedures is to bring the aircraft to a hover over the intended landing spot and then gently lower the helicopter to the ground. The second is to continue the approach all the way to the ground without bringing the aircraft to a hover over the point of the intended landing. In the heavy sand and dust areas of Lebanon, this was virtually impossible. If a pilot were to attempt the first of these types of landings there, he would quickly find that rotor blades and engine would be smothered with sand and his visual reference lost, ending in probably destruction of the aircraft and possible injury or death to the passengers and crew. Due to this concentration of dust and sand, His aviator wisely took the second approach, the fast and direct route, picking a spot from distance and taking a continuous approach to the touchdown point, without bringing the aircraft to a hover over the point of the intended landing.

Moving across the wind because of the turbulence, strength and changeability of the breeze, entirely down to the pilot's knowledge of the terrain and the capabilities of his aircraft, the passenger moved to the lowered cargo ramp at the rear of the aircraft and alighted softly into the wind-whipped sand. The bird has gone and He is alone now, time to find his contact and to plan for the assignment ahead.

The Lebanese Shiite Muslim group, Hezbollah had caused outrage here in recent days. They had launched a surprise attack along the Lebanese-Israeli border, resulting in the capture of two Israeli soldiers, instantly turning what had been a localised conflict into a full-blown conflagration. His assignment on this mission was Search and Rescue (S&R); difficult enough in any conditions, but especially so in this tinderbox of the Lebanese-Israeli-Syrian tri-border area.

In the four years since the second Lebanon war, Hezbollah had turned over one hundred villages in South Lebanon into military bases. They had created weapon stores near schools and hospitals and residential buildings, essentially using the residents as human shields in direct contravention of UN resolutions. The utmost care would have to be taken if his assignment were to be completed without military or indeed collateral casualties. Fortunately, his government was very well supported here by the Americans and the Israelis and recent and constant satellite surveillance had now revealed the exact location of where the hostages were being held.

Moving into position well before dawn, his S&R patrol hunkered down in the cold of the early morning, high above the southern Lebanese village of Al-Khiam, He took a moment to summarise the plan in his mind. His weapon of choice for this mission was the US manufactured Saber Forsst modular rifle with custom shoulder stock, measured and fitted exclusively for him and chambered for the .338 Magnum round, it was fast and deadly, ideal for these conditions, designed to be transportable, durable, reliable and of course, highly accurate.

He was too big an asset to be part of the snatch team that was to go in to locate and free the hostages. His role in this risky mission would be to take out as many insurgents as possible above the killing ground in a carefully prepared hide. He was supported by Israeli snatch specialists and with a small squad of local elite troops from the Lebanese Army. At exactly 0400, the pre-planned rocket attack on the village commenced. Launched from inside the Israeli border to the south, the rockets were not designed to cause death and destruction in the village, their purpose was to create panic and confusion, to provide just enough time for the ten-man posse to move in, execute the release of the hostage and move out, without casualties. Crashing in for a full fifteen minutes, the unearthly noise and chaos of the rocket barrage preceded what turned to be a full-scale gunfight down on the ground, but high above, visibility was good. At a range of between five hundred and seven-hundred-and-fifty-yards, it would later be confirmed that He had made fifteen clean kills in less than ten minutes of high-intensity action; there were zero casualties on the S&R team. The NO-STOP pick up by the Chinook chopper later that morning, was also a walk in the park.

C IS FOR CHERRIES

"The real voyage of discovery consists not in seeking new landscapes, but in having new eyes." Marcel Proust

I have been privileged to travel the world in search of the finest cherries. I don´t have space or time to tell all those stories here, but I can list you some of the places to which I have travelled. The best cherries in the world come from the hills behind Beirut, in Lebanon, but that can be a difficult place to go to! Aside from Lebanon, I have hunted down the best growers and the best fruit in Canada and the USA, Spain, Italy, France, Belgium, Germany, the UK, Portugal, Hungary and all of Eastern Europe in the northern hemisphere. Chile, Argentina, New Zealand, Australia, Tasmania and South Africa amongst the countries I have chased down cherries in the southern hemisphere.

Some say that the mango is the king of fruits. Others argue that in fact, the king of fruits is the durian. Interesting factoid here - the durian is the only fruit in the world banned from airline cabins, hotels and public transportation. Any ideas why?

Basically, the smell, to those who don´t like it, it is absolutely disgusting!

Personally, I believe the sweet cherry to be the king of all fruits. I admire cherry growers more than all other fresh produce growers. One must have tremendous balls to even consider planting cherry trees and huge nerve to live through the period from flower, fruit set and ultimately to harvest. Crops worth millions in any currency are often lost entirely at the last moment before picking. Rain, hail, freak heatwaves or cold snaps, anything can destroy a crop that requires huge amounts of love and care and expensive treatments in that critical period of approximately three months of worrying! Birds especially can wreak havoc in minutes. In Australia, where most cherries are covered with nets to protect against the worst of the weather, a single parrot finding its way into a protected cherry crop can cause devastating damage in no time at all!

The sweet cherry originated in the area between the Black and Caspian Seas in Asia Minor. It is likely that bird faeces carried it to Europe prior to human civilization. Greeks probably cultivated the fruit first. Later, Romans cultivated the fruit as it was essential to the diet of the Roman legionnaires (their use likely spread the fruit throughout Western Europe).

The cherry has also been associated with virginity from ancient times to the present day. The association may be derived from the fact that the red coloured fruit that encircles a small seed symbolizes the uterus of Maya, the virgin mother of Buddha, who was offered fruit and succour by a holy cherry tree while she was pregnant. Fragrant cherry blossoms are a rite of Spring. Cherry wood is used in high class furniture production and a little-known fact is that parts of the cherry tree itself have long been used for medicinal purposes. The bark, leaves, and seeds of the cherry tree contains cyanogenic glycosides - poisons that are lethal if ingested by children or animals. Native Americans and others use the leaves and carefully prepare teas with them for the treatment of colds or coughs. Others have experimented with cherry stalk tea in the treatment of kidney diseases.

I had to go to Belgium some years ago to audit a cherry farm and packhouse. The company brand was "Royal" and they were superb in everything that they did. The owner and I got on very well and at the end of my visit, he asked me if I'd like to take a box of cherries home. He presented me with a 2kg open carton of his best fruit. 32mm plus sized, gorgeous red cherries with bright green, fresh looking stalks. Despite this only being Belgium and bearing in mind that I lived in Malaga, my journey home was complicated, via Brussels and Madrid to get to Malaga. An airport official in Brussels stopped me in a queue for security and demanded to see the paperwork for my cherries. I'm convinced he just wanted to steal them from me, as did virtually everybody else that travelled with me that day – they were that good. I told him that they were from an EU country, that I was travelling within the EU and that I did not need a phyto-sanitary certificate, a goods manifest and a commercial invoice. I watched him make the call as I gradually zig-zagged my way to the security check. I watched him get the confirmation that I knew he would and I blew him a kiss as I left his view.

Fairly typically for me at the time, I drove from Malaga airport straight to my hometown, an hour away, and straight to my favourite bar, box of cherries still looking crazily artificial in their magnificence. I love to bring samples of my fruity world home for my chums to taste. It's like having my personal taste panel and this habit has helped me enormously over the years in judging what people want to eat and what would change their habits. My pals were in the bar but more importantly, so was a large group of attractive women, deeper into the bar. I walked to the girls and I distributed several of these enormous, glowing with health and freshness, kings of fruits to each girl. I recounted my tale of where I had been and some entertaining cherry facts. I could have taken any or all these ladies home there and then, they were smitten with the fruit and the stories of how they had come to be. An hour or so later, my friends had by now scoffed almost all the cherries. There were just a few fruits left in the carton and one of my pals decided that he would have a go with the girls. He took the box and approached the table. Not to be sonny, I am afraid, they want the cherry man, so buzz off and leave us alone!

C IS ALSO FOR CHILE

Chile, Chile, Chile,

One of my favourite countries in the world. Brilliantly professional, honourable, straightforward and direct, and endlessly optimistic and positive - I love these people and this unique country. Despite exporting hundreds of millions of cartons of fresh fruit all over the world each year, agriculture is not in any way the biggest contributor to the Chilean economy. Copper is the most important export commodity here. Incidentally, for my golfer friends, one of the highest golf courses in the world is here, built many years ago in the Andes by American copper miners to occupy their leisure time, and there's also air-freighted fresh salmon and lobster, timber and the amazing wine. Don't forget the wine!!

As diverse a country as one could find anywhere in the world, Chile occupies some 4,270 kms of Pacific coast (more than 6,000 kms if you followed the coastline), and yet its average width is just 177 kms! From the oldest and driest desert in the world, the Atacama, right down to Tierra del Fuego and the polar icecap in the south, Chile has almost every climate possible in between and all the rich biodiversity that goes with that.

Summer is in full swing, so for a sun follower like me, it's an essential destination if we cold dwellers in the northern hemisphere want some of the world's best summer stone fruit. Have you ever seen cherries at 30mm plus in diameter or sumptuous nectarines that melt in the mouth? Maybe a rich and nourishing avocado harvested at the perfect moment, or perhaps a crunchy, delicious apple? Perhaps some sweet and succulent table grapes? All of these and much more are available now.

Chilean fruit production, a marvel in the modern world of fresh produce. Largely due to its central region possessing a Mediterranean climate, but in no small part assisted by being the longest country in the world, giving huge diversity of climate and therefore extended seasons of key products. With protection from pests and diseases provided by the Andes to the east and ever present along the entire length of the country, and a maritime climate from the Pacific Ocean, Chile's central fertile valley produces huge volumes of some of our favourite fruits. This week I am looking at table grapes and at cherry farms. However, Chile is also renowned for its production of avocados, apples, pears, stone fruit, kiwi, berries, citrus, and other widely consumed fruits.

For professional reasons, I won't mention names, suffice it to say that the companies I have seen here are world leaders, pioneers and incredible farmers - it is my honour and pleasure to work with them. Don't talk to me about "seasonality" - if this fruit isn't "in season," I jolly well don't know what is!! This is not just any old run-of-the-mill fruit; this is YOUR summer fruit but from the other side of the world.

The Hyatt Regency in Las Condes, Santiago de Chile. One of my favourite hotels in the world. I am asleep in my suite on the thirtieth floor. I am awakened by a strange sensation; a vibration, growing to a wave-like rocking feeling as I lay shock-still in my bed. I know instantly that it is an earthquake. There is nowhere to go, for some reason I dare not move and for what seems like an age - but is probably no more than a couple of minutes - I lay still, rigid with terror until calm resumes.

Later that day, I have an orchard visit to an intriguing new source of plums. Leo Romero is a pioneer. He grows only plums and he has been experimenting with some common global varieties, crossing them with some spurs of his own. His orchard is difficult to find and even more difficult to inspect. He has constructed ditches all through the planted areas in an effort to protect his jewels from unwanted eyes. In fact, crop theft, or even more seriously, theft of plant material for later grafting and proliferation, is common in the fruit world. New varieties these days are often registered and patented as intellectual property; the fruit's actual DNA is used in the registration and patenting process and there have been several high-profile court cases brought against individuals and companies accused of stealing plant material for gain.

Leo asks me if I can ride a quadbike. I give him the affirmative answer and we set off for my first look at his secrets. Five minutes later, I am towing Leo out of one of his own ditches, but we proceed and after a heart-rushing climb on the quads up a steep hill that overlooks his orchards in order to get an aerial view of the land, we descend and dismount, ready to meet the family and to have lunch on a majestic lawn beside his farm hacienda. The family wolf, really, a dirty great big WOLF, and several German shepherd dogs join us and I am at peace with the land, the orchards, the family and their pets. Without warning, my legs turn to jelly as the very ground I am standing on starts to become liquid. I know again instantly that this is another tremor. All I can do is weather this and it soon passes. My memory will never allow me to forget the surreal combination of the eccentric Chilean plum grower, his pet wolf, the quadbikes and the tremors that day.

I have another mission to Chile later that year. I am again based in the Hyatt Regency and this is an important client visit. I am to host a visit by the British supermarket chain, Safeway. My mission is to showcase some of our farms here and I have to look after the buyer for grapes and stone fruit, Abigail Barnes, and supporting her is her technical manager, Derek Reacher. My support comes in the form of a good friend of mine, a gentleman called Bill Todd. Bill is a fruit trade professional, an artist in fruit procurement and in this case the man responsible for making the trade agreements with the growers we are to show to the clients. Bill is an accomplished pianist, trombone player and singer and I know that the fruit trade, for him, is just a means to an end.

I have the fragrant Ms. Barnes for a week on the ground and our time is spent in a blur of travel up and down the famed Trans-America highway, AKA dead dog highway for obvious reasons. We see numerous farms, orchards and vineyards all in the metropolitan region of Santiago. I am obliged to play golf with her boss on one day and end up playing for a deal worth ten million dollars a year in trade with Safeway. (See G IS FOR GOLF.)

The week culminates in a dinner with Abigail and Derek in the Hyatt and I plan how to close my deal. The previous night and on several nights before, as I have been in Santiago a lot longer than my retailer colleagues, I note that there is a live band on in the main bar in the hotel. They are good and I can´t resist making a plan for my deal-breaker dinner the following night. I approach the leader of the band during their first break and I quickly come to a working arrangement with him.

Dinner is a major success. Abigail is dressed to kill, and I can feel the electricity between us, despite the off-putting presence of chaperone Derek. As we finish dessert, I suggest a night cap in the main bar, and we are soon ensconced in a cosy booth just above the band and next to the dance floor. Our drinks order arrives and we 'cheers' all round, all of us comfortable with the work we have put in that week and with the likely deal between us coming closer and closer. Now it´s time to relax and I catch the band leader´s eye at the right moment and we wink at each other.

"Ladies and gentlemen," the band leader announces. The audience in the bar are paying attention now. "Tonight, we have a special guest who´s going to play with us. I give you, all the way from the United Kingdom..." I am looking at Bill now, he´s completely unsuspecting, "...please give a warm welcome to... Meester BILL TODD!"

Bill mouths an inaudible obscenity at no one in particular, Abigail grins at me as I revel in my trickery and Derek stares into outer space. My pal and colleague gets to his feet and makes his way down the few steps to the band, he approaches the band leader and a whispered conversation takes place. Bill takes a seat at the baby grand piano, counts to four and opens with the sweetest melody I have ever heard. It is Bill's own take on the Gershwin classic, Summertime, and the Livin' is Easy, and as the band click easily into Bill's sumptuous piano playing, the saxophone kicks in, I take Abigail's hand and lead her onto the dance floor.

We got that deal, although I suspect it had a lot to do with my golf match against the boss. But that is another story...

C IS FOR COLOMBIA

My favourite country. I've been out looking at farms all week. Some of the most amazing people on earth in a country of 55 million inhabitants, occupying a land mass the same size as Spain, France and Portugal combined and a land that is divided north to south by three serious mountain ranges. Travel in Colombia, if not by commercial aircraft, is a time consuming, nerve-wracking and sometime hazardous affair. I've been in Pácora, 50 miles due south of Medellín and it's time to get to the city, to a good hotel (I've been staying in a tiny but acceptable hotel in the town and my last three nights, including dinner, has just cost me approximately €11 Euros!). Pácora is isolated. It's a five-hour drive to the nearest big town to catch a bus. The car journey is impressive, scary and tough. We drive over a tropical mountain range on single vehicle lanes, down to the Pácora River, along a dirt track for hours. If you've ever driven a motor vehicle in Colombia, you'll know that the country produces crazy drivers. Think Juan Pablo Montoya, ex F1 Driver, in a powerful Toyota Hi-Lux pick-up, the driver only slowing or yielding reluctantly, as if there's a loss of face involved.

We arrive suddenly from the country into a bustling market town, there's a bus, we hail it from the car. "Medellín?" asks our driver.

Affirmative, confirms the bus driver. We have thirty seconds to grab our bags, load them underneath the bus and we jump on board. I´m with my pal, Jimmy Patrón, local assessor and auditor. We are tired. We sleep fitfully and awake at dusk as we pull up on the outskirts of the city. We climb down from the bus. The next phase of the journey is by taxi. In Colombia, taxi sharing is a common practice; an economical way to cover distance, so they have taxi 'stops' where one can opt to share and to keep prices reasonable. It´s not happening, however. I am standing by a football pitch with kids playing a match, in the rain, and I'm waiting for Jimmy to order an Uber. I´m using my travel bag as an umbrella.

The Uber comes and twenty minutes later, we are at our destination. I am at the trunk of the taxi to extract my bag. Right there on the top of my bag is a child´s toy spider, made from pipe cleaners. I go to swipe it off into the boot of the car when it stands up on its back legs and sticks it´s fangs up, straight at me. Now, normally I hate spiders, but this thing is so alive, so big and so beautiful, I am fearful but also staggered by its presence. Jimmy lifts my bag from the car´s trunk, the spider´s going nowhere, it refuses to be coaxed down from its new home – my bag – and I think, she must have 'boarded' my bag from the luggage compartment of the bus. Meanwhile, the taxi driver, a young Colombian man, is in a state of absolute panic. He really is scared. Jimmy and I are trying not to laugh. We get the tarantula into the verge of the hotel´s tropical garden in the soft rain that´s still falling. She looks content. We admire her beauty one more time. I turn to the driver to settle our debt and I can´t help saying to him, "They always travel in twos, you know…"

He had been in deep cover in the reed bed for over a week. Holed up in his den on the banks of the Palomino River, in the heart of the tropical rain forest of the Santa Marta district, north Colombia. Three things concerned him: firstly, but not least, the risk of detection by his objectives. However, as far as He knew, they were not aware of his presence and save for avoiding their daily patrols on the far side of the river and the occasional passing Rigid Inflatable Boat, usually crewed by heavily-armed fighters, he was able to remain undetected, reserving his observation times to dawn and dusk and on the occasions that new patrols arrived at the guerrilla camp that he had been monitoring for the last seven days.

Heavy-headed ground snakes were also a problem. Not venomous, but aggressive and hard-biting, they had pestered him constantly since his arrival in the night all those days ago. Sand flies or biting midges were the other issue that he had to deal with and since his observation times were governed by the need to stay invisible, it seemed that the midges were always waiting for him, rising in a cloud to surround him whenever he left his camp to take up his watching position.

He had chosen his weapon carefully to suit this jungle warfare assignment. There are three main challenges that a jungle brings and these will determine which gun can handle the job at hand.

A jungle comes with thick foliage, humidity, and mud.

Foliage means that unless you get your bullets to magically fly *around* the leaves and branches, you'll need a calibre that can go *through* them, and still do damage to whatever it is you're shooting at. Any bullet can go through a leaf or two and still deliver hurt to its target. But when you're fighting in a jungle and you see rustling in the trees 50–60 yards ahead of you, you don't have time to find a clear line of line of sight, you immediately start firing. And if the bullet must go through a small tree and some branches, it needs to maintain its ballistic capabilities. For that, a heavier bullet such as a 7.62 is called for. Anything firing a bigger cartridge will be cumbersome, and anything smaller will only be effective through volume of fire.

Unless you plan on storing your weapon out in the open, humidity is more of a problem for personnel. The need to keep feet clean and dry is obvious, but so is the requirement to maintain a neutral odour in order to avoid detection.

Mud means that your rifle needs to be reliable despite the gunk that'll end up on it when you accidentally drop it or when for some God-awful reason, you need to crawl through a jungle alongside all the creeping and crawling insects and reptiles that call the forest floor home. It's been proven that a weapon with a good seal from the elements is superior to a weapon with looser tolerances (He had rejected the otherwise excellent rifle, the AK pattern for this reason). In other words, it's better and easier to design a firearm that keeps the mud out than to design a firearm that can run with some mud inside.

His weapon of choice, the FN FAL, fitted these requirements

The "right arm of the free world" fires a 7.62x51 NATO round that will easily go through branches and foliage. It's been tried and tested in the Rhodesian Bush War and in the chaos of the Vietnam War by Commonwealth forces. Simple, reliable, and affordable full-automatic fire.

Because this weapon is a battle rifle, one drawback is that it is significantly heavier than most modern weapons, especially AR-15's and modern AK pattern rifles. Marching and fighting for long periods of time would be a pain in the ass. But if you were put in a jungle and needed to fight a battle-royal style of conflict and were granted a weapon along with its ammo, you'd want one of those rifles.

The light was fading as he heard trucks approaching the camp across the silent river. He had already carefully mapped and charted his distances, factored in the prevailing wind speed and taken into account the elevation in the killing ground ahead of his gaze. The Mark was there, the leader of this FARC group. They were highly dangerous enemies, funded by kidnap and ransom, by illegal mining, extortion and the production and distribution of illegal drugs. The UN had estimated that twelve percent of all civilian deaths in the Colombian conflict, were committed by FARC.

Zeroing his telescopic sight's cross hairs onto his objective, he knew that he had one opportunity, a miss would be unacceptable, a kill shot would be required and He breathed in deeply, oblivious to the midges all around him and close to invisible in his gilly suit, constructed from the natural materials of the river and its banks all around him. He exhaled slowly through his nose, now applying slight pressure though his right index finger to the trigger, already well adjusted to his firing preferences. A CRACK, muted by his rifles fitted silencer and a half a second or so for the round to traverse the six hundred yard plus range to its target. A burst of red mist from the head of the Mark confirmed that he had taken the kill shot and, as if in slow motion, the target folded and was down. Calmly, but urgently, He packed his essential kit into his bergen. Shouldering his weapon, he pressed the call-in facility on his satellite location finder and he headed to his pre-arranged pick-up zone. The chopper would be fifteen minutes. Time enough for Him to turn his thoughts to his other role and to think of a plausible explanation for the scores of insect and snake bites that covered his body.

I am on a week-long mission into the campo in Antioquia State. "It's a market garden," I thought, as we arrived on what was really just a small-holding. My job was to look at the farm from the point of view of the M&S protocol or standard that I was auditing against. Known as Field to Fork, it had ten sections covering everything from risk assessment, through land selection and planting, irrigation, water source and management, harvesting, packing, cold storage and logistics.

This was a small piece of cultivated land and I was there to look at Tamarillos or 'tree tomatoes'. A strange fruit that grows on small trees and is hand harvested and packed. The farm also had some Granadillas, another exotic fruit that grows from vines, much like a kiwi fruit does. The small holding was owned by a lady farmer, perhaps in her sixties and fiercely proud of her achievements. I completed my detailed inspection of the various cultivated areas, I made my notes and we made our way to the "cabaña" or cabin, in the centre of the farm to sit down to discuss the paperwork and physical systems that they had in place that would ensure that the food was safe, the environment was in good shape and that HACCP (Hazard Analysis and Critical Control Points) have been put in place and are well monitored. It was clear that they were not going to meet the standard this time. She was backed up by her receiver and distributor's technical team, I was supported by my Colombian team, comprised of my TM, Jimmy Patrón and my logistics director, Sara Toro. They asked me to give my verbal report and where they stood and that I should do it in Spanish for everyone's understanding. I'm doing my best to be understanding and positive, but my message is clear: There was just too much work to be done to pass them as things stood. This dear, sweet woman, hard-working and rightly proud of her production, was getting a NO from the Man from Del Monte. "Not good enough. Too weak in too many areas; risks apparent; poor systems and procedures." She stoically maintains her very dignified silence and attention as I'm reaching my conclusions. "I am very sorry, you are not currently up to the standard of good agricultural procedures and I therefore cannot pass you to F2F standard at this time. I will put a plan together that should allow you to address these issues and then I will return in twelve months for a second assessment."

She stares at me intently for a while and then she starts to cry softly, fat tears running down her sun-scorched cheeks. It is all I can do not to join her.

C IS FOR COSTA RICA

Liberia, Guanacaste province. On the ground on an exceptionally large and very special mango farm here in Central America. Summer. Temperatures are in the high thirties and it's the start of a harvest in another part of the world.

After all the care through the wet season: Nutrition, irrigation, pruning, soil maintenance and renovation; the flowering period, busy bees and crawling insects doing their job; a prayer for a good pregnancy or fruit set; and then nurture and love again until it's time to organise the harvesting gangs, fire up the tractors, clean the bins into which the fruit will be placed directly from the trees and prepare the packing station for an intense period of sorting, grading and packing for export.

I am here on the ground with my good friend Marcos Vinicio Morera, agronomist extraordinaire and the man charged with the huge responsibility of getting the best crop possible from this unique farm. Mangos are just like peaches or nectarines or apples in that when the fruit is mature on the tree, it must be harvested or it will rot and fall from the branch. In the same way, each mango variety will last for two to three weeks of production, therefore, in order to make a seasonal offer, you would need several varieties of mangos that flower one after the other. Then somewhere between 100 and 150 days after flowering, the fruit is ready for harvest and the spread of varieties gives consistent and consecutive production over a summer season.

On this farm, fantastically named varieties give us the season we need. Here on the farm, I am looking at the first fruits ready to be picked. This variety is called Alphonso and it's going to be followed closely by a fully green coloured one called Ataulfo. Mainstream varieties will follow in volume and these include Haden, Keitt, Kent, a fascinating Thai variety called Nam Doc Mai and then finishing with the very common and not much liked variety, the Tommy Atkins. I say not much liked because mango breeders and growers all over the world have really changed the game in the last twenty years. More traditional mango varieties such as the Tommy, can be astringent and quite fibrous, often delivering a strong turpentine flavour and aroma when consumed. Modern varieties, such as the ones I have named, are melting flesh types, non-astringent and with outstanding juice content and flavour. Older cultivars like Tommy Atkins still have a massive presence in global consumption because European retailers have joined, as always, the push for innovation in better eating fruit and they will sell this range of mangos as 'Premium' whereas a Tommy would now be retailed as 'Value', targeting a less-discerning client or a purchaser with a smaller budget.

So, a 'normal' mango harvest occurs once a year, usually in late summer and after approximately four months from flower bloom.

A newly planted mango tree will usually begin to bear fruit after year three and it will come into full production in year five and then be able to give a full harvest for something like the next 40 years. All modern mango production uses a rootstock onto which the true variety is grafted in a nursery before being planted in a well-spaced orchard. The rootstock is the base and root ball of either another species of fruit or a different variety of mango that possesses the characteristics so desired by today's growers. These characteristics are often related to the vigour of the tree (the speed of growth) and to the size to which the tree will naturally grow, so what you are looking for in order to plant your orchard as densely as possible, therefore gaining as much production in kilos as you can, is a tree that is naturally dwarfing and less vigorous than it would be without the control that a well-chosen rootstock will provide .Without the use of a rootstock, it is possible in some varieties to have a tree that will grow to more than 100 feet tall and with a canopy as large as 35 feet across – clearly not ideal when it comes to harvesting your crop. It is also possible that a pure mango tree on its original root base can produce fruit every year for 300 years! If you didn't know, global production and consumption of mangos is very big business. In 2020 the world produced more than 55 million tonnes of fresh mango, with India remaining the world's largest producer. Amazingly, India has over 1,000 different mango varieties. However, it is South and Central America where the real spike in production is coming from, which is why I have spent so much time in Mexico, Peru, Ecuador, Brazil and Costa Rica. There are some pockets of production Europe too. Spain has a thriving mango industry on the south coast, a region known as The Axarquia, and Portugal has invested heavily in large scale farms that will come into production in the next few years. I also hear that there are new experimental farms in

Sicily, which if successful, will change the norther hemisphere season all over again.

I so often hear tales about lack of seasonality in stores these days. Oh, how we long for the good old days when new potatoes were available for three weeks in May or the strawberry season that started in June and finished in July. Do not forget that somewhere it is summer or autumn or winter or spring and somewhere it is harvest time. This fruit deserves to put into fruit lovers' hands.

Small tip here in case you have shied away from buying a mango because you are unsure how to prepare it. Botanically a mango is a drupe, consisting of an outer skin, a fleshy edible portion, and a central stone enclosing a single seed. So having purchased your mango and having checked that it is ripe by giving it a gentle squeeze, you would then take a sharp knife and cut vertically down both of the widest sides of the fruit, carefully avoiding the central stone so that you have two "cheeks" of fruit. Then simply score each of the cheeks horizontally and vertically into small squares, without breaking the external skin. Once scored with your knife, you then just press from the outside so that the cheek of fruit turns inside out, your chunks of fresh, juicy fruit, like a mango hedgehog, are now right there in front of you and ready to scrape or to spoon off and onto your serving dish of choice.

Some mango home truths:

Mangos are the succulent, aromatic fruit of an evergreen tree called Mangifera Indica.

Mangos were first grown in India over 5,000 years ago.

Mangos are related to cashews and pistachios.

The Paisley pattern you will see all over India is based on the shape of a mango.

The mango is a symbol of love in India.

So, now you'll easily be able to tell me what kind of fruit is this, pictured below? Clues: same family as the mango, comes from the tree in the second photo, it is two types of 'fruit' in one. One is known as an accessory fruit in that it grows from the other one, which is in fact a seed. The fruit part is a light reddish to yellow fruit, whose pulp can be processed into a sweet, astringent fruit drink or distilled into liquor. Grown commercially in exceptionally large quantities and I am sure that most of us eat them! It's the seed I'm interested in, by the way.

D IS FOR DEREK REACHER

We are in big business with the UK supermarket, Safeway. We have done a deal that involves brand-new and large-scale production of white seedless grapes in northern Argentina. I am tasked with securing the technical accreditation of the farm and new packhouse in San Juan province. I am also heavily involved in the commercial side of this deal and it is quite new in many ways. Seedless grapes are sold in millions of tonnes around the world. I once read that penetration – that is what percentage of each shopper's basket contains the product in question each time they shop – in the case of seedless grapes, the number is 66%. That is exceedingly high. On the other two ends of this scale, I can tell you that stone fruit, let's say again, peaches, nectarines, plums or apricots, the number is 11% and that goes down in winter, whereas seedless grapes is a year-round consumption. Interestingly, note that a big branch of a major multiple retailer might have upwards of forty thousand individual lines for sale. Which one is the biggest contributor of cash into the tills? No, not grapes. It is petrol. But second biggest of all products sold, in term of cash contribution? Bananas! Nudging 85% penetration! All year round. No wonder there really are such things as banana wars!

Which is why nearly all supermarkets plan to have their fresh produce department as soon as you enter the store. It is obviously there to create a fresh market effect, but it's also a massive contributor to the store's sales.

This grape project is an innovation because it is in a new production zone in the world and it will produce earlier fruit than other, established areas — that's always good. You want to be either early or late. Prices are better and there is less competition. We are going to fill sea containers with the grapes but before that we will open the first three or four weeks of the season using air freighted fruits. My procurement guy in this case, Bill Todd, has come up with a most innovative solution to fly the grapes to us. Since the end of the cold war, a new availability of air cargo transport has emerged and, in this case, Bill has negotiated and agreed for a Russian Antonov cargo jet to move our grapes from San Juan in the desert north of Argentina, all the way to Manston airport in Kent. I'm told that the Russian pilot and his comrade are mad. They wait to load, and this thing is a beast, it can take eighty full pallets of almost one tonne each. The two pilots drink chilled vodka all day, until they are loaded (both individually and as a cargo…) and receive clearance to go. Nostrovia! And they fly!

We have sold the entire crop at fixed prices and everything is coming together. It is now my task to get Derek, the Safeway fruit technologist, from London to San Juan and back. I also have to ensure that our partners on the ground have finished the construction of the new packhouse and that all protocols and procedures needed to pass an audit are correctly covered. I know Derek well, from many years of working together and I know that he is a good technical manager.

I also know that he has a particular fixation on toilets and that he has pulled many a supplier over an issue with a packhouse washroom. Mirrors not registered on a plastic or glass breakables ledger, would be a favourite. Poor quality of insufficient number of hand washing signs, lack of cleaning register or poor storage of chemicals might be some other examples of reasons why Mr. R. is a specialist in toilets, so amongst the top things on my list of things to do in the next week of discussions with our partners in Argentina is to make sure that the new block of worker toilets and hand-washing stations for the packhouse are totally faultless. All the above-mentioned potential issues and a dozen more are noted and a plan to get Derek out there starts to come together. Lads, lads, whatever you do, make sure that the toilets are amazing!

I am in a passenger van travelling north in deepest Argentina. The previous night, I have spent with our man in a luxurious hotel in Buenos Aries after flying overnight, business class on British Airways. Derek had given me his requests some days earlier – must fly BA, must sit in seat 26B, upstairs in Business Class, here is my BA Executive Club card number for my air miles. Nothing unusual here and I get his request passed and the trip organised. We are four in the van: our driver and host, the commercial representative from the grape farm, Señor Derek and me.

It is a nine-hour drive and we converse sporadically throughout the journey. We note how the scenery changes as we go farther and farther north, pampas becomes desert and after an age, we finally arrive at the gates to the farm and packhouse. We pass through the security barrier and we fill in the visitor questionnaire and register. Derek turns to his left and spots the brand-new toilet and handwashing block just there and he prepares to disembark.

"Oooh, is that a toilet facility there? I'll just go and have a pee and a freshen up before we start the visit" he says, heading off to the new block, in his blazer and slacks. Tie on and shirt buttoned, his freshly polished shoes glinting in the afternoon sunshine. I note that it is 45 degrees Celsius. I am laughing inside, because I knew that this would happen, I am just surprised that Derek has headed immediately to his specific point of interest. My partners and hosts are looking at me in a state of disbelief and nervous anticipation. After fifteen minutes, the man himself emerges, walking towards us as we wait in the shade at the farm entrance. He is still semi-airdrying his hands as he approaches. "Fabulous toilets. gentlemen. I'm not going to have any problems passing this farm," he states.

My partners and I stifle our laughter as we exchange knowing looks. "Told you," I'd say a day later to the hosts. "Get the bogs right and Derek will pass you!"

E IS FOR EXCUSES.

If you have ever sourced and supplied anything to anyone, you will know that the path never runs smoothly. In fresh fruit and vegetables this is especially true. There are just so many factors that influence the supply chain and that is not even considering the vagaries of demand. Demand is created by the client and it is influenced by several factors. In salad crops, or berries for example, demand can fluctuate wildly depending on the weather where the product is marketed for sale. It can also change slowly. Over a period of time, the consumer begins to understand the product, the offer, whether it is being promoted in store or not and, of course, if the product delivers what the consumer expects.

On the other hand, supply is even more complicated. When one is servicing a large retailer with fresh fruit, you would normally expect to be providing supply year-round and that you would "own" the category, meaning that for a twelve-month period you would have to understand the changes in demand, as seasons change, both in all the source countries of that particular product, as well as in the country where the fruit is being sold.

Things often happen to disrupt that supply chain and therefore, one must always be prepared to offer an explanation or an excuse as to why constant supply to a varying demand is going to be interrupted. In my first sales job at Saphir Produce, I learned quickly to develop my "book of excuses." Now, it's important to understand that all excuses are based on facts; on events that actually happened. Although, it's important to point out that "***based*** on actual events" is the key phrase here. I am now going to give you some excuses that I have used in my career. I want you to tell me which of these are real and which are made up stories take from my Saphir Book of Excuses.

Weather is the suppliers' favourite excuse. After all, we are all in Mother Nature's hands when it comes to planting, growing and harvesting. I remember a time in my early twenties, we were supplying fresh spring greens to Tasbury's; a weird looking product that is a bit like a large and loosely formed cabbage. I think you chop it up and boil it, but anyway it is popular and we have a weekly programme to supply a good few thousand crates of greens, cut fresh, bagged and labelled for retail sale. It is February and the weather is freezing. Nobody - not even the hardiest "Gang Master" - is going to put his crew into the field to cut and pack. Apart from the fact that the air temperature is below freezing, the greens are frozen too. No cutting this week. It's a freshly sold product, cut and bagged to order each day. My boss, my mentor, Rob Sayle makes the call to a particularly obnoxious buyer in his warm office in London.

"Chris, Rob Sayle here. I need to update you of our supply status for spring greens. The fact is that all production has stopped as of today. The fields are frozen solid and we can't cut. We are hoping to see a rise in temperatures later this week but as of tomorrow, there will be a zero availability until further notice."

I watch Rob as he moves the earpiece some six inches away from his ear as the buyer goes apoplectic at our pathetic excuse. He refuses to believe that way down south on the Isle of Thanet, in mid-February, there is any chance of a freeze. He is going to send his senior vegetable technologist down immediately and when he finds out we are telling lies we are all for the high jump.

Another time, I recall making the call myself. We are procuring fresh mangos from Brazil and we have a weekly contract to deliver one full sea container of mangos each week to the various main distribution depots that the retail chain uses to send product to each store. The shipping line that is contracted to transport the containers to Europe has a weekly arrival into Dover and normal procedure dictates that once our container has passed customs inspection and it is cleared for collection, we can send in our truck and pick up the container for its short journey to our warehouse in Kent. We have a problem, however. My boss takes the call from our shipping agent in Dover.

"Bad news I´m afraid. Big storms in the Channel yesterday, you´ll have seen the news. We have lost several containers from the ship and one of them is yours. Gone straight to the bottom of the English Channel. Suggest you begin to make a claim against the shipping line immediately. I´ll be in touch."

I make the call to the buyer – come what may in this trade, professional reaction and instant and honest communication are the orders of the day. His reaction is one of complete disbelief; I can feel his rage and I can picture his face as he gives me the verbal thrashing of my young life. We are liars, thieves, rogues. We are incompetent suppliers and there will be serious consequences if we don´t immediately locate the missing container, which of course did not actually fall off the front of a wildly pitching ship. Come up with a better excuse than that or else!

Another day and another issue. Brazil at this time was still being discovered as a major source of fresh produce for European retailers. We are involved in new sales development in several products: Royal Gala apples from the south, limes from the tropical north. Melons of all types from all regions.

I recall watching a melon container being unloaded by hand in our yard. The 10kg cartons of fresh melons are hand stacked into a forty-foot refrigerated sea container. They are not even on pallets so I watch as a team of workers are physically "hand balling" around two thousand cartons of fruit onto roller conveyors placed in the back of the container and then to the ground where a second team is stacking them onto pallets, according to the fruit size which is marked on the ends of each carton. From there the pallets go into cold store, ready for examination and sorting to order over the next few days. As I watch incredulously, a very large four-legged furry creature with massive incisors appears in the back of the container, behind the men now working at the front on the last of the hand loaded boxes of melons. I know straight away that it is a capybara but I can't for a second work out what on earth it's doing here. It stares at me for two seconds, then it leaps out of the container, to the concrete of the yard and it makes a run for the orchards at the bottom of the yard. I never see it again!

We are also involved in supplying guava and papaya from Brazil and these too are sent to us weekly, by boat.

We have a problem and I must once again gird my loins and make the call.

"Morning David, we have had an issue in Brazil with papaya," I begin.

"What's the problem?" my buyer asks. "Can't you do anything right?" he continues, already on my case before I've had any chance to even begin my rehearsed speech.

I explain that the papayas come from the Amazonian basin in Brazil and that they are cut freshly every day until there is enough fruit to fill a bulker lorry. This is an open trailer and it carries around fifteen tonnes of fresh papaya. It is an articulated lorry and the unit to pull it to port is open. This is because of the heat and because of the economics of this particular supply chain. The drivers of these trucks are used to a four-day journey from the papaya plantations, down through the rain forests on unmade roads and then on to the port in Rio de Janeiro, where the papaya are sorted, packed and chilled, before being loaded into a container for onward shipping. The whole chain takes five weeks, so to give a buyer this kind of notice is good in a way: at least he may have some time to organise covering supply.

I continue: "So the bulker didn't arrive in Rio as planned at the weekend. There are no mobile comms - no GPS tracking in place to locate the truck - so we had to send a team back up into the rain forest in search of the truck. We find the truck, we find the fruit: it's rotten, gone west, totally unusable. More importantly, we have found the driver and… he's dead, I'm afraid."

I go on to explain that the driver has been the victim of a terrible attack by a vicious and dangerous indigenous tribe whilst en route to the port. He's been blow darted with a poisonous dart and robbed and left for dead in his open cab. All that's left is a skeleton and fifteen tonnes of rotten papaya, so I'm telling you now, that in fives weeks' time, we will not have fruit to cover your orders for one week.

I wait for the inevitable tirade of accusations, satisfied that I have given my excuse as well as I can, but nervous, always, of the backlash I was about to receive.

There is silence on the line and I know to wait. He speaks: "Steve. That is such a ridiculously poor story. What a bunch of lies. I can't believe it!" I wait for the assault to continue and for the threats to manifest themselves. "However," he goes on, "That is so good, such a brilliant lie, a story the likes of which I have never heard before that I'm going to take this one on the chin. I need to make plans to cover, speak in a while," and he disconnects. Phew, I think, got away with that one!

Another day, another issue. Guava is the new kid on the block. We are selling it in volumes to all the major retailers. It's a strange fruit is a Guava; small, green and roundish, but wizened, a bit like a quince in that respect. It may well be a tasty and refreshing fruit to eat but it also smells distinctly of cat's piss. It is also unusual in two ways: One, it grows at the very top of extremely tall trees in the rain forest. Two, only one creature can pollinate the flowers of the guava tree and that is the Flying Fox or common Fruit Bat. Now, from where we are taking our guavas at this point in the season, there is a small village. We use local labour to harvest the fruits and to help us load them for transport to port, but therein lies the problem. The bats are considered pests; vermin even, the belief locally is that the bats cause damage to the fruit crops (in fact it's much more likely to be birds) and over a period of time, the villagers have exterminated the fruit bat population. You know what comes next: no bats, no pollination, no fruit, supply problems coming up....

This excuse actually gave me a great deal of pleasure to deliver.

So, I want to know which of the above is a lie, from the book of excuses as it were? Which stories are genuine and which are fantasy? The answer of course, is that they're all true. As Frank Carson used to say, "It's the way you tell 'em!"

E IS FOR EGYPT

Since the 1950's Egypt has been irrigating the land bordering the Nile River north of Cairo. By constructing canals and permitting water extraction and at no detriment to flow or water level of this magnificent waterway, it has literally been possible to turn desert into fertile farmland. In this particular area around Badr, roughly halfway between Cairo and Alexandria, the availability of good water, sandy and well drained soils and a high diurnal range - that's the difference between day and night temperatures - have enabled farmers to produce, amongst other crops, very high-quality table grapes. In this case, a range of mainly seedless varieties that are on the market from early June until October. Many of these varieties are red or black in colour and they are early and develop their colour quickly after flower and fruit set. That is where diurnal range comes in. Hot days and cooler nights help nature to give us colour in our fruits - you will find this all over the world where colour in fruit is key, whether this is in bi-coloured apples, grapes or citrus, the best fruit comes from the areas that have hot days and cool nights. Brazil for example, is a huge producer of oranges but they are not big in exports of fresh oranges because it is too hot for the fruit to change from green to orange! Anyone for a green orange? Errrr...no, I hear you say.

What I did not know was just how expensive it is to prepare and to plant grapes for fresh consumption. This grower spends up to €175,000 per hectare to get to a crop within perhaps two years of planting - that is one hundred and seventy five thousand euros per hectare in case you use commas or decimal points in your maths.

Assuming a grape variety is not fazed out or superseded by something better, the grower may get an average of fifteen years of production from his vines. That's not a lot of time to get your money back, and to farm over three hundred hectares here takes serious decision making and some pretty big cojones. There is also little point in being average at this game as competition is fierce and guardianship of one's secrets is almost impossible. This is why I am bursting with admiration for this grower and his formidable team here. I cannot mention names or brands for professional reasons, but I will note for posterity the professionalism, the optimism and the dedication to their art that I have seen today in the vineyards of Egypt.

Interesting factoid and in case anyone is wondering why my head appears to be close to my posterior in the photograph below: the best way to check properly on the status of a grape crop, is to bend at right angles and view the fruit bunches from between one's legs. It's the only way to get a proper view of the bunches of grapes beneath the canopy of leaves.

F IS FOR FIGS

"Travel makes one modest, you see what a tiny place you occupy in the world." Gustave Flaubert

Around 3000 years ago (1100BC) the Phoenicians reached Andalucía, founding the town of Cadiz. Their culture reached across the Mediterranean. They were also involved in trade with the British Isles. Tin from Cornwall in England was smelted with Spanish copper and the resulting bronze traded on. The olive tree reached Spain at this time, brought from the eastern Mediterranean.

A mere thousand years later, the Romans took control – their province of Hispania Baetica covers much of modern-day Andalucía. Andalucía was a renowned source of many products for the wider Roman Empire, including silver, olives, emperors, philosophers and dancing girls.

After the slow collapse of the Roman Empire, the next major influx of change in Andalucía was the Moorish invasions. The Islamic Moorish army conquered most of Spain between 711 and 718AD, in time creating a kingdom of Al-Andalus with its capital in Cordoba. Once more, Andalusia was part of a multi-national empire with good trade links. Valuable crops from further east, such as figs, citrus and pomegranate were introduced for the first time, as were sophisticated irrigation systems, some of which are still in use. It was common practice to plant a fig tree at the end of stone irrigation channels. Not requiring too much attention, the figs thrived on the overspill of water not used to irrigate more needy, short term crops.

Today the Colar variety of figs is cultivated across Andalusia, but specifically in the Province of Alicante. Known as Brevas and Higos, the trees unusually produce two crops: The first crop, the Breva, comes from the end of May until the end of June. The Higo - or Fig - is ready to harvest from the middle of July until the end of August. Highly prized, it is my pleasure to be involved in putting this amazing fruit to market. So how do figs get fertilised? They rely on wasps. Each species of fig – and there are nearly 1,000 of them recorded – has evolved with its own species of pollinating fig wasp. They are small – less than 2mm long in most cases, and their lives are short and unpleasant.

When the female flowers inside the immature fruits are ready for pollination, the fig emits an enticing aroma that attracts only female wasps of the specific type for that tree. The wasp finds the fig by its scent and then struggles inside through a tiny hole in the bottom of the fig called an ostiole (from the Latin ostium, 'opening'). The female gets pretty badly beaten-up squeezing into the ostiole, losing her wings and other non-essential kit like antennae. It doesn't matter because she will never need them again.

She runs around the interior of the fruit visiting many flowers, laying eggs inside the seeds that will nourish its progeny and also spreading the pollen collected from the previous fig where it was born.

This pollen will allow all seeds to grow, not just the ones where it has deposited eggs. The ovary of some flowers is safely out of reach of the wasp, so it can't lay its eggs in them and those seeds can reach maturity. Having fulfilled her life's mission, the female wasp dies inside the fig.

The eggs become grubs that grow inside the seeds. After completing their full development, in a few weeks they emerge from inside the seeds. The males emerge first and start looking for females to mate with. The males are smaller than the females and don't even have wings; they will never fly and are basically a penis with big jaws. After mating they, like their mother, die inside the fig that was their home all their lives. When the females emerge they are already fertilized and ready to find another fig in which to lay their eggs. At this point, the male flowers inside the fig are ripe and loaded with pollen. Before abandoning their home the females will remember to take a supply of such pollen to carry to the next fig.

This incredible partnership requires fine tuning and synchronicity on the part of the plant and of the pollinator. It is often mentioned as a fine example of coevolution.

F IS FOR FLYING

I have taken over three thousand commercial international flights in my fruity career. I have only ever missed two and even now I am a stickler for an early arrival at whichever airport I am flying from. I missed a flight in Greece once, on a grape mission, but it did not cause me a big problem.

At the other end of the scale, I was in Morocco, escorting a buyer on a stone fruit visit. Morocco is a valuable early source of northern hemisphere peaches and nectarines for climatic reasons. We landed in Agadir in the south, our objective is Taroudant, approximately 100 kms to the east. I have a story about Taroudant, I must dig it out. Our host is Moroccan, American university educated, young and handsome. The buyer and I know his father Mohamed well, and it's clear that Number 1 son has been charged with escorting us on our four-day journey. We are to cover his two orchards of early peaches and nectarines, firstly in Taroudant and then north to the second farm in Marrakech. The son has been given the use of his father's Porsche Cayenne 4x4 and I note that it's the S, petrol, version. This is a beast of a car and we pass the four days in this thing without a single hitch. I don't mean a hitch mechanically or with timings and schedules. What I mean to say is that to drive long distances, well any distance at all really, in Morocco, is an experience. We nearly died fifty times, I swear. The highways are actually quite good and of course, we were in just the right vehicle for what would turn out to be a five-hundred-mile trip. The problem is who is driving the car, what else is on the road and how you encounter it. Chickens, donkeys, tuk-tuks carrying various live animals to market and a plethora of mainly crappy vehicles, driven either by madmen or very old men. these were the normal things we would come across every day. The scary incidents seemed to occur in the mountains: The story of a near-death experience on a one-hundred-and-eighty-degree curve, high in the Atlas Mountains, springs to mind. A 50-year-old, 35 tonne truck. At the wheel an obvious lunatic, coming at us head on, on our side of the road at a combined sped of well over 100 miles per hour. One of many!

That trip was also unusual in that it was my first farm audit as a newly qualified auditor or assessor / information collector / advisor / best friend / worst enemy / route to victory, and I am convinced that the buyer was sent along to check my work. In some cases, these assessments can take two days on the ground for just one farm. There are over six hundred questions, divided into ten sections that contain subjects such as Risk Assessment, Hygiene, Water, Microbiology, Worker Welfare /Ethical Practices, Planting, Growing, Harvesting and Use of Chemicals. Fascinating stuff, eh? No, really, for me, this is the heart of what I do and where the biggest part of my passion for the fruit trade lies. I just fundamentally love being on the farm, always learning, but also sometimes able to help a grower to improve. Anyway, the audit went great. Probably my best one ever. Since my first audit, over ten years ago, I have had the honour and privilege to have done over 400 farm assessments all over the world across a huge range of different fruits and vegetables and in some of the most diverse growing and farming conditions on this earth.

The flight, the flight I hear you say… Sorry! It wasn't a huge deal in the scale of the universe but it did bother me somewhat at the time. The 500 miles in the Porsche had led us on a big loop. On the coast from Agadir, into the interior to Taroudant and then up to the Atlas Mountains and to Marrakech and then back to Agadir for our flights home. The buyer was flying home, to the UK. I was heading home, to Malaga, Spain. A mere forty-five-minute hop from Casablanca, which was the flight I had checked in for now, twenty-minute ride but unusually, due to its popularity, on a jet, a 737.

He left and was home in his house four hours later. I didn't get home for forty-eight hours and I was more than a tad stroppy during that hideous two-day ordeal. The flight from Agadir to Casablanca was six hours late in departing. I missed my connection to Malaga and had no option but to spend the night in a nearby motel and catch an early flight the next day to Barcelona and then to connect with another airline to Malaga. Air Morocco (wonderful airline, always a joy to travel with them) kindly agreed that everything was their fault and rather than have me wait three days for the next Malaga flight, they could get me to Barcelona and home that way. Of course, I took that option and I recall throwing myself out of bed at 3.00 a.m. the next day for my first flight.

This after queuing for three hours at the airline desk the night before, and another two hours arguing my case for a schedule to get me home. I make it and I arrive in Barcelona. All is well, but I must run. I run, fast walk, nearly die, but I get to my gate for my departing flight home on the other side of the airport and in a different terminal. I get there, it's fine although people are beginning to board. I sit to catch my breath and to prepare to board, my passport and boarding pass in hand I prepare to stand, to join the queue of embarking passengers before me. I look up. Our eyes meet as a tall, familiar looking gentlemen, stops to allow me to leapfrog him in the line of passengers. He's instantly recognisable, it is Sven Goran Eriksson, the former England football manager and I shake hands with him and thank him for his gesture. I can't help but ask him for a photo; my brother Kevin is an avid collector of celebrity selfies and I know that this one will hurt him. Sven shakes his head sagely. "No, we wait until Malaga. Better opportunity there. No rush." Jeez he's so wise, I think, and I step up to the girl on the gate, thinking I've met a new chum here.

"Please wait over there, Sir" were the unforgettable and often repeated words she said, as she scanned my ticket fourteen times and then gave up, clearly having no choice but to bump me, albeit temporarily, while she checked through the rest of the passengers. Sven grinned a goodbye. I thought the guy looked just like a shark at this point, as I felt my gander rising for more than the first time on this trip.

Eventually we came to the end of boarding and I was there by the desk waiting. "Air Morocco have issued you a boarding pass, Sir, but they haven't paid for the flight. There's a payment system in these cases where connections are missed and I'm sorry but you can't board because they haven't paid for the flight."

After a minor tantrum and some self-important stomping up and down at the desk as I watched the staff close the gate and pack up their stuff, I knew that I wasn't going home on this flight either. The mist left me after a while. It became clear that the obvious thing to do was to buy another ticket. I could claim the cost. Let's do it. To cut a long story short, the only daily flight to Malaga had recently departed that morning and the next one was tomorrow! Well, another airport night out, another stupidly early rising, and I do eventually make it home two days later than a forty-five-minute flight that I never took. Never take anything to do with flying for granted.

I think my friends think that I am an impatient man, and I know that I can seem short-tempered on occasion. I can't suffer a fool and I don't like sweaty, tattooed men without shirts in my bar, in summer. But I am a good listener, a great secret keeper and a storyteller. I have seen the world in many of its guises and a lot of the people who inhabit it. I can tell you categorically that anyone that travels the world by jet plane for a living has to be a deeply patient person, or you would never get anywhere. Maybe, one day, I will write a book about my other life as an airport transient: "Musings from Terminal 4."

It is 5.00 a.m. local time, still dark outside and I awake as I feel the Boeing 747 change gear below me. We have switched to descent mode, the engines changing note, the balance of the aircraft changing slightly, previously hidden lowlights now subtly lighting the cabin around me, I can feel us begin to turn downwards, at an angle greater than the curvature of the earth which had been our previous trajectory this long night, now passed. The cabin crew are emerging from wherever it is that they go, the mood in the cabin changing from slumber time to breakfast time.

I am on a British Airways flight from London Heathrow to Sao Paulo, Brazil. I am on a mission and I am travelling alone. At thirty years of age and with the wonders of cheap flying years ahead of us, I am something of a big dog these days. I say that not in a big-headed sense, I mean that in those days, business class for long haul flights of a work nature was considered essential. After all, how was a man expected to get to Chile, overnight to the other side of the world and then go straight to work upon landing in Santiago de Chile at seven bleedin' a.m.?? Funnily enough I've been to Chile fifty times at least and I probably flew business class about twice! Bucket seat, sleep for twelve hours, arrive, clear customs and have a fag. Collected or taxi to first destination. Either way, work first, rest later.

I must make another note here. On these birds, thirty years ago, you could have a smoke. In fact, if you were seated in the smoking area, you could smoke yourself to death on a fifteen-hour flight to Chile. The last three rows from the tail of the plane, next to the bulkheads at the back, were usually designated as the smoking zone. I would always have a seat here. Vodka and tonic or some wine (to relieve my nerves and to help me to sleep, obviously) and four packs of Benson and Hedges would generally see me through a long flight. I always thought it odd indeed that the guys sitting in the fourth row from the back were just getting smoked out there. I'm Puffing Billy behind them and I am happy as Larry. Nowadays, it doesn't bother me one bit that you can't light up in the air and I think those that do are selfish morons that deserve to be flayed. Not being able to find a place to have a smoke in an airport, however, is a very different story indeed. See later book "Musings from Terminal 4".

Another great flight I remember was SAA Airlines out of Johannesburg to London Heathrow, some twenty-five year ago. We were on the tarmac, in the queue to hit the runway and take the bird home. It is a night flight and I am in seat 54B at the very back of the Jumbo, toilet to my right and a very scared looking steward, a boy really, just behind me strapped into his jump seat and alone as we prepared for take-off. I've never been afraid of flying but this was nerve-wracking. You see, this was a night flight and we can't take off. There is a huge electrical storm all around us. Forks of lightning hit the earth in the distance as I marvel at the theatre through my porthole to my side. Thunder rents the air and Nature gives us all her juice as our three-hundred tonne man-made bird is battered on the ground, sheets of driving rain now peppering the flimsy fuselage all around us. The captain turns on the intercom; they're so reassuring these boys (and girls); I am sure that a big part of their job is to develop a smooth and calming voice, to create a personality that you believe in; our guides, our leaders. A bit like a doctor with a good bedside manner.

"Ladies and gentlemen," he begins. "This is a major storm and it appears to last all the way up to and over The Congo. That's three hours flying time from here. However, the storm is worse over Jo'Burg because of the quantity of metal in the ground in this part of the world and the fact that we are high above sea level." Everyone is all ears as he goes on, "We've been in touch with the tower and we're going to give it a go, as it's only going to get worse. I advise everyone to remain in their seats with their seatbelts on. It's going to be bumpy, I'm afraid, so there will be no bar service or food until further notice."

"Well," I think. "Let's give it a go," as I glance to my right to meet the gaze of the boy-steward almost next to me and just behind me. He doesn't look happy as we taxi out to the runway and then, on, on, on, that surge of power and then the feeling of weightlessness and in this case a degree of helplessness, as we leave terra firma and begin battle with Mrs. Angry up in the heavens before us. I am suddenly and thankfully mindful of being strapped into our paper dart as we climb and enter the storm proper. The aircraft is like a rag doll and we are tossed and blown and flung all over the night skies, a palpable sense of foreboding pervades my cabin section of perhaps two hundred people. There is no talking, but the cabin is far from silent. Perhaps as frightening as the storm, I hear sobs and screams, prayers are uttered, and babies scream. It is merciless.

I turn to my steward, I nod. He acknowledges me. I make the universal sign for a drink and I wink at him reassuringly. There's nobody but us. We are in a relationship that the other five hundred passengers can't comprehend. "What can I get you Sir?" he mouths above the mother of all dins going around us.

"Vodka and Tonic, please," I mime back. With two-foot slack of seat belt and with a job to do that had previously looked toasted, my man gave me a personal five-hour bar service that remains unrivalled to this day. I am certain that I was the only person on that plane to get a drink until we hit the shores of northern Africa, four hours from home. My man's smile on receiving his tip on landing safely, was worth a thousand journeys like that one.

My Bird to Brazil shifts down another gear and I glance around me. I am in British Airways club class. Unlike today's modern pod-type individual seating found in most business class cabins, I am seated facing forward and next to a fellow passenger. I have my TV screen and my space, some nooks and crannies to stow my stuff and there's even a lightweight screen that I can put up between us if I want to be extra private. We haven't spoken a word to each other, not even on boarding.

As the crew busy themselves around us, serving up breakfast and taking care of passengers' needs, without warning, there is a terrific BANG! The aircraft jolts disturbingly at the same time as the far starboard engine explodes in flames, in clear view to my right. We veer alarmingly to port and I frantically watch the engine management systems kick-in, and the flames quickly extinguished, streamers of smoke and oil the only evidence of a serious engine shut down. I feel the pilot at the controls, I can sense him on the rudders, struggling with the pitch and roll, the yaw of his beast. We right ourselves and calm resumes.

Our captain reassures us over the intercom. "Ladies and gentlemen. Captain Morris here again. No doubt, you've seen and felt the incident that just occurred. Please remain calm. This is a Boeing 747-800 series and it's the safest aircraft in the world today. Starboard number one engine has gone down, but we are in no danger. We are approximately one hour from Sao Paulo and we are descending at a rate of four hundred and thirty knots. ETA on the ground in one hour. Crew, that is landing in one hour, one hour."

I turn to my breakfast tray and I try to put some sort of order into my sausage and omelette breakfast, now "Á l'Orange" flooded with my morning aperitif.

BANG! Bugger me. Only my seat belt stops me from hitting the roof as we dive off to port again, this time on much more of a yaw than previously. I am hanging on for dear life as the skipper tries to rein-in this out-of-control fairground ride. I am on a giant albatross as we swoop left and down towards the earth. Bizarrely, as we yaw groundward at a forty-five-degree angle, I can see lights below us through the cabin windows, on the far side, opposite me. I do not find this comforting in any way.

I feel us pulling up, our tilt angle in the cabin now coming back to normal, some normality resuming, and I look to starboard, and I see engine number two now shut down, still smoking and now a brother to his compadre on the same wing. ON THE SAME WING! Jesus help me, I think as El Capitán clicks his cabin mike to "ON".

"Ladies and gentlemen," his voice at once commanding, calming, soothing but authoritative. "My apologies for that. In forty years of flying, I have never experienced two engine-outs. But please don't worry. With our current airspeed and the descent angle we have at twenty-nine degrees to the horizon, we have enough lift, even if the other two engines go, to glide home. Stay seated. Seat belts on. Crew prepare for landing; I say crew, prepare for landing."

I am in a daze as I watch the screen between me and Mr. No Talking slowly sinking into its mount. The guy leans in. I stare at him like a goldfish as he extends his hand, in which is clearly a business card. I take it as he moves to shake my hand, I accept. "Robert Thompson. Allianz Life Assurance: Do you have time for a chat about a policy?"

F IS FOR FRANCE

We get the call. The director for food, Marks and Spencer, wants to visit our peach and nectarine orchards in the Rhone Valley, southern France. For years, we have been supplying them with some of the finest summer fruits in the world from these parts and we have invested heavily, financially and personally, in our grower base and their farms. To supply M&S with fresh fruit is a pinnacle in any trader's career. Of all the UK retailers I have worked with, M&S and Waitrose were the only ones that I would consider fair. When a retailer puts their name on fresh produce, I am often riled by their arrogance. Most of them, I would consider to be shopkeepers with shelf space. I recall a TV commercial in the eighties where Tasbury's had contracted the star Dudley Moore, to play a roving fruit buyer and in this case, he was in Italy buying Italia seedless grapes. The advert was funny and successful but, in reality, they were only "our grapes" because Tasbury's bought them from us. We were the guys that travelled the world in constant search for innovation. We were the guys on the ground pioneering new varieties, searching for new areas, micro-climates, new production techniques and I could be resentful of supermarkets claiming ownership of product just because they were paying for it.

What work had they done to get to a supply offer, what risks had they taken in buying the land, preparing and planting and then caring and nurturing the plants and trees in readiness for harvest? In the case of the aforementioned two retailers, however, they worked differently. They employed the best staff and they trained them and gave them time to accumulate specialist knowledge of the fruit and vegetables they were charged with buying. This applied to both commercial and technical personnel and I cannot ever recall a time or a visit when they were anything but brilliant at their jobs.

Mike Taylor, M&S Director of Food. A very big cheese indeed. He had agreed to come to Montélimar to commission our very first "ripen at source" packing operation for peaches and nectarines. This was new to the game. The idea being to harvest selected varieties at optimum size and maturity and then to bring the pressure of individual fruit down to a ready-to-eat status using our newly completed pair of ripening chambers before packing them in four or six-pack biodegradable trays and film, and then transporting them by road directly to depot in the UK for onward distribution to the stores. Mike was to make a speech to the owners of the facility, to the growers that contributed to the supply program, local investors and various dignitaries that had supported the project. It was a nervous time as I prepared for the visit. A lectern was purchased from where Mr. Taylor would give his speech. The speech itself was translated into French and food and refreshments were ordered for the day. This was my baby and I was in charge of all organisation, including flights for the clients from London to Lyons and then collection and delivery to their hotel on the day prior to the speech.

In fact, the day went smoothly; Mike did make his speech in
French, despite not being a French speaker – I had the original English
version, translated into French and then inserted into the program
notes for guests on the day – He was commanding and authoritative
as we progressed from speeches to the tour of the facilities and then on
to champagne and canapés in the sunny yard. What struck me most,
however, were the events that took place on the preceding day. I knew
Mike Taylor only by reputation at this point. Indeed, he had worked as
a young man for the same company that I worked for: Saphir Produce,
quickly making his name as an English fruit specialist and going on
to be head-hunted for the M&S fruit department and then upwards
to take control of the food division; probably M&S's most successful
area of business ever. Mike had his own office in Baker Street, with an
imposing desk and dining furniture, several large couches to provide
comfortable seating for visitors and a well-stocked bar. There was even
a butler on call for anything that the director or his guests would need.
I remember well, a couple of years after this visit, an invitation to
dine in the Marks and Spencer board dining room, on the top floor
of Baker Street. All of us involved in French stone fruit supply from
my firm were to be there for luncheon with the board and it did not
disappoint. Full silver service was the order of the day and each of
the diners, perhaps twelve in all, had a personal, individual waiter.
I have dined in some of the world's best restaurants but this would
surpass anything before or after. Pierre Deranger, the owner of the
French peach company, NectoFruits, a scruffy-looking individual with
a hippy-like dress sense and a laisse faire attitude to every aspect of
human life except for growing peaches (which he more than made up
for first appearances) remarked on a magnificent painting, dominating

the dining table from the wall at the far end of the room. "Très bien!" opined Pierre, gesticulating towards the painting. "Ça c'est la meilleure copie d'un original Monet que j'ai jamais vu - 'Ow you say ? Ze best copy of un Monet original zat I 'av ever seen!"

In typical under-stated M&S fashion, Mr. Taylor, who was seated alongside Monsieur Deranger, replied, courteously and professionally, "Lovely to have you here with us Pierre. It's an honour to have the House of Necto here at Baker Street, I hope that you are enjoying your lunch." He said in his unmistakeable low and gravelly voice. "That is in fact the original painting. Magnificent isn't it?"

I am on the road early with my boss. On the road from Montelimar to Lyons airport to pick up our guests. I am driving and it is an S-Class Mercedes, a V8 S-500 to be precise; a vehicle that I have hired for this visit and a car that I think is appropriate for the status of the clients we will be entertaining over the next couple of days. Beside me in the front passenger seat is Gordon Winterbottom, newly installed managing director of my firm. The plan is that Gordon's role is to square off to Mike Taylor throughout the trip and mine is to manage the young superstar buyer that Mike is mentoring. Their flight is on time and soon we are shaking hands in arrivals and heading out to the parking area to begin our 200-kilometre drive south to the hotel that we have booked for the next couple of nights. Despite it being June, the weather is awful; torrential rain and high winds lash us as I find the right junction and motorway toll entrance and I accelerate smoothly to begin our journey south.

Robin, the buyer, is now in the front seat beside me, I can see Mr. Taylor in my rear-view mirror, behind me on the right and my boss is tucked out of view, directly behind my seat. There is a constant verbal stream from Robert; a non-stop commentary about Necto, the innovations we have made, the investment put into the business, the new ripening chambers and pre-packing facility, he goes on and on until I silence him with a motion of my hand. There's trouble ahead on the autoroute. In the filthy conditions, we are still making good progress, well within the car's limits and notwithstanding the heavy rain outside, we are making a healthy 80 miles an hour: safe in our cocoon, alert and aware of traffic at all times, I can just overhear the two VIP's in the back chatting softly to one another as Robin, for once, stops talking I indicate ahead to him. We are coming up to a line of heavy trucks in the lane inside of us, keeping a safe distance from the cars in front, we begin the execute an every-day overtaking move. 500 yards, 400yards.

"BOLLOCKS!" I shout to myself in my mind, as I clearly see the end of a juggernaut's exhaust pipe, on the cab itself not the trailer of course. It is rattling itself to death and I can see that it will soon be heading down the motorway on a lethal trajectory to those following. I don't want to scare my passengers but I have no option but to shout, "BRACE!" as the object does indeed detach itself from the engine of the truck. Two hundred yards, one hundred yards, the thing, about two-feet long and cylindrical metal, bounces in the road and launches into a high downward-curving arc on a direct path to impact the front of our vehicle. I have zero option but to judge the flight and I make an instant decision. I boot the car towards the incoming missile; my best chance was to hit the exhaust with the lower front of the Mercedes; smack in the middle to try to avoid wheel impact and to survive. If I'd stayed where we were, it's coming through the windscreen.

SMASH, we're hit big time but it's all good. I swear I have trapped it, right underneath the number plate sideways on. Hit us, huge bang, two clatters as it went straight under the car and gone! I find a stop: A check, a calm-down and a coffee and we are back on the road. I sense that our clients are happy to be alive but that they want this journey from hell to end ASAP.

We get back on the autoroute and resume a smooth rhythm. This car is the perfect mode of transport for big businessmen and, Robin soon gets chirpy again, picking up effortlessly his non-stop chatter about the business and the days ahead. We hit heavy rain and traffic speed is down to forty, it's dangerous. My co-pilot doesn't care and there is now a monopoly of one person in the conversation in the car as I am forced to slow again as I drive into the intensified storm ahead. This is bad. I cannot see more than twenty feet as I bring the car to a crawl, desperate for something terrible not to happen to us from front or rear. "Necto this, Necto that, stone fruit category this, margins up, cost chain shortened, blah, beautiful orchards, blah, unique harvesting method..." he continues as we three, in a state of near-terror stare out of the impossible-to-see-out-of-windows-because-of-the-rain.

The director screams....

"FER FUCK'S SAKE ROBIN, SHUT THE FUCK UP AND LET THE LAD DRIVE!"

In silence and as the rain subsides, we arrive at our country hotel. I am in familiar surroundings and as the sun begins to shine, I whoosh the Merc into the gravel front drive and into parking area, well off the road and in amongst pine trees and well-kept gardens. We park and I walk around and open the rear passenger door. A very, very direct look in my eye, "Well driven lad," in tones like an aggregate in treacle. He turned away and marched purposefully away from me and into the entrance to the hotel. Unruffled and smooth in his blazer, tie and summer slacks. Marks and Spencer Divisional Director. On duty quintessentially English.

That story is amongst many of the great memories of Mike Taylor that I hold dear. I would go on to have more adventures with him and he was a brilliant man (albeit very scary to me at that time!). I ended up working with him at Keeling's in Ireland; he was on their board of directors as an advisor and I saw him again but from the other side. He was incredibly kind to me and I liked him very much.

He died a few years ago and I think that the whole fruit world mourned.

F IS FOR FEAR AND FLASHBACKS!

Years and years ago, it was a 3.00 a.m. wake-up for a Heathrow flight to South Africa when He first felt the paralysing fear that could destroy him, should he be in-country and on a mission. The ball of pain and anxiety in the pit of his stomach prevented sleep and the alarm, when it came, had been expected for some hours. On this occasion, he would fail to make the flight, a lame excuse about a tree blocking his route from home would have to suffice and it was 24 hours before he was able to bring himself together and to make the flight and begin his mission.

Unacceptable as this clearly was, it was far from being the last time that he would experience this paralysis; the fear of starting a mission would never leave him. Even worse, he knew that fear and all its manifestations could kill him, and others, in the field. There was no room for hesitation or doubt in the areas of conflict and situations that he would find himself in. Trust and reliance on his training and handlers gave him the solution: the knowledge that EVERYONE has this fear and the acceptance that fear is a tool to be used – recognise it, embrace it, suck it down and turn it into focus, into commitment, into EXCELLENCE in what you do. This is a hard skill to learn and involves very serious simulated and real potential situation training activities to master it. But, once mastered, it is an incredible advantage in pressurised situations; repetition of critical tasks, weapons maintenance, survival, camouflage and concealment, escape strategies… these are all essential activities, but under the most severe pressure of all, can you cope with the fear? Can you breathe that in and turn it to your advantage? Can you execute the mission without letting the fear cripple you and leave you vulnerable and exposed to danger?

As a fifteen-year-old boy, live ammunition training with the Army Junior Leaders at their barracks in Folkestone in Kent was an early exposure to fear. Barbed wire, mud and lots of it, pain and endurance, all under live fire, red-hot lead inches above his head as He fought the fear. He had completed intensive weapons training that week, graduating as a marksman – that is five rounds from one hundred yards to hit the target within a radius of a two pence piece – with the Lee Enfield bolt action .303 rifle, no telescopic sight. Standard issue to the British army from the mid-1800s until 1957. In fact, a sniper variant of this rifle was still in use into the 1990s, which makes it the second-longest serving military bolt-action rifle in official service.

He also trained extensively on the Lee Enfield's replacement, the L1A1 self-loading rifle, also known as the SLR. Standing in a firing pit, head, arms and shoulders above ground, elbows in the gravel, rifle in automatic firing mode. This weapon is a beast. Recoil is huge and although it is expected, it is still a shock. It will slam backwards, upwards and sideways all at the same time and it packs a hell of a punch using the NATO 7.62mm round. He quickly became an expert with these tools and many more One remarkable thing standing out above all, and the one thing that marked Him as special against other trainees – He had a resting heart rate of less than fifty beats per minute and an uncanny ability to bring his BPM down to His resting rate in seconds, regardless of how challenging the mental or physical tasks that were put in front of Him.

Soon after these early discoveries, His training schedule and levels of difficulty and pressure were ramped up several notches: Street and jungle warfare, Sniper School at Bisley, psychological training, fast jets and helicopters, torture resistance, concealment and escape, all of these became second nature to him. He was to become the archetypal agent. Highly efficient, deadly, silent and with seemingly no conscience, He had learned early on all about fear and how to use it as a weapon, forever able to go back to his training to find the way through. Whatever the situation.

G IS FOR GUATEMALA

Today has been one of the best days of my 37 years and counting in the international fruit industry. I could have been on Discovery Channel or perhaps Lonely Planet - I've been privileged to see some amazing farms all over the world, but today, I've seen something incredibly special: Tropical fruit farming on the border of Mexico on a farm of some 6,500 hectares; that's around 13,000 soccer pitches!

I won't tell you what fruits this producer grows - please have a go at identifying them if you can - but I have seen a fabulous mix of maize, rubber, hardwood, coffee and several established fruits alongside some new stuff that we are sure to develop. I woke this morning with my usual sense of nervous anticipation and excitement, knowing that I was going to look at fresh ground, so to speak. I was expecting a six-hour drive on crappy roads; pretty normal for me, so no problems expected, but no. My fabulous host (I won't name him or his business for professional reasons) picked me up punctually and then drove us to the airport to board his private plane, piloted by his personal pilot, Luis, another new "life friend" I have made.

We flew up and away, directly past El Fuego, one of Guatemala's active volcanos, and then on to Coatepeque on the border with Mexico and in plain sight of the Pacific Ocean. (Just a note here, the plan was to fly in his helicopter but it was out of service!)

My job today was not to audit the farm and packhouse for British retailers or to look at procedures and protocols or potential risks, it was to assess who they are, what they do and how they do it, and I mean every aspect of what they do; an absolute honour and privilege for me. I can tell you that you may well see some of these products for sale near you in the near future and if I can assist and advise in any way at all in this process of learning and continual improvement, then I will be very proud indeed.

So, Guatemala...beautiful country, beautiful people, marvellous agriculture and I sure am coming back as soon as I can!

I was 54 years old when I wrote the above. My first visit to Guatemala and an unforgettable trip. First impressions of Guatemala City are very positive and I find it easy to make friends in and around my hotel, both with the staff and clients and with owners and patrons of some good local bars. I had been told that this country can be dangerous and I did note on my first farm visit, the 'protection' that always seemed to be around my growers, my hosts. There were always guys with guns around. Now, I have never really been nervous about my immediate environment wherever I found myself in the world. I have come close once or twice to a sticky end, I will admit, but my attitude has always been firmly focused on the earth, the soil, the environment, Mother Nature, the trees, the fruit, the grower, the chain. I never once let politics, personal opinions or local activities divert me from my primary purpose: to do my best to get the most from the production, working hand-in-hand with the environment as I see it in order to get that fresh product to market in the most efficient way possible. Doesn´t always run smoothly.

I am still in Guatemala. I have two farms to assess and audit today. The farmers are cousins, they both grow tropical fruits and they both want to export to one of the key markets in the world: my market. I work diligently for a long morning on Farm One. He´s good, he´s taken his time to call in external consultants, the fruit location, the care of the soil, the land, his risk assessment and controls are all first class. I pass him to a good standard and we shake hands as I am collected and driven to my next appointment. I spend all that afternoon and evening assessing a similar farm. Only, it´s not good. I see holes in their systems, I don´t fall in love with the orchards, I am worried about the safety and the quality of the fruit and I have a problem that needs addressing. That evening, I am due to cross the border into Mexico, to begin the next leg of a long trip. I must address the situation and I am standing with the grower and his team as my time is running out. I say directly, as I always do, one way or another, "I´m sorry Señor Gonzalez, there are too many unacceptable issues here for me to pass your farm today. Let´s identify exactly what needs doing over the next few weeks and I will come back to reassess you."

Señor Gonzalez stares at me expressionlessly. He turns to one of his men, standing with all of us with his fleet of farm pick-ups, his bodyguards and his commercial and technical aides. An AK47, commonly known as a Kalashnikov, appears in his hand, he cocks the gun and he waves it, kind of directly but indirectly in my direction. "I think you had better think again, Señor Askham."

I am not intimidated at all. I look at El Señor waving his gun around and I know I that I could disarm him in a second and put him and his team in immediate mortal danger. I have encountered situations far more threatening than this one, in my training from my early years and subsequently in real life. Fear, for me, is a welcome, almost comfortable feeling, a tool to be used to create commitment and excellence. I will not back down and after fifteen minutes of diplomatic but firm negotiations, we agree that the farm has failed its assessment and that I will review their improvement actions over the next three months.

I felt good that night as I crossed the border into Mexico. I had assessed and passed all the farms but one, on this trip remit. Nobody gets El Señor Askham to change his mind. Integrity, openness and honesty. Hard work and my best efforts for the land and the fruit. These are my mantras.

G IS FOR GOLF!

Golf games in business are marvellous things. Where else would you be able to get an uninterrupted meeting with your client, whilst sharing a mutual passion and doing business?

Chile, Campo de Golf Los Leones in the centre of Santiago de Chile. A city of six million people, the heart of which is full of skyscrapers and a Central Business District that is the envy of many a modern world city. I am playing against Jason Farringdon-Smythe, the Buying Director of Safeway supermarkets. On the line is a grand prize of one American dollar. In reality, the prize is an annual ten-million-dollar supply of fresh fruit from our growers in Chile to the stores of Safeway in the UK. I am early and I search out my caddy for the day, eager to get on the course and get our match started. My caddy is local; a stout Chilean chap called Nelson, no doubt because he possessed just the one arm!

I have met Jason before and he is a character. We have a shared love of motorcycling, golf and smoking. I consider myself to be a professional smoker, I can make a roll up cigarette one-handed, in the dark, in a canoe on rapids. Jason on the other hand is a quintessential

I-smoke-everything kind of guy. During our round, I watch him smoke his pipe (he's a great pipe-lover), billowing great clouds of aromatic smoke around, tucking into some rough smelling Belgian fags and of course, sampling several of my rollies as we battle our way around the golf course. With the help of my man, Nelson, I produce my finest ever round of golf and we arrive at the eighteenth tee, all square, an imposing par five ahead of us. Only one man can win the dollar, and the honour of course, as we tee off. My drive is long but off the fairway, right and under the branches of a young tree, the green still some 265 yards away. Jason is on the fairway and looking good. I look to Nelson, my one-armed caddy, for guidance.

"Driver," is all he says as I look at my ball sitting up nicely in the light rough under the tree. I have never hit a driver "off the deck." I strike it well and I hop, skip and jump out of the rough, Sergio García style, in order to track my low-flying ball as it scythes right and then straight and comes to a halt on the left-side green fringe, some twenty feet or so to the hole and with a putt for an eagle coming up.

Jason plays. He hits his ball well with a fairway wood and he too makes the front of the green. We stride together up the fairway, comfortable in each other's company and puffing happily on our chosen smokes. We reach the green and Jason is to play first. He putts up the long slope towards the pin. It's good but just short, leaving him a tap-in eighteen-inch putt for his birdie, which he duly makes. I stand over my putt for eagle and send it in towards the hole. It breaks right to left, goes towards the hole and past, settling two and a half feet from the hole on the other side. I mark and walk away a distance to squat down and look at the putt to halve the match and to save paying out on our one US dollar bet.

It was a putt that I feel I would make nine times out of ten. Straight, just inside the right lip, firm hit required. I hit it. My legs buckle at the knees as the ball moves towards dropping in the hole. Jason goes into knee bend mode too and we hear the two caddies, standing respectfully and until now, quietly, behind us, noisily suck in their breath in unison. The putt hits the hole, dips in as if to test the water, but does a perfect 180-degree U-turn around the lip of hole and comes to rest a couple of inches out on the wrong side of in. I can only make par from my two-inch tap-in, thereby giving a win for JFS and, of course, the honour and a whole dollar in his bid for winning.

As I settle our debts in the bar afterwards, I hand Nelson a secret 50-dollar tip and buy him a coke. Jason graciously accepts my crisp one-dollar bill. We shake hands firmly. He wins the dollar. We win the fruit supply deal for the next ten years. Just a game of golf.

In the nineties, the firm that I worked for were big on corporate entertainment. We had an annual golf day at Woburn, one of the UK's premier golf clubs. All the senior trading staff had the opportunity to invite client guests to the golf day and as it turned out, mine was a tough ask. I am just thirty and I am asked to invite and play with Lee Clayton, Marks and Spencer Divisional Director of Food. Lee wasn't a great golfer but he sure was a big-hitter in my world and I was nervous as I pulled into the car park early on the Friday at Woburn. I had never met LC but I knew what he looked like and he was instantly recognisable there in the car park, busy putting his shoes on, boot of his car open and golf bag ready to go. My nerves were worse when I noted that his company car was a spanking new super-charged Jaguar XJR, but I was calm enough to know that the day ahead would be fine. All possible needs would be met. We had a freebie all day, a great meal with after-dinner speakers later and a free bar all day.

We played unspectacularly and made it into the club house in the late afternoon for beers and then a shower and change before the evening kicked off. That morning, I had left home very early. I had checked that I had all the required golf gear and dinner attire. I had my wallet and some loose change and, as is my habit, I had counted exactly how much I was carrying – it was 43 pounds and 50 pence – some notes and a lot of change. I thought at the time that it wasn't a lot of money, but I knew from previous golf days at this venue that I wouldn't need a penny, so I set off and didn't stop for a withdrawal from an ATM.

Dinner was a success. I was on form and I felt a part of the evening. My guest was in his element, the food was superb, the after-dinner speaker, an ex-cricketer called Dermot Reeve, had us in stitches and coffee and choice of digestive were being served.

I felt myself relax, as a great day and evening were coming to a close.

"Gentlemen, cigars?" said a voice next to me and I looked up from my self-satisfied gloating to see a pretty waitress hovering next to my guest and me, proffering a very professional and comprehensive range of cigars from a large display held in her hands. "Hmmm, lovely. I'll take a Romeo and Juliet," Mr. Clayton utters. I am pleased he feels relaxed enough to take the most expensive cigar in the tray and I motion to the cigar sommelier to put it onto my account please, if that was possible. Discreetly, but within earshot of my dining companions and my guest, she says to me, "I'm sorry, Sir, cigars are the only thing that you can't put onto an account today, I can only take cash."

I melt slightly and have to ask in a less than fully confident manner, "No problem. How much do I owe you for the Romeo and Juliet?"

Lee is already lighting up and is savouring his first puff of his Cuban smoke as I search for my wallet and reach into my pocket full of change. "That's forty-three pounds and fifty pence, Sir."

As I unloaded my few notes and two handfuls of the exact amount of change required into her hands, I knew that I had dodged a bullet and I vowed never again to under-estimate how much cash I may need for a day out with a client.

I took a buyer from Tasbury's to a great course in the UK, Walton Heath, for a day's golf. Corporate entertainment, a bit of bonding, forge that close relationship with your client, call it what you will, golf is a great way to do business. On that day, I had a good budget, I was able to invite a couple of friends to make up our four-ball and we arrived in good time and in good spirits for an early tee time. I oversaw the purchase of souvenirs for all of us in the pro-shop, including a nice rain jacket with club logo for the client - a good start for what would hopefully be a "normal" day for him, being entertained at zero cost by his suppliers. Three holes later, we would see what being entertained on expensive golf courses had done to this guy by sycophantic customers, desperate to gain favour with a powerful and influential buyer.

The third hole is a par three of some two hundred yards. Tree-lined and out of bounds on the right, a small target and a one-shot requirement of accuracy and power to reach the target, our high-handicap, but enthusiastic guest, strikes his five-wood well, but right, into the trees and probably lost. We advise him to play a provisional ball in the likelihood of not finding his tee shot. For non-golfers, that means that if and when he fails to find his first ball, at least he has a second one in play, albeit under penalty of one shot for losing his first ball. He declines the provisional and strides purposefully off in the direction of his first wayward shot. Clearly looking in vain for a lost ball, he decides to select a new ball from his bag and to drop it, correctly it has to be said, at shoulder height and facing the flag. He then selects his choice of club in preparation to hit his second shot to the green. Errrr....no, we say. That's a lost ball, out of bounds, Stroke and distance penalty applies. Because you failed to play a second provisional ball from the tee, your only option now is to go back to the tee and to hit another ball as your third shot. Nothing like upsetting your client in the first hour of a day out, but we stood up to his bluster. He was actually pretty angry that we were penalising him. Despite only playing golf for the last two years, he had already notched up rounds of golf on some of the great courses of the world, all paid for by suppliers of course, and not one of them had the cojones to tell him the correct rules to play having lost a ball!

Having breakfasted well in the sumptuous clubhouse, our names had been announced through the Club's tannoy system and we are now stood on the first tee at the majestic Stellenbosch Golf Club in RSA, eager to tee it up and strike our drives down and onto the first fairway, sun-drenched and glorious, snaking away in front of us. We are a fourball: myself, my good friend, Colin, MD of a major UK fruit importer, his pal Dave, a used car specialist from London, and a British supermarket fruit buyer called Clive Buntley. Today we have a starter, a short dark-skinned Indian gentleman. His job is to ensure that we understand the local rules and etiquette of this prestigious club and that we keep up with play. He looks us all up and down, short but stern and authoritative, I can see him noting our attire. I am in long lightweight slacks, polo shirt tucked in with belt, glove and hat, newly purchased from the club's pro shop and all gleaming in the early sunshine. Colin is dressed similarly, as is Dave but in tailored shorts. Our guest is in polo shirt and shorts, smart but his shirt is outside of his shorts, possibly a nod to more modern fashion trends, and certainly a little different from us three veterans.

"Keep it on the fairway, stay up with play or wave players through, if necessary," our starter guy gives us no-nonsense instruction in his clipped South African accent. "Rake the bunkers and repair your divots," he goes on. He turns to glare at Clive, continuing to address all four of us, "Enjoy your round, gentlemen," he concludes, jabbing his index finger directly at our buyer and turning smartly to begin his walk back up to the clubhouse, he finishes, "AND YOU CAN TUCK YOUR SHIRT IN!"

H IS FOR HELICOPTERS

"Twenty years from now you will be more disappointed by the things you didn't do than by the ones you did do."
H. Jackson Brown Jr.

Guayaquil, Ecuador, late summer of 1995. I am on a mission to meet and form new partnerships with mango farmers in Ecuador. Mango consumption is rising and we need new growers, new supplying countries and I am pleased to get to Quito, to be able to leave the aircraft and the airport and to have a smoke before catching my bird for the last leg of a long journey to Guayaquil. I arrive in the middle of the night into the city. I am tired and, on first impressions, a little disappointed with my lodgings for the next two weeks. The hotel is clearly a substantial and historical edifice; it is well positioned but it is shabby and in need of an upgrade. I sleep soundly until breakfast and I make my way down to the dining rooms.

It is immediately clear that my initial disappointment in my hotel is misguided. All the lobby areas and dining rooms, and up the first two floors too, are full of beautiful young women in various states of dress / undress. I amble into the breakfast restaurant and I have some difficulty in getting a table, such is the volume of girls competing for space. There are groups of people scattered everywhere, an eclectic mixture of nubile females cramming all available space. I make an enquiry of my waiter as to what is going on here in downtown Guayaquil and it transpires that for the next five days, my hotel is the focal point for the finals of the Miss Ecuador competition. How rubbish. Some of my missions are SO brutal, I think, as I am met and collected for my first day on the ground in another of my favourite countries to be.

That day proves to be most interesting as I am guided around what is effectively a secret mango farm, and it is great. A five-hundred-hectare plantation of very acceptable varieties and high-quality production. What is cool however is that the mango farm is totally secluded by the surrounding farm of five thousand hectares of cacao, better known as cocoa to us English speakers and what is of course, the fundamental ingredient in making chocolate. These guys give me a cocoa lesson that day – they have the holy grail of cocoa beans, the unique variety that the best chocolatiers in the world queue up to buy, but my hosts have a secret. They have pioneered a way for the plants to produce high yields and year-round production that match the yields of the other main cocoa plant of lesser quality.

I spend a week in this area, and I cover half a dozen mango farms. A whole new supply window is coming together for me and for our clients. Going forwards, we will be able to supply fresh mangos into the European marketplace in November and December, just in front of the established Peruvian season and ensure continuity of supply.

As I reach the end of my first week on the ground, my audits and farm visit summaries are more or less up to date and I begin to get that feeling of job satisfaction that is such a great sensation in my world. I have made my contribution to the mango supply world and I have identified and communicated all the issues I have found on the farms to the farmers and their teams and to the people that are responsible for providing me with my employment, my goals and my reason for being. There is however, one more surprise in store for me in Ecuador. I am informed that that night, I would be flying across the border to Peru for one final farm visit. I am cool with this new and unexpected plan: it was not the first time that my itinerary has been changed mid-trip and it sure wouldn't be the last, I reason. I receive basic details of that evening's jaunt and I head up to my room to get some sleep as I now know that I am to be collected early that evening and that the flight would be a night flight.

It is January 1995 and as always, I have done my research on the countries that I am visiting. I always check on certain key things; the political climate and any civil unrest, GDP data, population and social demographics, key natural resources, water quality and availability and so on. And I always do my research on the local wine!

Studying wine production in whichever part of the Earth I found myself in, gave me one or two advantages. Firstly, I would generally know that if good wine was available in the area I was visiting, then good fresh fruit production would also be highly likely. Secondly, as a young world fruit traveller, and despite my intensive training in my 'extracurricular' role for Her Majesty's Government, I could be nervous company, especially at dinner with owners of large-scale agribusinesses, very often much older and much smarter than I was then. I was not always a great conversationalist and in my early career, I often felt my age and lack of worldly experience could expose me in key situations such as dinner with business owners. But by studying local wine, vineyards, grape varieties and soil / climate types, I was now armed with serious "dinner table knowledge." Knowledge that empowered me and enabled me to overcome difficult situations. To take this to another level, some years later, I was on an important trip to the Loire Valley in France, my task to accompany a VIP from Tasbury's supermarket on his mission, as director of food, to meet a large group of influential apple growers who were key suppliers to the Tasbury's apple business. To give you an idea of the scale of this business, I was the commercial account manager for one of several fruit suppliers to this chain and we had pioneered not just the redevelopment of this retailers apple business by bringing a refocus on the inherent qualities of varieties that were becoming less fashionable such as Golden Delicious or Granny Smith, we also proposed and backed new production of traditional varieties such as Egremont Russet, Worcester Pearmaine and a good old English Bramley. We were also, of course, heavily involved in the newer apple types coming onto the scene at that time, varieties such as Gala and Royal Gala, Fuji and the now universally known, Pink Lady. In any given week, I would move around fifty full trucks of apples to one UK retailer – twenty-six pallets of fruit per truck, fifty trucks… that is in the region of seven MILLION apples. Per week!

My job on these types of trips would be a multi-role, in that I would be the client's PA, his diary scheduler, liaison officer for all visits, dinner and event or farm / packhouse visit planner and of course, his constant companion. The client in this case, was a very distinguished gentleman called Ian Mitchell. In my research on him prior to the trip, I was delighted to discover that amongst his many and significant business achievements, he was an accomplished sommelier and Master of French wine. I had no hesitation in passing on this information to my counterpart in France who had the responsibility of organising a grand dinner in honour of their auspicious English visitor, but I did not expect what came to pass on that special evening.

Our French hosts had surpassed themselves with the dinner – haute cuisine of the highest quality and variety. Six courses, all accompanied by some of the finest wines that the most famous viniculture in the world could produce. There was Chablis, Sauterne, Burgundy and Bordeaux. There were wines from The Loire and Languedoc, Alsace and The Rhone, each a masterpiece of the art of winemaking and of course each one was perfectly matched to the food in each course. Whilst I expected that wine would be a central part of dinner, especially given that we now knew that our VIP guest had earned the right to be called a Master-of-Wine, I had not grasped that my hosts would expect Mr. Mitchell to identify each wine as it was served. If you want to impress people, do what IM did next! From the first wine to the last and over a three-hour dinner, my guest not only easily identified each one by variety or "sippage" if it was a blend, he also correctly and without seeing a single label of a single bottle, named the year of the wine, the producer and, remarkably and in every case, he spoke eloquently and at length about the actual producers of each wine. He knew them all personally, and their particular and very individual "terroirs" (that is to say the exact location, orientation, soil and climate types of each vineyard) that gave the wines their exalted status. We certainly cemented our Tassbury's apple supply contract on that visit.

Anyway, I have moved away from Ecuador and my night mission to Peru, so I'm going to finish that story now.

I am collected at midnight from my downtown hotel. I know from my pre-trip research and from world news that Ecuador is currently in conflict with Peru at this time (later it will become known as the Cenepa War 26 January – 28 February 1995). I am accustomed to visiting military air bases in the dead of night but still, in my civilian role I wasn't expecting this lift to the base north of the city in a convoy of armoured cars, and to find myself boarding what was clearly a heavily armed machine of war - a Gazelle helicopter in full combat mode - a camouflaged and missile-carrying gunship, ready for one specific and top secret job: to get me over the Cordillera del Cóndor, a range of mountains that was the centre of the area of military dispute and conflict, and onto the mango farm on the other side. I have been shot at many times before, but to be taking hostile fire from large calibre weapons in the air in a lightweight attack helicopter in the pitch black of night takes one's breath away, and this was something else. If you can imagine fifty calibre rounds (that's a full half inch of white-hot solid projectile travelling at 2,700 feet per second) thumping into the aircraft's fuselage and even pinging around the interior… death by ricocheted bullet had not been high up on my list of imaginary ways to die until this point in my life. Strangely, my biggest fear at this time, was not just the terror of taking fire. No, my nightmare realisation was that here I was, caught up in a war, dressed as a civilian in a military aircraft. I knew that even if we survived, if we made it to ground, here

I was wearing my every day working get-up of field boots, thorn-proof slacks and bush coat, topped with my Panama hat as per usual, the strong likelihood was that we would be taken prisoner and that I would be summarily tried and then shot as a spy. How ironic that I might die in a war zone, on civilian duty!

We did survive and amazingly I was able to inspect the farm and give it a big green light to supply. Slightly perturbed going in, I was much more relaxed coming out. It was a three-day journey 'home' through the jungle, across ravines and gorges via rope bridges and rickety crossings. Long treks and short nights. But, as I always say to my daughters about this crazy, enormous and yet tiny world of ours: You're never more than three days and three plane rides from home! That's the fruit business sometimes and South America all of the time!

I have had many other helicopter experiences in my life apart from this story of guts and gunships, but most were because of business needs in the sense of customer care or more commonly known as corporate entertainment.

One was a day out to watch the British Grand Prix at Silverstone. A pre-dawn start, a long drive to a field in Northamptonshire and a breakfast of Champagne and bacon sandwiches followed by a dash to our four-man chopper. As a twenty-eight-year-old commercial manager of a successful supermarket fruit supply business, I had begun to enjoy the benefits that come with being good at one's job. I had a great salary, a beautiful car, frequent global travel and regular exposure to some of the great characters in our business; men and women with power and charisma, people that were accomplished in their fields and able to command immediate respect as soon as they uttered a word. I admired these characters enormously, but I felt in awe of them so much. If anything, they hindered my upward progress in the industry for a while. I felt shy, inadequate and unworthy in their presence because I was never really trained in a business sense. Although mentally and physically, I could be nerveless, ruthless and highly efficient in the other world, I did feel powerless on occasion in the business world. Ultimately, I couldn´t shoot a businessman in cold blood as a response could I? Even though I often wished that I could! That was until one of the great epiphanies in my career occurred two years or so before the grand prix experience.

I was working for one of the fastest growing fruit companies in the UK. The firm was called McLeod McCombe and it was owned and managed by a husband-and-wife team – Norman and Jackie. I have to say that these two were probably the greatest influence on my career. Easy to say in hindsight, hard to comprehend the magnitude of their care for me at the time. Jackie and I are in London, we have stayed the night at the family apartment in town and we are attending a huge gala dinner hosted by Capespan, easily the biggest fresh fruit exporting company out of South Africa following the deregulation of the South African fruit industry in 1992 and the business that emerged as the powerhouse after the demise of the old Deciduous Fruit Board (The DFB); responsible for annual global exports of fresh fruit approaching two hundred million cartons per year. They ran two major brands from this era you may recall: Outspan for Citrus and Cape for all other deciduous fruits.

That morning over breakfast, I had confessed to my boss, Jackie, how inadequate I felt when in the company of industry players and leaders, how under prepared I always felt and that my lack of "worldly experience" and knowledge of current affairs was a burden I struggled to deal with. She gave me one of the greatest pieces of advice I've had.

"Steve, every Sunday morning, get up and go and buy a copy of the Sunday Times. Sit down and read it cover to cover. That'll set you up for whatever comes your way each week."

That evening, as we sat at the top table, dignitaries included Leon Kruger, the Chairman of Capespan, a distinguished gentleman and a great business leader. Alongside him, sat Louis Kriel, dynamic, handsome and charismatic general manager of the organisation. My familiar feelings of low self-esteem in exalted company returned, although I did feel bolstered by Jackie's pep talk that morning and was eager to follow her advice at the earliest opportunity. Jackie could sense that I was having difficulties in keeping up a conversation with the other guests on our table, even though it was clear that she was fully occupied in dealing with the relentless attentions of young Mr. Kriel, who clearly knew Jackie well having seen her company become established as possibly the biggest panellist or receiver of their fruit over the last few years. To me, LK was flirting with Jackie and had been since greetings were exchanged a couple of hours earlier. He appeared to be drinking heavily too, even though he was due to make the biggest speech of the night in a short while.

Jackie simply told me to watch and listen to what Louis was doing and I duly noted that this remarkable man was able to hold onto four different conversations at once. He was able to focus on the first speech, now beginning on the stage behind us, and throughout all of this, without once reducing the level of his charm offensive on my boss, he was writing occasional words on a small piece of paper in front of him.

The next speaker was up: a brilliant after-dinner speaker paid to entertain us. This unknown guy had held three extraordinary positions in his working life, as a paratrooper in the Parachute Regiment, a Trappist monk and a mental care nurse and he regaled us all over the next thirty minutes with tall tales of his amazing life. In many ways, he was the perfect entrée to the real power behind this behemoth of a fruit company, Capespan's General Manager, Mr. Louis Kriel.

With his Post-It note concealed in the palm of his hand LK bewitched everyone in the room. He was razor-sharp with his wit, telling two quick jokes about the RSA / England rugby and cricket rivalry that drew us together more than any business deal could have. He was insightful, ruthless, commanding and chivalrous all at the same time and I could not help but marvel at a man at the top of his game absolutely shining, with what seemed like little or no preparation for his speech. A brilliant speech from a brilliant orator and a massive inspiration to me today as much as he was then.

My point of this digression is that you must take inspiration and learn from your leaders. You must always stay true to your principles and beliefs and, above all, you must try to be as informed as possible at all times so that you can interact and perform at your best, no matter what the circumstances are.

So it was, armed with my new sense of self-awareness and self-worth, that I had no hesitation at all when called by the tannoy from our breakfast of bacon sandwiches and Champagne in a temporary marquee in a grassy field just after dawn in the middle of

Northamptonshire. "Mr. Askham and party to board aircraft number four, now arriving in Paddock two."

My guests that day were big-hitters too: Mr. Ray Crammond, Head Buyer, general fruit world guru and spokesman for the whole of Waitrose supermarkets, and my old adversary, Jason Farringdon-Smythe, Director of Fresh Produce for Safeway, a young and highly intelligent, chain-smoking dude who was also punching way above his weight in our world.

The next thirty minutes was a stomach-churning, gut-wrenching thrill of a ride over fields just lit with the early morning sunshine. At tree-top height, we roared into Silverstone, swooping in and then rising slightly, to hover over the starting grid of the racetrack. After permission was granted, we proceeded to land and disembark from our ferocious beast of transportation. We were collected by a limousine and we were soon seated at our elegantly decorated table right at the front of the hospitality suite and overlooking the starting line. I was clear that day what my primary responsibilities were going to be: I was not to pretend to be the witty host, nor the great raconteur of stories past and present. I did not need to talk too much about current affairs or world events or even too much about the fruit trade. No, my tasks were simple: firstly, to make sure that our guests were appropriately refreshed with good food and plied with plenty of alcoholic drinks throughout the day. Secondly, and you'll know this if you have ever been to a live motor racing event and have no access to a TV screen, to make sure that we knew at all times which driver and which team or car was in what position in the race. My third task that day, was to spend as much money as I could on Formula 1 merchandise for our esteemed guests.

The afternoon passed without issues and the short ride back to our departure point was quick but uneventful. I made one mistake that day however and I knew it as I sat in horrendous traffic on the A-Road leaving Northants, knowing that I faced a five-hour journey home. Mr. JFS grinned at me, as he pulled alongside me in stationary traffic, clearly very pleased with himself as he sat astride his 1000cc Triumph sports motorcycle. With a jaunty wave, he revved his machine, clunked it into first gear and just fucked off into the distance, scything his way through the cars and into the twilight!

The other chopper ride that springs to mind happened because of a job well done and it was a reward for a very successful advertising campaign that I had coordinated and managed in my position as head of stone fruit for Hunter Saphir back in the nineties. I was thirty, in charge of a thirty million pound per annum business unit. I had a dozen staff, including traders, procurement staff and administrators and I was reporting to the Group MD and the chairman of the whole company, a very scary and very impressive individual, Nicholas Saphir himself, son of the owner, successful farmer and accomplished businessman. In later years, I would accompany him to the south of France to oversee significant investment in ripening chambers for peaches so that we could pick, ripen and prepack, label and barcode four-packs of ready-to-eat French peaches and nectarines that would then go directly to stores in the UK and therefore bypass expensive UK stages and deliver greater value to the customer.

My invitation was issued to me by the magazine that I had advertised with for the past year: the Fruit Trades Journal, later to become the Fresh Produce Journal.

The invitation only specified that I was to be at the Royal Lancaster Hotel in south London at 09.00am to meet and to breakfast with other invitees.

I arrived safely, mingled and chatted with other people from the industry and was soon called to the lobby of the hotel where a coach was waiting to take us to what we though would be our final destination on our surprise day out.

Within ten minutes, we pulled into the London Heliport, Battersea, on the banks of the Thames. It was clear that we were in for a treat and soon we were boarding a huge passenger helicopter, quickly rising from terra firma and soon above the river and then roaring out through London in a westerly direction, directly above the Thames and all its iconic bridges and landmarks. I was in a state of near ecstasy as the City of London disappeared behind us, suburbs and industrial parks gave way to green fields as we continued to follow the great river below us. Within 40 minutes, we began to descend and it was clear that we were deep in the English countryside, although no one had a clue exactly where.

As we disembarked the aircraft, four waiters carrying trays of Champagne and orange juice came to greet us. From their uniforms, we knew where we now were – this was Le Manoir Aux Quat´Saisons, Chef Raymond Blanc's masterpiece deep in the Oxfordshire countryside.

The day was a wonderful treat and something that I would recommend for that very special occasion. After arrival, Champagne and canapes, we were invited to meet the great man and to tour the herb gardens and the Japanese water garden that were features of the exterior of this magnificent country house. My day however, wasn´t really about the helicopter ride, although the departure and completely thrilling ride over the Thames and through the City of London remain etched into my memory for eternity.

No, the thrill was in the genius and the freshness of the food, the location and the brilliance and pure humanity of the man himself, Monsieur Blanc. Having completed our tour of the gardens and now getting ready for lunch, I was in one of the bathrooms, down near to the kitchens and a little bit disorientated. Standing at the sink, washing my hands, I was surprised by the master himself. Monsieur Blanc emerged from one of the stalls and had proceeded to wash his hands at the sink next to me.

"´Ow are you today Monsieur? Are you ready for your dining experience today?" he asked.

Seizing the moment and with inexplicable bravado that came over me in an instant, I told our famous host that I was indeed looking forward to lunch and that it was a doubly special day for me. Not only was a lucky enough to be here in Le Manoir, but I had met a girl on the helicopter ride in and that I was keen to impress her over lunch. "Sacré bleu!" exclaimed the master, rising to affairs of the heart with typical French enthusiasm. "You must come with me." And he gestured for me to follow him into the vast kitchens next door. One or two glasses of exquisite Chablis later, we had concocted a cunning plan. At some point during lunch Monsieur Blanc would come out to greet his guests and then he would recognise me as on old acquaintance and approach me with a personal greeting.

Lunch was superb. Passionate cooking, wonderfully chosen

ingredients and several mouth-watering courses later, each accompanied by the finest wines, I was deep in conversation with my new belle. Things were looking good, but they suddenly got even better. Raymond appeared from the kitchens in full chef's whites and he was now diligently passing by each guest, stopping for a word here, a word there, always subtle, discreet and very unshowy in his demeanour. Now five yards away and without pausing from his duties, he looked up and our eyes met. He winked, I winked, and he headed straight for me at the next table. "Monsieur Steve!" he exclaimed with genuine fraternity, "'Ow lovely to see you my old friend. Tell me, 'ow is your fazer, Raymond? 'Ow are your beautiful daughters? 'Ow is your golf these days? It was just ze ozer day that I..."

I raised my hand. "Hang on a second Raymond, old chap," I said. "I'm just finishing a conversation here, I'll be with you in just a tick..."

I turned away from him and refocused my attention back to my shocked lunch companion. In mock exasperation, hands on hips, and with bulging eyes hanging out over his pince-nez, he gave me that indignant, really offended look that only Frenchmen can master. Shock soon turned to laughter, however, as both RB and I quickly cracked. Guffaws of laughter gushed from deep inside of both of us as we realised that our little joke had gone to plan. Of course, I had never met him before, but he played his part in the ruse willingly, beautifully and with a generosity of spirit that only truly kind people can.

In answer to your next question, No I didn't!

,

H IS FOR HUMILIATION

Let's rewind a bit. Back to the beginning. I am nineteen years old and I am travelling the south-east of England every day in my work as an agricultural engineer for Kent Fruit Services. Our field of interest is anything to do with the UK apple and pear industry and we are importers and suppliers of trees; fruit and windbreaks, picking buckets, entire grading packing lines and orchard sprayers - designed to apply a preventative or curative treatment in droplet form to the fruit bearing trees in an orchard. Usually these are tractor-towed and operate off the tractor's PTO (Power Take Off) system, using a connecting shaft. Sometimes, for small crops, perhaps bush type plants, a sprayer would be tractor-mounted or carried in a backpack type, known as a knapsack sprayer. Later in my career, on a well know French peach and nectarine farm in the Rhone Valley, I would see the world's most advanced orchard sprayer: a self-contained, self-driven space-age vehicle that enabled the operator to work free of his tractor / trailer responsibilities and to focus completely on the job in hand: an accurate and correctly measured application of product to the trees.

One of my roles was to provide spares and servicing to our range of Dutch-made Munckhof sprayers. Typical works could involve cleaning and changing broken blades in the fan housing at the rear of the machine, perhaps a change of the nylon milled valves in the forward-mounted pump, and occasionally, a fibreglass repair to the one thousand litre tank that formed the main body of the sprayer.

Clearly, a damaged and leaking tank was bad news for the farmer / owner, so essential repairs were a necessary part of my skill set for work and I cringe now when recalling stories of entering a tank to locate and repair the leak, usually with fibreglass patches that would set hard, straight after application. In that era, H and S, - Health and Safety - was not a first consideration and I cannot remember an occasion where I would even think to wear a mask or - God forbid - independent breathing apparatus. Because these sprayers are usually used to apply a dosage of a particular chemical, a pesticide or an insecticide or whatever, and even though the chemical would be well diluted in potable water, they would invariably stink of chemical residue with the only relief of fresh air coming in and out through the "tank turret" lid, which was also the only means of entering and exiting the tank.

This particular day, I am local to our Kent office and I am to repair a leaking tank on one of our largest tractor-towed machines. This is a big farm, operating at least half a dozen tractor / sprayer combinations. There are six farm engineers and tractor operators gathered, as I lay my kit out on the hard-packed dirt outside the farm workshops. Some weeks earlier, I had been given a wonderful incentive to convert my service and repair appointments into sales of our products in return for a generous commission on anything I sold. At that time, the industry was going through a huge change in the way we used chemicals on crops. Traditionally, we used vast quantities of hugely expensive treatment products, diluted of course, but still pumped out of the array of nozzles, positioned at the rear of the machine, in serious volumes through a small but very visible hole in the ceramic plate that formed the jet from the nozzles. Now, all sprayers were now going through a revolution. Studies had shown that by using a much finer nozzle plate, therefore giving a much smaller droplet size, application of the "active ingredient," the actual chemical contained in the spray mixture, would be much more effective on treating the plants to which they were applied. The result was a much lower and more efficient usage of the very costly chemicals, but it did involve having to remove the existing factory-fitted nozzles in order to accommodate the new mountings for the recently released ULV (Ultra Low Volume) setup and new nozzle.

Our machines were well-priced, quite robust and easy to operate. We had lots in the field, but there was competition, the main one being from a well-known local agricultural consultant called Mark Burnett. Although Mark was an independent operator, he was linked with many other manufacturers and suppliers. His plan was clearly to offer advice on all tree crops, in this case the same area as us, apples and pears, and to make gain from choices made and equipment and machinery sold.

By now, I have donned my one-piece overalls, I have located the leak and have begun to prepare my patch in readiness for application. I am inside the tank, almost overpowered by the chemical fumes inside but maintaining a steady conversation with the six or seven engineers and operators that now surround my disabled machine.

The conversation has turned to the benefits of ULV spraying and following my new sense of freedom in my sales / service role, I am confidently extoling the advantages of our machine and its ease of conversion to the latest nozzles and spry plates. A faceless voice brings the subject around to Mark Burnett and his advice that the machines and equipment that he was marketing were superior to ours. Without real knowledge of our competition and with never having met Mr. Burnett, I bridled immediately at this suggestion and went further.

"Mark Burnett, Mark Burnett? Who is he, what does he know? He's talking rubbish, doesn't have a clue! His products are useless and the brand of sprayer he's selling is a bag of shit!" On and on I went, invisible to the exterior and fixated on pushing my now prepared patch into the leaking bottom of the tank, I was oblivious to the fact that the conversation had stopped and there was silence all around, save for my diatribe concerning the never-encountered but highly respected Mr. Burnett. Finishing the patch up and by now desperate for clean air, I rose from my cramped position inside the tank, head out of the turret and I exit the filthy machine. The operators and drivers were still standing around the machine, most with arms folded at the chest and all silent, all eyes on me as I watch my footing on the rubber tyres of the sprayer and I step down onto the dirt in readiness to continue my "sales" conversation with my captive audience. Except that there is another figure in the group, a smartly dressed blonde-haired man of around 35 years of age who meets my gaze immediately.

Although unsmiling, he does not hesitate to approach me purposefully, striding forwards, right hand extended in greeting. "Hello Steve," he says. "I was listening to your conversation with the boys here. Pleased to meet, you, my name is Mark Burnett."

I IS FOR ISRAEL

"Like all great travellers, I have seen more than I remember and remember more than I have seen." ~ Benjamin Disraeli

I have been to Israel perhaps 20 times. In one year, I was back and forth every month, working on a citrus deal with one of the world's best-known brands of fruit. I was taking Hebrew classes, I was beginning to understand the culture, the attitudes and the uniqueness of this remarkable nation of people. I was to help take them from a national selling board, into a private company scenario. It was huge business. With one client, a major UK supermarket chain, at the end of the first season's supply of citrus, we gave back in the form of a rebate (a kickback paid directly to them by cheque that they said they'd use as "below the line marketing". In other words, it went straight to bottom line profit. The bastards), nearly five million pounds as a direct percentage of the total sales we had made to them. Not only had they given us the worst average prices throughout the whole season, we had had to endure one of the worst possible supplier-customer relationships ever and we also had to give them a monster cheque at the end of it.

But that's not the first story that comes to mind.

We are in the car, on a highway travelling north to south. We are heading to a large citrus farm and packing station, north of the sea of Galilee. The highway is divided by mature gum trees, Eucalyptus. It becomes noticeable that they are almost ever present, exceptions coming for turnpikes or exits. Our driver and our host explains that although they are commonly used to drain swampy ground so that concrete can be laid or construction started, they are actually used in Israel to provide cover from the air for columns of troops and vehicles, which is a regular sight here.

In the car with me is my partner in crime, Mark, the boss of the UK office, my pal, an eloquent and very smart guy. Incidentally, Mark also took on my sick and whisky smelling BMW when I moved positions.

Also in the car is Tasbury's new citrus technologist, Harry Straker, straight from a very posh agricultural college and clearly the scion of someone important somewhere. He was maybe six feet five tall, big hair and the owner of a very likeable personality. Total mix of English landed gentry, the innocence of a young man (I was never like that at the beginning of my fruit career. Ha!) fresh from Uni and bursting with passion and energy for everything that's coming his way, at the same time blended with the sweetness and humour-bringing qualities of an almost grown-up Great Dane puppy. Making up our party is "The Captain," Andrew Sellar. I gave him this nickname after he arrived at our Sittingbourne, Kent, offices to start his first day as our new citrus technical manager; effectively covering Henry, his opposite number in our game of supply and receipt of millions of cartons of citrus. Everything from a White Marsh grapefruit, the pink ones, the Star Ruby, Shamouti oranges, brand-named and patented clementine varieties, even gigantic pomelos. The captain walked into the main office where Mark and I and the team worked, carrying a dirty great big black Pilot's case. He just looked the absolute business! I know that he's still working and he has carved out a great career.

So, we are driving north. Harry is full of questions about everything: the country, the weather, the language, the politics, the wars. The climate, the citrus. It's a non-stop barrage, an inquisition. It's great fun also because he is so keen, he's got the passion, the bug, the enthusiasm for life and for the fruit! We approach a gap in the gum trees, a junction coming up. The highway sign looms into view. NAZERETH, clear as a bell, there at the top of the sign, some other destinations listed below, some Hebrew, some Arabic words. We all see it. We pass it going north. It is unremarkable to us as we've passed it before many times.

Harry turns, makes boggling eye contact with all of us, including Meir, our boss, host and driver. "Nazereth!" he exclaims, almost agog with excitement at what he has seen. "Nazereth!" Again… "Are there any old buildings there?" Harry gasps with sheer delight and incredulity. Honestly, it was all we could do…

Now I'm not implying that our guest on this mission is dim, in fact I know that the delightful Harry went on to have a highly successful time in the business and I believe he's still going strong. But our H did give us another good laugh later that day at the packhouse. Andrew is in charge, this is his territory, processes, flow of fruit, critical control points, use of fungicides, water quality and checks, worker clothing and welfare. Harry is loving it; this is his first big overseas trip and he is in awe of The Captain as Andrew effortlessly bats away question after question about everything a man with a childlike craving for knowledge on his new subject could possibly think of. Mark and I are impressed. Meir is impressed. We come to an exterior part of the set up. The path is concrete, it's in good condition. There are no weeds or rubbish, the wall of the packhouse on our right is made from acceptable materials and is freshly painted in a pleasing dark green colour. I can see what's coming. There is a large plastic rodent baiting station coming up. Maybe a foot square and five or six inches high. There is a lid on it, a hole in one side and it is tethered to the concrete base on which the packhouse walls are mounted. We all know what it is (later I would be in Andrew's position many times and I can still immediately recall exactly what happened next). Harry pauses as he sees the 'trap'. A puzzled look comes over him and he rubs his chin, clearly searching for a penetrating question about the trap with which, like a man in a duel, he would vanquish The Captain. Nothing comes, Andrew can see it, we can all see it. He is stumped. Lost for words. Cat has got his tongue. Andrew waited. He's got this, I thought, he's cool, he's educated, polite, knowledgeable and professional.

He gives Harry just the right amount of time and he says "it's a rat trap, a rodent baiting station. It's part of a planned and mapped pest control system. Look at the identification on the wall, matching the one on the trap. They must be the same. It's tethered, so that it can't be knocked away and become a possible contaminant somewhere else in the production process. I'll note the number, so that when we return to look at documentation in the office, we can see that this one has been visited and checked recently and that it's in the right place, according to the map." He's got it, I think.

Harry pauses again, almost physically stepping back with the force and the power of this new knowledge he's been given. I can tell he's unsure what to say. We are all silent, waiting for a response. Eventually, H blurts, "So, it's a rat trap, a rodent baiting station you say?" Andrew nods, we all give off affirmative signals. "So, we kill the rats then?" Harry asks.

Andrew nods, expressionless. We continue to accept Harry's direct gaze at all of us, giving him the positive responses he so clearly needs as he moves in with the killer question he has so obviously been looking for, as he has for the last two hours on every single step we have taken on this citrus packing tour.

"So, how does it work?" H asks. "Is it poisoning?"

To this day, I will recall what Andrew said and just how smoothly he delivered it. Without a hint of sarcasm and with patience and in total charge, despite the barrage all day and the fact that it was still incoming. Meir, Mark and I are almost smug. This is an easy one, even we know the answers, us commercial jockeys, really only making up numbers on this little tour. I swear that I am nodding as The Captain begins to answer: -

"Poison? No. Actually, we are working far more ecologically these days." Henry is nodding, we are now all nodding. "In fact, what we do these days is to lure the creature inside the station with a treat and then it finds itself in quite a roomy space. Note the size of these modern rodent stations."

Harry is entranced, fervently nodding and now softly rocking back and forth on the balls of his feet, I think I hear him softly humming as he continues to absorb the lessons.

"Do go on. What happens?" prompts our man, as I, for one, realise that The Captain hasn't got this, that's he gone off piste and that he is now winging it. He's expressionless, the tone of his voice is the same.

"There is a free wheel inside, much the same as you'd find in a pet hamster's cage at home, but slightly larger and in a space that is conducive to the rodent's well-being. Basically, we just let them be happy and run themselves to death."

I imagine the ground opening up, eternal damnation coming our way at a rate of knots, but no. Harry scratches his chin, mutters whilst making swiftly scribbled notes on his clipboard. "Brilliant, quite brilliant," we all clearly hear him utter as we observe him finish his notes, re-attach his Mont Blanc to his clipboard and then stride purposefully away and up the path ahead of him, in his chinos and brogues, blazer on, clipboard tucked under his arm.

Another time and another trip to Israel. My task is to escort three UK supermarket clients on a three-day mission to inspect Persimmon orchards and to plan a season-long supply campaign. This is a unique variety of Persimmon, known and sold as "Sharon Fruit". It is a sweeter variety, small and succulent and equally tasty eaten soft and ripe or sliced hard and crunchy. We are the pioneers of this product and we sell it to all the British retailers in large quantities. I remember this story well as there is subtext to it in that shortly before this trip, I was driving home to Kent around the infamous M25. I have Radio 4 on in the car and there is a fierce debate going on about the mighty Tesco selling volumes of a small and exotic looking fruit called a "Sharon." The theme was about Tesco insulting the lovely girls of Essex who were suffering in the UK press at the time for apparently all being called either Sharon or Tracy! Guests included the Bishop of Essex, the Mayor of Basildon, a local prominent feminist and the radio host. It was a furious affair, insults flying backwards and forwards, accusations of blatant sexism just to sell more fruit, how the poor women of Essex had a hard enough time as it was dealing with a myriad of crude Essex-girl jokes and that there their reputations as fine English maidens were being yet again sullied by the corporate monsters of the land.

I pulled into Clacket's Lane services and I stopped my car. I called the BBC and I requested an opportunity to put in a point about the live Sharon fruit debate. I was connected to the producer of the show and in about half a minute I had made my point. I finished my call and resumed listening to the show which was now reaching fever-pitch levels of angst and vitriol, when just like that the show's host stepped in and said that the debate was stopped with immediate effect. You see the idiots had gathered in the studios, prepared well for the clash of opinions and were ready and willing to do battle for the honour of the Sharon and Tracy's of this world. But what they hadn't known, they hadn't bothered to research to a man and a woman, was that the little orange exotic looking fruit being marketed by Tasbury's (and in fact all of the other retailers at the time), was not named at all after a Sharon. No, this beautiful piece of fruit is in fact named after a fertile coastal plain in Israel between Jaffa in the south and Mount Carmel in the north. Yes, that's right, it's called the SHARÓN PLAIN! (Accent on the O.) I had to laugh as the show ended in farce. Moral of the story: For Gawd's sake, get your facts right.

It is the morning of the first day of the Sharón Fruit trip and we are late and in heavy traffic on the gorgeous sea front of Tel Aviv. Our guests are awaiting collection in a nice hotel on the beach. We are running late and Meir, my boss and driver for the day, and myself are nervously edging towards the hotel entrance. We are picking up two technical managers, Tom and Sarah, and the commercial manager for buying exotic fruit, Rachael. I know them well and they are young, knowledgeable and good at their jobs. We must be on our guard for the next couple of days. These guys know their stuff and there cannot be any holes in our presentations, orchard visits and packhouse tours. We make it into the crescent-shaped hotel entrance in our bottle-green Mazda 6 sedan and there is a queue of cars all waiting to stop and collect people from the hotel. Rather than wait our turn in the traffic outside the hotel, to save time I disembark and head to the main hotel entrance to meet our guests. I see them immediately and we exchange greetings. I can tell that they are tetchy as I am more than fifteen minutes late. That's never good when dealing with supermarket personnel; they want you to be on-time and I feel their annoyance with me as I escort them out of the revolving doors and towards our car, which Meir is now holding at the front of the queue, directly in front of me. I open the rear doors and the front passenger door and I hurriedly settle our clients into the car. I am last in, jumping into the front spare seat and as I close the door, I confirm to Meir that we are ready for the off, "We are all here boss, we are ready to go, let's drive." and I turn, engagingly to the passengers in the rear seats, sitting there like three little ducks in a row.

Nothing happens and my world goes into slow motion as I turn towards my man for answers. It is not my man, it is an elderly Israeli lady, staring at me in disbelief and looking as if she is about to go into shock as her vehicle is highjacked in plain sight. Of course, I have loaded the clients into the wrong car as I catch sight of Meir, four cars back and waving at me helplessly. I want the ground to open up and swallow me as I exit the customers and reload them into the correct car. We set off out of Tel Aviv and towards the Sharon Plain and I can feel the clients´ minds all focusing on the same thing: Steven Askham is an idiot.

To finish this story on a positive note, I can tell you that from a regrettable beginning, we went from strength to strength and the visit was a major success. On the Friday afternoon, when the mission had come to an end, the two incredibly attractive ladies thanked me for my time and efforts, their Sharon Fruit business was prepared and they were confident of creating more sales and further establishing their business plan. They explained that they were heading to Eilat, a resort on the Red Sea coast, for the weekend and would I care to accompany them? Their companion, Tom the technical manager would be travelling home this evening and they would like the pleasure of my company.

Two morals of this story then: Firstly, just because you make a clown of yourself in the first ten minutes of a trip, does not mean that you are going to fail: after all, in my situation at that time, the only way, really was up! Secondly, when you have earned the prize and the prize is not quite what one expects always accept the prize with a smile and good grace. The customer is always right. But I never crossed the line…

Though I would have for Abigail Barnes…

I IS FOR ITALY

One of my favourite places to visit, Italy is unique. The best food? The best clothes and shoes? Best cars and motorcycles? Women? Well… Buenos Aires certainly, but even that's down to the large-scale Italian immigration from the mid-nineteenth century until 1940 and Italians remain the largest ethnic origin of modern Argentines to this day. The scenery, the people, the passion. Tick the box on all of those. Even the national airline, Alitalia, has an elegance and style about it that is often copied but never matched. But I never went to Italy on a mission for any of these things. My world is the world of fresh produce and Italy always delivers in quality fresh fruit.

I land in Bari, just above the heel in the Boot of Italy, at 2.00 a.m. It's a strange, isolated airport and my lift hasn't arrived. Fedora-wearing, suspicious looking men, seemingly clad exclusively in a uniform of white singlet vests and pinstripe suit trousers, patrol the empty arrivals area; sharp eyed and clearly on the make, these men seem to be the only human life in this remote outpost and I am on my guard as I decide what to do. I take the sensible option and I get lucky as I find what must be the only taxi in the airport and I take the ride to my lodgings. I've been in much more dangerous situations than this, but I know that to travel is to have encounters and to travel frequently is to inevitably find oneself, from time to time, in 'situations'. I recall as I write, some 'situations' in my working life: Crocodile attack in Brazil, near murder in Cape Town, Snakes everywhere I've been, aircraft engine fires, tropical storm survival and guns, all come to mind. And me meeting a guy called Andrew and, in a two-hour meeting about lime supply from Brazil, calling him Colin, Peter and Frank (but never Andrew!) – how embarrassing - and as I faced myself in the mirrored lift going down from the fifth floor in Tasbury's HQ that day, a lesson learned in how to remember people's names. Get it right the first time and then word associate their name with whatever fits you! That guy incidentally was a complete bastard. At that time, I was possibly 26 or so. More confident of my place in this industry and now less afraid of my peers and of the titans of the industry that were around at that time. My company was big in Brazil and we were hooked up with a massive agricultural cooperative there called Cotía. This firm was second and third generation Japanese owned. There is a huge Japanese population in Brazil, I'm guessing from something to do with the end of World War II, but that's not my story - Cotía farmed everything in the fruit world and with them, we were pioneers in the UK importing industry because of the immense volume of Brazilian produce we offered and the types of fruit that were grown. To name three, Gala and Royal Gala apples, yellow melons and limes. The lime was of course why I found myself in Tasbury's HQ on a wet Tuesday afternoon. We had an availability of thirty x 40-foot reefer container per week for eleven months of the year. That would be twenty full pallets (in each container) of perhaps 100 cartons of limes per pallet. Each carton container between 150 and 250 limes. That's

400,000 limes per container, or *twelve million* limes per week. For eleven months of the year! "How many do you want?" was basically my sales meeting preparation, knowing that this was a deal I couldn't fail to land and that it was a multi-million-pound, long-term order: this was a gun that was already loaded and cocked; all I had to do was point and shoot. So, I failed to prepare, and I prepared to fail.

I had set up the meeting earlier with the buyer, John Valensberg and although I had never met him before, I knew him to be smart and a very tough cookie, like all Tasbury's people were. I just focused only on John. John this, John that, John, John, John, as we sat and talked in a small corner of Tasbury's giant fifth floor produce department. "I've called my Technical Manager, Alan Thompson, over," said John, halfway through the meeting. "I want him to quiz you on the technical aspects of this business. Pesticide usage, worker welfare, HACCP's and stuff."

I gulp as I realise that I am unprepared. I haven't gathered any information on technical, I'm a racehorse thoroughbred, why would I prepare when all I had to do was flog five hundred million limes a year to John? Alan joins us and John does the introductions.

"Steve, this is Alan. Alan, Steve." We shake hands. My amazing eye for detail takes him in immediately, my other mind is automatically curious about this fellow; the way he carries himself, the shape of his head, his haircut, his clothes.

"Nice to meet you Colin," I say confidently, mind number one now going into Red Alert mode in the knowledge that I am about to be slaughtered by the eager and hungry-looking fruit technologist in front of me. Of course, he killed me. I went to the gallows and I was executed slowly over a forty-minute period, made even worse by me calling dear Alan, Peter and then Frank. Thankfully, I didn't call him Colin again.

That wasn't the end of my encounters with Alan, however. He came down to Kent one day, to our packing facilities, to review our latest arrivals of containers of yellow melons from Brazil; Tasbury's were having lots of problems managing the quality of fruit in our daily deliveries of melons into their national depots and they were rejecting them.

"We've had a rejection" are the worst words an office-based fruit trader can hear when his logistics manager gets the call. So, Alan is with us today to look at a large quantity (I mean hundreds of pallets of fruit put into cold store following their arrival into Dover the previous day). The problem is that the melons are out of specification. The second worst words a fruit trader can hear are: "They're out of spec." All supermarkets have a written specification for every type of fruit or veg supplied. They are highly detailed, and they will have photographic and written examples of acceptable and non-acceptable defects, minimum and maximum weights or dimensions and so on. In some cases, there is a calculation to follow that is designed to add up the total amount of scarring per fruit and then give a percentage total over a box, a pallet and then the whole consignment. So, Alan spends about four hours in a cold store, aided by a couple of our yard staff, basically pulling out boxes to inspect at random, sometimes ordering whole pallets to be de-stacked so that he can get at the lower stacked cartons and inspect the fruit therein. This is good practice as there were exporters that would put poorer quality fruit in cartons placed first, at the bottoms of the pallets, the theory being that quality controllers, or QC's, wherever they were in the supply chain, would only trouble themselves to look at the top few layers on a pallet of fruit when doing their inspections and calculations as to whether the delivery or consignment was 'in specification'.

So, scarring. Completely natural in the fruit world. Imagine a tree fruit. A plum, say. A scar, a cicatrice, a patch of rough skin; healed and non-progressive in a decay sense, on the surface of the fruit, that's what I am trying to describe. Perhaps caused by the plum growing against the branch, possibly wind rub against leaves. Acceptable defect if it falls into the tolerance percentage given in the individual specification. In the case of these yellow melons, they don't grow on trees, they grow on the ground and it is inevitable therefore, that a small area of the melon's skin must touch the soil. They grow in rows, beneath a plant that looks like a weed. They are harvested by hand, the stalks cut to an inch in length and they are transported to a shed for sorting and cooling. Pick up any melon, turn it around in your hands, and you will find the one spot where Mrs. Melon has been in touch with Mother Earth throughout her life.

Our yellow melons are yellow – a good sign - we have no problems with sugar levels (an essential measure of the melon's maturity and likelihood of delivering taste to the consumer). Our melons are firm, we have no soft fruits, no problems with rots. No, the problem is the level of scarring, so we await Alan's return to the offices to give us the results of his deliberations. We gather round as he places two open cartons on the table set up for him. Each carton contains seven plump melons, placed in a nest of straw for transit protection. They look fresh and clean. Alan moves the boxes two feet apart and he goes for carton one. He picks up each fruit and he turns it over and over in his hands to show us the full surface of each melon, noting for us the brownish, small, scarred patch on every fruit. He moves into carton two and he repeats the show.

"Now," he says imperiously and indicating carton one, "this carton of melons is out of specification for excessive scarring," he turns ten degrees and takes a step, "This carton of melons is in specification for scarring."

I'm looking at the two cartons of fruit and, honestly, there was no blinking difference between them and I knew that Alan had spent four hours looking at fifty thousand melons to come up with these two examples of "ACCEPTABLE" and "REJECTED." I knew because I'd been out to the stores to try to chat to him a few times that afternoon. I knew that he was doing an absolutely correct and professional job in there, but, like everyone else involved in the affair that day, I knew that what he was doing was futile, impossible to implement as a standard and pointless. Every melon, every single one of the things, had a mark on it. We are standing there silently, in shock. My boss, Jackie, co-owner of the business with her husband Norman, unlike me with the limes, had done her preparation. Struggling to keep control of her emotions and probably in the knowledge that her half-million-pound consignment of fresh melons was now not suitable for supply to Tesco, she knew, as we all did, that Alan's idea of an acceptable level of scarring and the calculation required to be within it, was impossible to comply with. How could we possibly teach our line workers, tasked with a second manual inspection of each melon passed down on a conveyor, that they must grade and select to a certain percentage of scarring and no more?

Jackie produces a third box. One that she had spent time selecting hours before Alan's arrival. She places it between the other two on the table and she gives him the look. "In or out of spec, Alan?"

Our man examines each piece of fruit carefully. Almost in a religious manner, he rolls the rugby-ball shaped fruits individually in his hands, carefully inspecting the brown areas where the fruit has grown on the soil. "Out of specification Jackie, the same as that box," he states authoritatively, pointing at box number one.

Well, I've never seen an angrier woman. Jackie erupts "How can they be out of spec, Alan?!" she screams, "THEY ALL LOOK THE FUCKING SAME!!!"

Colin, Peter, Frank, whoever, got banished from our premises that afternoon. Soon afterwards, we resumed full supply of great quality fruit and with a newly agreed specification for acceptable levels of scarring. We successfully delivered millions of fruits to the consumer. I presume that most of it was eaten. Incidentally, I did get the lime deal.

Around this time, He met His second handler, a New Zealander in his seventies named Ken Milne, a tall, striking man with a heavy build, a pronounced limp from an undisclosed injury, and a shock of pure white hair. As a senior fruit technologist, Ken's knowledge of all things tropical was unsurpassed. He would spend every day by Ken's side for months on end; white-laboratory-coated together in their fruity world, one imparting knowledge and the other sucking in and devouring every single morsel, every scrap of information in order that His education would be completed so that he could be assigned to work.

Mr. M's (or 'M's) other role was in counter-espionage, specialising in several areas, including resistance to torture and pain endurance, knife and hand-to-hand combat, and survival in impaired visibility conditions. Through more than a year of training with 'M' he mastered all these dark arts; an A-Grade student, diligent and hard-working, He knew that he would need all these skills in missions to come.

What happens later that day in Bari is a reminder to me to be ready for anything. It is 7.00 a.m. and I am up, breakfasted and on duty, ready for the days ahead of me. I am to collect my client, a top buyer with the best supermarket in the land. I am to drive him north, some three hundred kilometres to a motorway service station where we will meet my agent, Luigi. Our mission is to view a newly discovered specialist peach farm run by two deeply passionate brothers with the intent to procure and supply their highly prized early fruits to my UK retailer client. In future years, this grower would become one of the "Story Growers". At that time, Marks and Spencer had a brilliant idea: they were (and are) the best at retailing fruit and vegetables. Brilliant buyers and technical staff, growers that are loyal and outstanding in their brilliance, exclusive supply deals for new varieties, the very highest standards, they punch above their weight in all areas of the fresh produce world. Their idea was to put a photograph of the grower, with a short story about their produce on the packaging of the fruit so as to get the consumer closer to "feeling" the life and the qualities of the piece of fresh produce they had purchased.

I am nervous as I collect Robin from his hotel. I am nervous, but not afraid, a 'normal' kind of nervous because I know that this guy is sharp and is highly regarded. I am nervous because I have never been to this part of Italy, I am in a hire car and I don't speak Italian.

It's seven-thirty and it is hot already. I settle him into my Punto, chatting easily but professionally. Later in my career, I find out that Mr. R is in fact a madman when off duty and that his peccadillos are wide-ranging and manifold. He's a dynamo, talking non-stop about the new farm we have discovered: "What are the harvesting dates? How many kilos? How many cases? What is the range of sizes? Good sugar levels? Can we pre-pack at source?" He's on a mission and I soak it up. I love his passion as I am the same. I am able to get into a lather very easily about more or less anything fruit-related so course, I get lost. I miss my rehearsed route to the junction of the autostrada and I lose my bearings (no satellite navigation in those days my friends!) and am lost. We are still heading north however, and I reassure Robin that I know where I am going and that soon we will reach the next turnpike for the highway. We don't. What I think is the "old" main road heading north, turns out be a country road heading for nowhere and I am forced to stop, turn and retrace our route. My man points out a hotel coming up on the right. There is no traffic, not a soul in site, and I have plenty of space to pull up in front of the hotel. We've been on the road for just over an hour, and as we exit and proceed up the stone steps to the entrance, the heat is noticeable. I quickly take in our surroundings and I note that, apart from being decrepit and remote, this hotel is not popular. As we reach the glass doors, there are two prostitutes in the shadows, ready to greet us with a cheery, "Buongiorno," and a knowing look. It struck me as strange that my companion seemed to linger for longer than a moment as I strode into the lobby to try to get some directions, perhaps a map and possibly a quick coffee to calm down my extremely alert client.

Robin joins me at the desk as I miserably attempt to speak Italian and to explain my predicament. I'm the supplier. It is my job to handle all 'situations' and I get there eventually after thirty or so minutes of battle. It is a hideous start to a tricky trip and I sense that my buyer is not at all impressed. I gird my loins as we prepare to leave back through the lobby and down to my car. After all, what more could go wrong now? I was freshly supplied with easy directions and a local map. "Chin up Steveo, you've been in worse situations then this before."

We pick up our work bags. We are not that stupid to leave those on view in a hire car in southern Italy, are we? The glass doors slide open. I stride through, side by side with the client. I am confident again, I am the leader, the supplier, the problem solver, the guide. Provider of innovation and amazing new supply of beautiful product from unheard of places... There's my car. Something is horribly wrong as I see it but don't see it. My car has no wheels. No tyres, no hub caps, nothing. I take in the scene below me. MY FREAKING CAR IS ON BRICKS!

The local hoodlums have stolen my hire car's wheels – things can always get worse! Eventually, after a couple of telephone calls and a long wait, we are rescued with a replacement car and I am able to restart our journey north, hitting the right autopista junction first time and finally catching up with Luigi. The visit is a major success and the peach brothers go on to become pioneers in early supply of delicious fresh stone fruit to our client.

I IS ALSO FOR IRELAND

It is 2003 and I am forty. A milestone in any life. Tony Blair is the Prime Minister of the United Kingdom and my babies are babies. The political climate at home has changed, New Labour is in power and we want to leave the UK. An opportunity duly arrives. I am contacted by a friend in the industry, he knows of a position in Limpopo, a northern state on South Africa, bordering Zimbabwe to the north, the mighty Limpopo River provides the seemingly impassable barrier. The job is a partnership with a well-known peach growing family. They want a marketing manager; someone to create sales of their early-harvested fruit and the negotiations are easy. We make a deal and we have three months to prepare for our new life overseas.

Except that it doesn't happen. With one month to go, my new partner withdraws from the deal and we are in limbo, but we remain determined to follow our dream to leave the UK and to start a new life with our two young daughters. It's Christmas and I receive a call from a business in Ireland that I have done business with for the previous five years or so. They want me to join them in north Dublin to work on developing imports and sales of fresh produce in the Irish market. I must say that this came as a surprise. I had never considered working in Ireland, but the proposition excites me and after some telephone conversations and an exchange of views I do receive a firm offer and I accept the challenge. Two months later, I drive across the UK, take the ferry from Holyhead on Anglesey and I find my lodgings for the next three weeks. I am in a fine hotel and country club on the northern outskirts of Dublin, late on a Sunday evening, ready to start my new adventure the next morning. I am nervous but comfortable in my new but temporary surroundings. I order food and savour a real pint of Guinness and I begin to chat with a young man in the bar. Inevitably the conversation turns as to why I am there and I explain that I am taking on a new role and that I am emigrating from the UK and that my wife, daughters and dogs will be joining me in a month's time. I am going to work for one of the largest fruit companies in Ireland – a family company – and that I am looking forward to the change and the new challenge. We speak about the fruit business and my career to date and it is a pleasant conversation, albeit that I don't have a clue who this inquisitive stranger is that seems so keen to know all about me!

I note that several other people are coming towards us as we sit chatting by a huge open fire in the bar. Two men in suits and a smart looking businesswoman join us and the introductions now come. My new friend extends his hand and he greets me, "Nice to meet you Steve, I am David Keeling, this is my sister Caroline, MD of the company, my father Joe, founder and owner of the family business and this is Michael Moore, our finance director." Well, I've just met my new boss and the whole of the board of directors by coincidence, the night before I start a new job. My mind is racing and I am thankful that I haven't dropped a clanger over the last couple of hours chatting before he revealed his identity!

I would go on to spend the next four years working for Keelings' and far from it turning out to be an easy ride in little old Ireland in the second half of my working life, the next four years turned out to be one of the most successful and enjoyable periods in my forty years in the fruit business. This is the story of me becoming an expat for the first time; a tale of an Englishman and his family emigrating to Ireland; of making a thousand new friends and of learning to adapt to a different marketplace and a different culture.

On so many occasions over the next four years, the first question (more a statement actually) I would be asked on meeting someone new, would be, "Are you English?" Sometimes the question would be posed aggressively, sometimes in a curious manner, but always that first question would be the same. I have to say that immediately on answering - getting it out of the way, so to speak - I never once had a problem in Ireland (although doing business in Belfast was once hairy!) and it wasn't just because I find the Irish people to be amongst the friendliest and cheeriest of this Earth (I have a theory as to why they are so, and that is because fundamentally, the weather in the Emerald Isle is so shit, if they weren't cheerful, they would be suicidal!) I think it helped me enormously by studying Anglo-Irish history before I embarked on my journey there and continuing to do so during my time as an expat.

I am not doing politics in this book, but this is my exception; my one and only political statement. I think that the English have been complete bastards to the Irish for hundreds of years, almost a millennium, in fact. My solution to 'The Irish problem' is simple: Ireland is for the Irish. We have no rights there and no role, then, now and in the future. All those that are for us, welcome to the UK. If you're not, then you're Irish. It is your island and your Ireland - no religious conflict, no borders, no bigotry. The border is the Irish Sea. If the Irish Rugby Football Union can unite the country, why can't the rest of the country unite?

So, my new place of work. Our offices are in Swords, a suburb of Dublin but a town in its own right, on the north side of the city and close to the airport. Keeling's is a business founded in growing Irish produce, including strawberries, raspberries, blueberries and a sizeable crop of traditional Bramley apples. The beginning of the business involved production of these crops and then sales through Dublin market, where they have their own wholesale stand. Later, business would expand nationally and with the rise of the supermarkets back in the seventies, new premises were created in Swords so that home grown and then imported produce could be packed, selected to order and despatched to depots across the country. This was to be my working home in St. Margaret's and it was an office set up: 'Upstairs' for the accounting and administrative staff and of course, the management. Below ground however was a different matter. My office was in the centre of a large fruit packing operation, staffed with perhaps a hundred or more commercial and support staff. It was effectively a stainless-steel box in the middle of a busy warehouse / factory. For obvious reasons, it was known as 'The Bunker' and I grew into a key role in the company from my tiny desk in the corner of the bunker. My day-to-day white noise was the cacophony of a hundred Irish voices on telephones, issuing orders, giving instructions to packing staff and supervisors and a never-ending series of impromptu meetings.

I was no stranger to a busy office culture and I am well practised and quite competent in the ever-changing and fast-paced world of fresh produce, but the difference was the change in the way the people behaved. Adapting to new sounds, new accents, even telephone etiquette was different. For example, as an Englishman, I would always finish a telephone conversation with a goodbye. Here, as is the case all over Ireland, the way to finish a phone call would be a gradual winding down of the conversation, leading to at least one, but more often several, "Talk to ya." Whether that means talk to you soon, we will talk again or something else along those lines, remains unclear but it was the way. My good friend and erstwhile one-of-many mentors at Keeling's, Maurice O'Sullivan was my role model in this regard. He would sit opposite me and be almost constantly on the telephone or having a desk-side meeting about the day's ongoing issues and problems. Maurice's MO to finish a phone conversation would be an almost unending but gradually decreasing in volume, stream of, "Talk to ya. Talk to ya. Talk to ya," before replacing the receiver onto the telephone body.

I quickly picked up this habit along with several other particularly Irish mannerisms, including the inimitable, "you know yourself," especially useful when making a sales pitch or in reinforcing an argument or a proposition. In this way, I quickly developed my own style of 'being Irish' and I had no problems fitting in with my new colleagues, in making new friends and in making a success of my new challenge.

My employers initially put me into a nice hotel. Eventually, this would become my golf and sports club and my kids would swim in the pool from time to time. But I needed permanent roots for my family, who would be making the journey across the Irish Sea very soon to settle with me in our newly adopted homeland. With the help of the firm, I found a house in Drogheda, a half hour's drive north of Swords, a town famous for more than one thing. For starters Drogheda was the scene of one of the worst massacres in the Anglo-Irish conflict. A certain Oliver Cromwell, in 1649, massacred nearly the whole population in the name of the English Crown and with the motive of conquering Ireland. In 1690, Drogheda was also the site for the Battle of the Boyne between the deposed King of England, Ireland and Scotland, James II, and the newly acceded King of England and Scotland, William III. Ultimately, victory for William helped to continue the rise of the Protestants in Ireland and has made the battle one of the best known in the history of the British Isles and is a key part in the folklore of the Orange Order.

So, Drogheda, my new home, was not a place to go out at night and sing, "Rule Britannia"! Rumour has it that Drogheda was also an IRA "Sleeper town"; a place south of the border with Northern Ireland that offered shelter and sustenance from the troubles in the north. The local Tasbury's store did not display merchandise with the Union Jack flag and an English accent was immediately pounced upon with the first question: "Are ye English??"

My faith in the good side of human nature always prevailed, despite the circumstances and despite the occasional sticky situation, we were rewarded with four and a half years of total happiness in the glorious country that is modern Ireland. I turned my hectare of rough field into an amazing garden, my babies went to the local school and I settled and grew into my new position with Keeling's.

My first responsibilities involved taking over a dormant stone fruit business, which soon expanded into handling lesser-known imported products such as kiwi fruit and avocados. At the time, consumption per capita pf fruits like plums, cherries, peaches and avocados, was low to say the least, and I took huge pride in growing sales in all these categories. I remember one of my greatest successes was in pitching for and winning the whole stone fruit account of a major Irish retailer (including avocado and cherries) from the biggest and longest established of all the Irish importers (think bananas and think of one of the most iconic and historic brands, Fyffes), and in radically changing the whole offer. I changed the size of fruits sold, I reviewed, challenged and changed the range of individual varieties used to make a seasonal offer and I introduced "ready to eat" peaches, nectarines and plums for the first time. At one point, to provide continuity of supply over the winter and, in particular, over the Christmas period, I flew in air containers of the highest quality, freshly harvested peaches and nectarines from Australia and despite teething troubles with petty theft of stock in our warehouse, the clients loved it.

Ironically, one of the biggest challenges and ultimately, one of the biggest upsets that I experienced, involved the supply and sale of an iconic product, the Irish salad tomato!

My bosses, the Keeling family, had challenged me to create a tomato supply offer for our newly delighted stone fruit customer, in the knowledge that the current English invader (in a retailing sense of course) the mighty Tasbury's PLC, had basically cornered the supply of all the Irish tomatoes. Now, it's important to understand here that the average Irish consumer is fiercely patriotic, and that any product grown 'at home' would always be sought after. To digress for a moment, sometime later, the family asked me to get involved in their very successful berry business. Marks and Spencer (another great British institution!) had 'invaded' Ireland at this time and full supply of Irish grown strawberries was paramount to their summer fruit offer. We were always 'over sold' or over committed and, in fact, the client base – fundamentally, the supermarket sector in Ireland, comprising Dunnes Stores, SuperQuinn, SuperValu and Tesco – would quite often have all-out wars over who was getting the lion's share of Keeling's Irish strawberries. One spring, I had promised the young buyer at Dunnes Stores some of the first of our strawberries. As supply began the following week, there was almighty fall-out as the Dunnes personnel had spotted our strawberries for sale in their local Tesco. Of course (of course!) they were expecting exclusive supply, which was never going to happen. They demanded my head on a plate and I even had to travel into Dublin City centre to explain my actions face to face with the buyer and his trading director, Complete arrogance on their part, and I never did get on with Dunnes after that. Balancing an under-supply situation, when there is more demand than product, is quite rare these days and it can be a nice position to be in, however the skill is really in the diplomacy needed to keep powerful customers satisfied while one waits for production to catch up with demand. I can also say, without hesitation, that the soft fruit, or berry, category is easily the most demanding sector to work in. There are just so many factors that influence change in demand. Quality of fruit, weather in growing or source country and of course, weather in country of sale, all make the management of a successful berry supply business the trickiest of all.

So, I'm in the front room, the parlour, of a very well-known Irish tomato growing family, the McCann family to be precise. I am in their home in Rush. If you know Ireland, you will know that the epicentre of tomato production is in Rush, on the east coast, above Dublin. A majestic landscape of green field, fertile soils and magnificent beaches. But this combination of factors is not the reason why Rush is the tomato home of Ireland. No, much like Motril, close to my home on Spain's southern coast, in the province of Granada, is the world centre of cherry tomato breeding, production and supply. Bearing in mind that tomatoes can be grown in Rockwool or other such man-made inert mediums that allow the flow of irrigation water which also contains the essential fertilisers and nutrients needed for the tomato plant to flourish and to flower and produce fruit. There are many crops that are farmed in this way and it can commonly be called 'hydroponic' production. Peppers, cucumbers, aubergines to name a few others are all farmed in this way, in that the baby plants will be taken from the nursery and then transplanted into the medium. As they grow upwards and flower and fruit, harvesting can take place in the lower plant area, and will continue moving up the plant as it grows ad throughout the whole season.

So why is Rush the home for Irish salad tomato production? Why is Motril the centre of world cherry tomato development and production? Is it soil? No, they are grown in an artificial medium placed on top of the indigenous soil. Is it climate? Partly, as heat is a requirement in the growing process, but greenhouses or glasshouses as they are more commonly known, can be heated, so no, not really. So, what is the reason? It is the quantity of sunshine hours and, fundamentally, the quality of the sunlight! Unpolluted, good light creates effective photosynthesis (the plant turning carbon dioxide into sugar or food) and therefore vigorous and healthy growth.

Interestingly, in Almería, easily the biggest area in the world for cultivation of salad crops such as the above, there is a phenomenon that goes some way towards offsetting the "sea of plastic" arguments that often crop up regarding this type of food production. Since the 1980s, Almería in southern Spain has developed the largest concentration of greenhouses in the world, covering 26,000 hectares. The greenhouses reflect so much sunlight back into the atmosphere that Spanish researchers have found they are actually cooling the province. While temperatures in the rest of Spain have climbed at rates above the world average, meteorological observatories located in the so-called sea of plastic have shown temperatures in the area moving in the opposite direction, with a decline of 0.3 degrees per decade. The strange phenomenon has not gone unnoticed in scientific circles, and now a study has suggested a plausible explanation: the white colour of the plastic reflects sunlight into the atmosphere as if it were a mirror, and it slows the warming of the surface. In this way, the greenhouses at a local level offset the rising temperatures associated with global warming.

All the family are there at the McCann's family home. The three brothers, responsible for all aspects of the family business. The mother is there, matriarch and boss of everything. Two of their senior farming managers are also present, as am I, alone and English in a very unusual environment indeed. A coal fire is burning in the grate, tea is served as I begin my pitch to win supply of their tomatoes for Keeling's client, my recently converted stone fruit pioneers, the SuperValu chain.

The reason I am with the McCann family now is because of another Irish tomato growing family, the Foleys. Matt and John Foley are brothers and they are committed glasshouse growers, again in Rush and again, focusing entirely on salad tomato production. I had become good friends with John, the younger brother, through our mutual love of clay pigeon shooting (John shot for Ireland at the 1996 Olympic Games in Atlanta) and I had had quite a few discussions with him concerning their supply and my client. However, they were long standing Tasbury's suppliers and they had already committed to a deal for the forthcoming season. What they did do, was put me in touch with Brian McCann, one of the two sons, and so here I am, ready to make them an offer that they couldn't refuse! In all seriousness, I think that they invited me over more out of curiosity rather than any real interest in changing the family business commitment to an 'alien' customer. "What could I possibly offer them that would make them switch loyalties to Keeling's?" was their basic question, but the unstated inference was who was this cheeky Englishman and what was he doing here, trying to shake up our established business?

I had done my research and I knew my numbers. I offered them easier distribution; in some cases, direct deliveries to local stores in place of supplying via a depot that involved extra costs. I offered them the benefit of reduced cost structures in the form of a better price per kilo. I offered them transparency of the whole supply chain – daily sales reports and stock positions. I offered them quicker payment terms and I offered them a substantial pre-season advance to aid them with their annual pre-production costs of planting and material purchasing. Two hours later, I smoked a cigarette outside with the two brothers. Nothing was said, but I could tell that I had impressed them.

It had been a tough meeting, but my message was crystal clear and I hoped that it had been well received. I drove back to Keeling's offices, nervous but satisfied that I had done my best to secure a radical new supply deal for SuperValu from one of the largest and best-known tomato producers in Ireland.

I had to wait just twenty-four hours before taking the call to go back to the house for news on their decision. Mother McCann and her two sons were waiting for me. Same scenario: coal fire burning, lino on the floor, tea on the table and expectation in the air. They took my deal, they accepted my terms and my offer and an agreement was reached to switch to Keeling's for the exclusive supply of Irish salad tomatoes to SuperValu nationally, from October to July – the full season. The deal was worth more than four million euros per season and naturally, I was euphoric. I loved my job and most of all, I loved my adopted country.

Two days later, the Keeling's board of directors took a conference call from the fresh produce buying director of Tasbury's Ireland. Under no circumstances would they permit the switch of supply from one of their key growers to an arch competitor. The penalty for such an act was the loss of the complete fresh produce supply deal to Tasbury's Ireland and given that this supply deal was worth approximately twelve million euros annually, really, the Keeling's family had zero option but to withdraw from the new offer I had agreed with the McCann family. An hour later, I took the call from a livid director of SuperValu. Business. Politics. Way above my pay grade, unfortunately, but better to have tried and failed, than never to have tried at all!

July 2007 and it's a gorgeous, sunny Sunday in Drogheda and I am in my garden, on my tractor mower, giving my hectare of grass some love. I am called to the phone and it's a pleasant and unexpected surprise. My old friend from Italy, Massimo Belotti, is calling and he has a proposition for me. He's been offered a job in Malaga, Spain, on the Costa del Sol working for an avocado farming company as a senior commercial trader, but Massimo has spent his working life in packaging and he knows that he can't hold down a commercial role in fresh fruit sales, so he thinks of me. Massimo and I have had many conversations about the fact that I always expressed a desire to work in a Latin or Spanish speaking culture – Spain or South America, I always said – indeed, to this day, I remain hopeful of one day finding my perfect life somewhere in Central or South America. So, I tell my friend that, yes, I am very interested in hearing more about this job offer and after a couple more minutes chatting, we say goodbye, vowing to catch up soon. No more than fifteen minutes pass and I am already back into grass cutting mode, when my phone trills for a second time. It's a Spanish number and I answer with all my senses now tuned to curiosity setting. It is the avocado business calling me to enquire if I would be interested in a commercial position with them.

We quickly find common ground and incredibly, just three days later, I find myself being collected outside Malaga airport. I have a one-hour interview with the owner of the business and his commercial director. They evaluate my skills and they set out their vision of my role in their organisation. There and then, they make me an offer of employment. It's a cut in salary - and a sizeable one as I have made a major success of the job in Ireland - but I recognise immediately that this is not about the money. I travel home later that day in a minor state of shock, semi-euphoric and apprehensive all at once, in the knowledge that I have just received a life changing offer.

That evening, when the babies have been put to bed, my wife and I sit down in the kitchen over a glass of wine, pen and A4 paper pad on the table, ready for a discussion about the day's events. It is pitch black outside, blowing a hoolie and hammering it down with rain. We do the conventional thing; we make a list of the pros of the potential move to Spain and an opposing list of the cons. After an hour or so of this, we have an epiphany moment: We realise that the pros and the cons are meaningless. We arrive at the same conclusion: We can't turn this opportunity down, for the sake of our children's future. We would always be looking back: "I wonder what would have happened if we had taken that chance to live and work in Spain?" So, on that conclusion, a light came on and we knew that we had to take the opportunity.

At the beginning of October that year, I started my new job with Frutas Montosa in Torre del Mar, Malaga. Moral of the story: Take your opportunities, look forward not backwards, give your children the best life path possible.

J IS FOR JAMAICA

"Traveling – it leaves you speechless, then turns you into a storyteller." Ibn Battuta

I am sent on a month-long mission to Central America, South America and the Caribbean. I am to visit, amongst other places, Honduras, Guatemala, Panama, Miami, Costa Rica, Mexico, Colombia and Brazil. The trip finishes with a three-day visit to Jamaica, which is one of my favourite stop-off points, especially after a long and arduous trip such as this one. It´s a rubbish place to be. Montego Bay is my location for the next few days and I am in an all-inclusive beach resort, as the farm is close by. I have been visiting this farm for three years now and I have seen many improvements. For my friends that enjoy "fruity" stories, this is the fascinating tale of the Sex Life of a Papaya. Papaya trees come in THREE sexes: Female, male and hermaphrodite. Hermaphrodite means that the plant carries the reproductive organs of both male and female plants, much like all avocado plants. This particular variety in Jamaica originated locally and is, I believe, the best of all papayas. Its name is Solo, and it is often sold as "Sunrise" papaya. One can only tell the sex of the plant when it flowers, which is why if you're ever buying a papaya seedling to plant, they always should come in threes.

What I find interesting about this species is that the Solo variety male plants do not produce fruit, so they are undesirable in commercial farming (bloody typical!). The desirable fruits come from female trees due to their uniform pear shape. The fruits from hermaphrodite trees produce more bulbous fruits and these are often lower priced in international markets. Female plants only produce female fruits but the flower needs to be pollinated (our friends the bees and other flying insects help us to achieve this) but a hermaphrodite plant is self-fertilising and will change its sex and therefore its flower type to male or female according to weather conditions. In this way, it will produce both female and hermaphrodite fruits. We also need these asexual plants to provide flowers to enable the insects to pollinate the females. Without this, female fruits would have no seeds! This business is a world leader. Aside from harvesting for export, the best trees are selected and the fruits are harvested and the seeds are removed and washed. Those that float are discarded because they are barren, and those that sink are selected and then propagated to produce seedlings which are planted directly onto the farms at high densities - up to 900 trees per acre! After approximately ten months, harvesting of mature fruits can begin and they are harvested by hand from the bottom of the fruit cluster upwards as each fruit attains size and maturity. However, papaya trees only have a useful commercial life of three years as they become too tall to reach the crop despite the use of hydraulic harvesting platforms to propel the pickers to the tree's canopy. In this business therefore, good planning of planting to ensure year-round continuity of supply is essential. Delicious and nutritious, Solo papaya is one of my favourite fruits -

try one sliced on a bed of mixed leaves with a vinaigrette dressing and some seared scallops! Yummy!

To close this Jamaican report, I want you to know that there is no fun to be had at all on this island. I didn't meet any girls or boys that I liked, I stayed in every night as there is absolutely nothing to do on this crappy island. The people are unfriendly and the weather is awful. I hate the local beer and I can't wait to go home. NOT!

J IS FOR JERUSALEM

I had undertaken so many assignments to Israel, it was inevitable eventually, for me to have time off to relax and to enjoy some of the tourist attractions of this remarkable country. I had been to the Dead Sea, taken a mineral and mud bath in its healing waters, I had travelled to the south, to Mount Masada and the ancient fortifications there. Up on the mountain and inside the ruins of the fortress situated on top of a rocky plateau on the edge of the Judean Desert, we were obliged to drink at least one litre of water every thirty minutes just to prevent being cooked alive in the furnace-like heat. I marvelled at the story of the nine hundred-odd Sicari rebels that took the agonising decision to choose their ten bravest warriors on the night before the Roman army would surely break through the walls at dawn on the following day, after months of siege. These ten men had the unenviable task of killing all their own people, before turning their swords on themselves, rather than fall into the hands of the Romans and the unspeakable horrors that that would have entailed.

I bathed in the spiritual waters of the River Jordan and of Lake Galilee and I saw the wonders of the Negev Desert and the Red Sea. I travelled south of Jerusalem to the limestone hills of Bethlehem and I placed my hands on the cold stone floor of the Church of the Nativity, the actual spot where the baby Jesus was laid; the feeling of the hair on the nape of neck rising and a sense of vibrant and surging life coursing through my body has never been equalled in any situation, anywhere. I remember clearly stooping to duck into and out of the entrance of the tiny cave, around which the church is built. And I will never forget boarding our bus to depart this holiest of places, outside of the walled gates at the entrance to the city, my curious nature forcing me to gaze all around me as I ushered the last of the pilgrims back on board. I note a group of suspicious-looking Arab men viewing our party with intent as I climb the steps at the front of the coach. Standing now alongside our driver, I can see the men in their ankle-length white robes, as we begin to move off, I see two or three men in the group unfurl their Tawbs and I see the unmistakeable sight of Kalashnikov AK47's rising in their hands to face us. I scream "Down, get down!" at the group of passengers seated behind me and I know already that the driver is on it, as the bus's engine roars and we surge to the left and away up the highway, thirty yards, forty yards, fifty yards, we are going to make it. The sound of gunfire, the unique report of the AK at short range, the impact of the 7.62mm rounds hitting the rear of the bus and the CLANG-CLANG-CLANG sound of the bullets striking the metal coachwork are simultaneous, but we have put just enough distance between us and the gunmen to make our escape and live for another day. I knew that Bethlehem had long been in the hands of the Palestinian authorities and I knew that it also been a Headquarters for Yasser Arafat and his PLO, but seriously!

A week or so later and the time had come to explore the capital, Jerusalem, and even with almost no religious convictions, I was soon in awe of the city, its biblical stories and its history. If you have never been, put it on your bucket list; Temple Mount and the Dome of the Rock, the Western Wall, also known as the Wailing Wall and the Armenian and Jewish quarters. The Western Wall tunnels which take you under the city, back to the level of the original city, are also not be missed. But my favourite place of all is the Church of the Holy Sepulchre. This is the ending point of the Via Dolorosa pilgrimage and the last five Stations of the Cross are inside the church itself. For Christian pilgrims, this is the holiest site of all, given that it is said this was the place where Jesus was crucified. This church is built on top of Calvary Hill and although the church is modest in comparison with other great cathedrals of this world, it is packed full of religious relics and other wonders that will amaze even non-believers.

I am part of an organised tour this day and our guide is a very impressive Israeli lady. Clearly a scholar, this incredibly knowledgeable woman is a joy to be with. Witty, sharp and informative, she speaks several languages fluently and she is patient with all of us in our group of perhaps fifteen curious travellers. Patience can be stretched however, and we do have one particularly annoying American guy in our party. We have been "upstairs" to the site of the Cross and we have seen the cleft in the rocks where Jesus's blood was supposed to have pooled below him. At this point and right in the middle of our guide's short talk on this major stopping point, the American pipes up: "So where's the body?" Clearly unimpressed, our Guide bats the question away expertly but the guy persists, "There must be a body," he grates.

"Sir," intones our guide, "These events took place over two thousand years ago, there is no body."

We move 'downstairs' to the tombs and we pass the Stone of Unction, on which Christ's body was said to be laid and anointed after his crucifixion. We move onto the Rotunda which contains the Holy Sepulchre, Christ's tomb, and we are allowed entry, just three at a time. Silent or at best our voices in a low whisper, we take in this truly emotional experience. The American is silent, at least for now, as we regather, ready to move onto the Chapel of the Syrian Christians which contains the tomb of Joseph of Arimathea. If anything, it is even more emotional than the tomb of Christ. It is unclad and cold, clearly cut directly from the rock. We take our turns to move into the tomb and to take our two or three minutes of reflection time within, before emerging into the half-light of the church. I am solemn and nearly in tears, as I take in my surroundings and the wonder of the stories that our guide has expertly imparted.

"So, who's this Joseph guy?" spouts the American, breaking the respectful silence of the whole group. It is unbelievable and the tour guide is finally out of patience. "How many Josephs do you know of, in a religious context?" she asks sternly of our unwanted guest. We can see him struggling with this one, "Well... there was that guy Joseph, you know the one, that guy with the Dream Coat..."

K IS FOR KIWI AND THE KRUGER PARK

Annual global kiwi fruit production in 2018 was estimated to be in excess of five million tonnes, with New Zealand easily the world's biggest producer with 42 percent of global volume sales.

The kiwifruit may be New Zealand's defining agricultural product, generating a handsome $1.05 billion in exports for the country in 2015, according to data from the U.S. Department of Agriculture. But how the South Pacific nation came to claim the exotic, fuzzy fruit with soft, green flesh and a unique taste is a story that combines considerable luck and a stroke of marketing genius.

The erstwhile Chinese gooseberry, as its archaic English name suggests, finds its root a hemisphere away in China. Its original name in Chinese, *mihoutao* — "macaque fruit" — refers to the monkeys' love for it, according to the 16th century Chinese medicine encyclopaedia, the *Compendium of Materia Medica*.

The kiwifruit's status as a transplant might not come as a surprise to many of you. After all, the story of one of the world's greatest marketing and botanical hijacks has been vaguely circulating for decades, from a

New York *Times* item about trade in New Zealand over 30 years ago to a TIME column about branding and psychology in 2010.

But the scant documentary evidence of *how* the fruit made it across the Pacific has given an apocryphal flavour to a tale that is, in fact, all too real. It all began in 1904, when Mary Isabel Fraser, the principal of an all-girls school in New Zealand, brought back some Chinese gooseberry seeds from China. They were then given to a farmer named Alexander Allison who planted them in his farm near the riverine town of Whanganui. The trees went on to bear their first fruit in 1910.

New Zealand's appropriation of the Chinese gooseberry wasn't inevitable. Around that same time, the species was in fact also experimented with as a commercial crop both in the U.K. and the U.S.

But, as luck would have it, neither the British nor the American attempt at commercializing the fruit was as... fruitful. For example, the first batch of seeds brought to Britain's Veitch Nursery all produced male plants, thwarting the growers' plans to produce edible fruit. The same fate befell the U.S. government's attempt. So, it seems ironic that the sending of seed by a missionary to an amateur gardener should eventually lead to a new horticultural industry when the efforts of the Veitch Nursery and the U.S. Department of Agriculture were so much less successful.

The gooseberry's rebranding didn't happen until almost 50 years after Allison's trees bore fruit, according to New Zealand's official history, when agricultural exporter Turners & Growers started calling their USA-bound Chinese gooseberries "kiwifruits" on June 15, 1959.

The fruit's importer told Turners & Growers that the Chinese gooseberry needed a new name to be commercially viable stateside, to avoid negative connotations of "gooseberries," which weren't particularly popular. After passing over another proposed name, *melonette*, it was finally decided to name the furry, brown fruit after New Zealand's furry, brown, flightless national bird. It also helped that *Kiwis* had become the colloquial term for New Zealanders by the time.

Demand for the fruit started to take off, and by the 1970s, the name *kiwifruit* took root across the Chinese gooseberry trade, cementing its popular image as the quintessential New Zealand product. All this happened while China was busy tearing its own social fabric to pieces, during the decade of terror that was the Cultural Revolution. Really not that long ago since the kiwifruit didn't even exist as we know it.

Some think it was a matter of luck and suitable climate that the fruit thrived in New Zealand, but it was nevertheless classified as a separate species (Actinidia deliciosa) as recently as the 1980s.

Large-scale cultivation of the kiwifruit can now be found in many countries, including the U.S., Italy and, ironically, China, which became the world's top kiwifruit producer by 2014, and where the fruit is commonly used to make jam. But much of the kiwifruit grown worldwide can be traced back to Alexander Allison's Whanganui farm — so much so that the Pacific nation had to try to halt the export of kiwi plants at one point, in order to reduce potential competition on the global market.

Today, even parts of the Chinese-speaking world call the fruit by a partial transliteration of its Oceanic moniker. In Hong Kong and Taiwan, at least, it's known as strange fruit — *qi yi guo* in Mandarin, or *kei yi gwo* in Cantonese.

And how deliciously ironic that unscrupulous Chinese traders have tried to pass off domestically grown kiwifruits as imports.

Then there is the Atlantic Kiwi - good name. Here in Aquitaine, in south-west France, there is a specific maritime climate that delivers little change in temperature through the seasons: Cool summers and mild winters allow a long growing season that produces sweeter kiwi than other European sources. Discerning buyers search for this fruit which is why I am here to check out production of this versatile and fascinating fruit. My customer, Besco in the UK, sells twenty trucks of fresh kiwifruit *a week* and I can't get that volume from here so we are going to be busy with other suppliers this summer. I will be heading off to Northern Spain directly after this trip and then on to Italy after that – if the client wants twenty trucks of kiwi a week, I am going to service that order.

There are more than fifty varieties in existence but by far the most popular in commercial production is the Hayward kiwi. First developed in New Zealand by Hayward Wright in the 1920's, it is oval shaped with brown, fuzzy skin. The vibrant, green flesh contrasts with a white core and small, black seeds. The Hayward variety is a tangy, sweet and sour combination of invigorating flavours. This amazing fuzzy, furry fruit has many nutritional health benefits and interesting properties. Amongst these factoids are that the kiwi is a brilliant digestive aid; although it also contains more vitamin

C than an orange, it also possesses an enzyme that breaks down meat - if you're suffering from a red meat overload, eat some kiwi! Try this trick to amaze your dining companions at home: halve a kiwi and squeeze the juice onto both sides of a fresh succulent steak the night before you plan to cook. You let me know how tender is that steak!!

Available now through the winter, try the green, try the gold, try the red varieties - try the new kiwi berries even!

I am in the Kruger Park in northern South Africa. It is a work mission and I am being interviewed in a most unusual way. We enter the reserve through the South Gate, just the northern side of the Crocodile River. There are no fences at this part of the park, so in theory, any wildlife crossing the river from north to south would very suddenly be in human territory and with no restrictions on movement. I know from my research that the park is approximately the same size and shape as Israel and that it is fenced only on three sides and not at all throughout its impressively massive interior area.

We park the car and we head into the reception area of the South Gate. We are to pick up our guidebooks, our maps and pay for our next three nights' lodgings as we plan to travel through the park, going north, and then exit into Mozambique on the other side. My guide and host is a Danish gentleman called Per and he is a large-scale citrus grower from Swaziland. I am thirty-eight years old and at this stage of my career, I am the boss of my own import company. I have contracts with supermarkets to supply fruit and a major weapon in my armoury is my contact book of quality growers in South Africa. Per is looking for a new receiver in the UK and he has invited me, with my English wife, to his farm in Swaziland to stay for the weekend and then to move to the Kruger for a three-night 'holiday' trip.

I must tell you first about our arrival into Africa and our subsequent drive to the farm. The light aircraft was descending rapidly, she banked and turned as the pilot lined us up for landing. I could see below the land rushing up to meet us. This is Tzaneen, in northern South Africa and I can see that we are coming into land on a grass airstrip. As we come to a halt at the end of the strip and as the pilot is doing his post-flight checks and is shutting down the aircraft, I can see a group of men approaching us. I assume, correctly, that the tall, blond man, leading the group, is Per and he greets us warmly as we step down from the small aircraft onto the ground. He is pleasant but authoritative and as he escorts us towards some vehicles, he is explaining that our plans have changed. Instead of Per driving us out of RSA and into Swaziland and then onto his citrus farm, we must now drive ourselves. He has an urgent meeting with his farm advisors here in Tzaneen and he will join us at his farm in the morning. He offers me a bunch of keys and he indicates that his Mercedes sedan, right here, is now at our disposal for the journey ahead.

"Steve, you see the robot up there on the highway?" he begins, pointing at a set of traffic lights on the main road that runs alongside the airfield. "Exit the airfield there, drive to the robot and turn right," he continues. "Stay on that road for approximately six hours, including the border crossing into Swaziland and until you come to cows in the road. That's the farm. Turn right there and drive a mile up to the house. My wife and staff will meet you there. I'll see you tomorrow." He said all this with such authority and conviction that I was almost convinced that this was going to be a doddle.

Six hours later and notwithstanding a very surreal night-time border crossing, we arrived unscathed at the farm. The next morning, Per has arrived and it's time for my first look at the farm. As Per drives me in his 4x4, he explains the history of the farm, what they grow and why it is where it is. As we approach the Crocodile River, some two hundred yards below us, down a forested bank, I ask him if there are indeed crocodiles in the river, he gives me strange look and says, "Of course!" and then he hesitates as if to try to find something that he can use that will mitigate my stupidity. "However, it's a good question," he continues. "In Africa, only in rivers that flow from west to east will you find crocs," and he begins to name some of the great rivers of this continent, "Congo, The Volta, Zambezi, Limpopo," he goes on. I lap this up as we come to a standstill and prepare to exit the jeep. I have used this story about crocodiles and African rivers many times. Of course, it's false, but you would be amazed how many people will believe you, if you tell the story with conviction!

We step down onto iron hard ground on a track running above the forested area that leads down to the river. I am still jabbering away with typical enthusiasm as I note a very large and scary looking reptile directly on the track about ten feet from where I am standing. I know from a lifetime of watching wildlife documentaries that this is a Monitor Lizard and it's a big one of perhaps eight feet or so in length. It is motionless, aside from its tongue which is flicking backwards and forwards, side to side, continuously.

"Is it dangerous Per?" I stutter.

"Move very slowly backwards and away," states Per in a low and controlled voice.

My introduction to the fabulous secrets of the Dark Continent had begun the day before and this would be the pattern every time that I took a step in this rich and fascinating place.

So, with our lodgings paid for, maps stowed, and fancy guidebooks to the wonders of the park in hand, we drive from the entrance and into the park. It is a clear and warm day. You can see the heat haze rising from the asphalt road in front of us as we begin our journey. Literally five minutes later, as we negotiate a long curve in the road, we have to stop. Before our eyes, a large herd of elephants has begun to cross the road. Maybe six hundred animals – babies, mothers, grandmothers, seasoned old tuskers and young bulls, all together, all crossing. We are unable to speak. It takes a long fifteen minutes for the jumbos to cross. What is almost as amazing as the sight of the elephants is the fact that on each side of the road, perhaps two yards from the kerb, the bush begins. Small, thorny bushes give way to larger plants and then to small, scraggy-looking trees. Nothing really of substance is there and it is certainly not a forest to give cover to the enormous pachyderm group that has, by now, almost crossed the road. What is unbelievable is that the elephants literally disappear in front of our eyes, as if they were never there in the first place. Thirty-eight years old, at the top of my game and with a career in fresh produce well on the go, I now know that I, in fact, am an inconsequential speck of dust in the universe.

The days pass in a non-stop blur of sights and sounds and smells. We see everything in the books and more. I am becoming an expert at spotting game: all kinds of birds, raptors, eagles, secretary birds, ostriches, reptiles, lions, leopards, hyena, hunting dogs, rhino, ibis, impala, monkeys and baboons – I mentally tick off and file every sight and every event. Per stops suddenly one afternoon between camps. He's seen something in the road. I can't quite believe it as he quickly steps from the car and crosses in front of us, stooping to scoop up a tiny creature into his hands and returning, thankfully safely, to the car. He turns to his two passengers in the rear of the car and he places a two-inch long chameleon onto my wife's head and I watch, transfixed, as it furls its tail, beady eyes upon me and moving independently of each other, and it changes to the colour of my wife's hair! A few miles later, we pull into our next camp and I am given the responsibility of re-homing our new friend. I place it gently onto a branch of a small tree and I watch it change again to the exact colours of its surroundings.

After supper we head out of camp on a night safari; something I would whole-heartedly recommend as a lot of Africa's creatures hunt at night, although I must offer a valuable piece of advice here – never ever, ever, offer to be a lamp holder on a night safari, you just would not believe the quantity, variety and massive size of the night-dwelling insects that want to be your friend, on your arm, holding the lamp!

The next day, as we continue our journey, we make a stop at a quiet-looking watering hole in the bush. It is quite a large pond, a small lake really, with grassy banks on the side opposite us, it has trees behind and there are low bushes scattered haphazardly on all sides. We sit in the car, binoculars trained. There is nothing there, or so it seems. Gradually, Per points out to us the wonders before us that are beginning to take shape and form from their hiding places.

"See the lions over there. See the giraffes cooling off in the shade there. Do you see the crocs there on the banks? The hyenas over there?" A warthog scurrying for cover with its hoglets in tow, takes our attention. It is like a landscape painting that requires one's total concentration to see all the details of the scene. Per motions for us to fix our gaze to the centre of the lake. We train our spy glasses onto the water. There's nothing there. "There" says Per. The surface of the water appears to be flat calm but no, there... there, we see something. It's a pair of ears, then two eyes, then four pairs of eyes and ears. Hippopotamus! We are quite unable to control our instincts and we blaze away with our cameras. "No, no, no!" our man says. "That's not the picture you want. I'll get you the picture you need, just wait." And with that he opens the electric window on his side of the car (definitely not allowed and certainly not recommended anywhere in this environment, by the way!). I can't quite believe my ears as Per begins to talk to the hippo. Grunting and groaning, gurning, yawning and grimacing as if in a trance, Per begins to attract the attention of the group of hippos there before us. They rise further from the water; we have heads now. There are maybe ten of the magnificent creatures, now clearly interacting with our host. Per begins to reach his climax, or so it seems, and as one, the hippos give us the photo of our dreams; mouths agape, grunting and growling like Chewbacca on speed, we capture a dozen images for posterity and I am in awe of the man beside me. He speaks bloody Hippopotamus and he's got them to pose just for us!

A day and a night later, we are coming to the end of my first Kruger experience. I have been grilled for a week by a Danish / Swazi citrus farmer. We have discussed everything possible about the fruit, the logistics, varieties that I can sell, what sizes work best for me, the terms of trade he expects, and the price returns he would be satisfied with. It's a quarter of a million cartons of fresh fruit per season and it's a big deal for both of us.

We drive slowly, all the while our eyes are peeled in search of new sights. Per stops the car. He points out several specks up in the sky, wheeling way above us in the azure heavens and he says in his unmistakeable business voice, "Identification Mr. Askham?"

I've been with Per for a week now. I think I have seen almost everything in the guidebook, I've identified hundreds of creatures and I am looking at these tiny dots in the sky and I am thinking, "Do you know what, I have not got the faintest idea what they are." I turn to Per and as I look him in the eye, I say clearly and confidently, "Yellow-billed Kite, Per."

He returns my gaze and without a blink, without any hesitation whatsoever, he proffers his hand to me, "Congratulations Steve, you have my business."

Whilst speaking about elephants, I must recount another tale that comes to mind, again in the Kruger but on a different visit. I am with a group of South Africans and I am in business with them. I am supplying Spanish avocados into RSA for the supermarket sector in their off season. We have become friends and the trip into the Kruger is like a post-season bonding session; some work, lots of chats and lots of beers! We rent a house in one of the main camps and we go out every day to search for game. We 'Braai' - a barbecue fired with wood, every night. One night after dinner at the house, I am called by the boys to the front door. It's open and I peer out of the door to the boys standing in the small yard there before me. I can immediately see why they have called me to the door: there is a coiled up, fat little snake there against the wall. I know that it is a Puff Adder, one of the deadliest snakes in Africa. I admire its beauty and begin to approach the beast for a closer look.

"Woah there Steveo," says my host, David. "Puff Adders can move and strike at three metres per second," he deadpans. By my instant calculation, I am two point nine five metres from the viper, and I back off with alacrity. You ain't getting me today, boyo!

The next day we set off in our car on safari once more. We head into the hills nearby, to a safe barbecue spot. The boys are South Africans; to barbecue - or to braai - is a South African's birth right. Always wood of a specific species, good meat and plenty to drink. These are the secrets of a good braai and the boys set up with no fuss. Steak and eggs follow with ice cold gin and tonics to wash it down, all the while settling ourselves into a peaceful afternoon overlooking a dam below us. It is literally teeming with crocodiles and we marvel again at Nature's bounty there before us.

We are on the way back to camp, driving slowly as we spot a solitary rhino taking shade beneath an Acacia tree fifty yards from the road. I don't know if you know, but rhinos are solitary creatures during the day; a female with a calf will be alone all day, as will all male rhinoceros. When night falls however, their inner social personalities kick-in and they will meet for a poop and a chat. You know that it's been a party the previous night when you come across a rhino toilet in the day. The animals poop in a big pile and then they push all the excrement outwards from the centre and into a giant circular shape. I want you to know this just in case, on your daily travails, you come across a three-metre wide, doughnut shaped pile of dried plant-based excrement and you're wondering what on earth it could be.

Just before we arrive at camp, I call the car to a halt. I've spotted some movement in the bush, ten or fifteen yards to my left. We stop. Yes, I am correct, there in the bush are two juvenile bull elephants. They are feeding and I can see they are devouring a sapling. They tear the branches from the young tree and are stuffing the branches into their mouths, seamlessly ripping the foliage from the branches, which are then discarded. I am in the front passenger seat and I am smoking a hand-rolled cigarette from the open window as I gaze upon the little scene before me. I am in awe as I watch the adolescent jumbos tear into their lunch and I can see them watching me. I am at peace with the world as I watch my cigarette smoke curl up and away from my fag and into the sunshine that beats down upon us. In slow motion, I watch the smoke take the light breeze and move towards the elephants as I exhale contentedly. I am still dozing with happiness as jumbo number one, perhaps two or three tonnes of young male tusker, moves his trunk from the task in hand, to the skies in front of him, as he takes in a sample of my cigarette smoke. My next word has a degree of urgency to it: "Drive," I say, as I watch the creature taste my smoke and it's clear that he's not at all happy with it. He begins to move towards our car, his trumpet up and out, scary tusks pointing my way as he speeds up now, crashing through the young trees and approaching us at speed. He wants a confrontation and this time, I scream, "Drive, DRIVE!" We escape to live another day. Lesson learned again that Mother Nature is easily the most powerful force on Earth and that we men are mere specks of dust in the detritus of life.

L IS FOR LYCHEE

Perhaps the most Chinese of the world's exotic fruits, the lychee, isn't just full of flavour and nutrition – it's also full of history.

Yang Yuhuan – or Yang Guifei, as she was also known – was the best-loved concubine of Emperor Xuan Zhong, whose reign of 43 years between 713 and 756AD was the longest of China's Tang dynasty. Yang was one of the 'Four Beauties of ancient China' and is famous for her love for the Emperor. She is perhaps less known, however, for her love for the lychee, her favourite fruit. She adored it so much that the Emperor had couriers ride night and day to bring her the sweet treat from Guangdong, some 1,900 kilometres away from her home in the capital.

China is, of course, the world's biggest producer of the fruit, accounting for more than 60 per cent of the global output. Guangdong ranks first in the country, with more than 266,667 hectares of lychee orchards scattered throughout the province. Last year, 1.5 million tonnes were produced in the province and its exports were estimated to be worth more than US$10 billion, with 80 per cent going to the United States, Canada and Europe.

Global production of the fruit has nearly doubled over the past

15 years – most, but certainly not all of it, in China. New and more sophisticated technology enables producers to store longer and ship over greater distances. Today's modern commercial volume growers of fresh lychees include Mexico, Israel, South Africa, Madagascar (where most of the world's varietal innovation comes from) and India.

Lychees are delicious and juicy. They are also low in calories and rich in fibre. A 100g serving of fresh lychees provides 86% of daily recommended vitamin C, hence their popularity worldwide. The fruit can be eaten fresh, dried or canned.

Lychee is a medium-sized tree that can reach up to 50 feet in height. It blooms from November to February in the northern hemisphere and from April to August in the southern. The flowers are fragrant and attract bees, the main pollinators.

It is a perennial plant and can survive for up to 1,000 years in the wild.

The seeds contain toxic compounds that can induce unpleasant side effects in the digestive system after consumption.

Lychee is a natural diuretic which can alleviate pain associated with kidney stones and can reduce the formation of blood clots. It can also prevent the development of breast cancer.

It is known across the world as the 'Chinese strawberry'.

Here in Veracruz province, on the east coast of Mexico, we grow the Mauritius variety, named after the island of the same name. With its strong character and disease resistance properties, this cultivar is ideally suited to a sub-tropical climate of heat and humidity. I love to talk about sustainability in my work and especially our relationship with nature. I always encourage growers to study and record carefully all aspects of their environment: Soils, erosion, biodiversity, flora and fauna and our relationship with them all. After all God isn't making any more of these things and our planet is a wondrous melting pot of all life. Farmers have a massive part to play in making sure that future generations have the same wonders to hand that we have now, and I admire them enormously for their efforts.

On this delightful farm, common creatures include the Caiman, Boa Constrictor, Blue Crabs and the local Jaiba Crab. Watch your back, mind where you plant your feet, look carefully before you walk! A true honour to be immersed in the joy of living Nature. ¡Gracias México, hasta pronto!

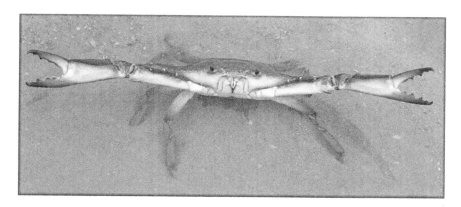

L IS FOR LOGISTICS

Logistics management is the part of supply chain management and supply chain engineering that plans, implements, and controls the efficient, effective forward and reverse flow and storage of goods, services, and related information between point of origin and point of consumption to meet customer's requirements.

To be a competent fruit trader, one must have a better than average understanding of logistics. What you may be grasping at this point in my tale, is that not many people have a good understanding of where their fresh produce comes from. What is in fact, a more difficult thing to understand is exactly HOW it comes. It's all very well to understand that pineapples do not grow on trees. It's one thing to know that apples are harvested in one go, usually over just a week or so, and that then they are marketed and sold from long-term cold storage. It might be useful to know that all citrus and avocado crops can be 'held' in a perpetual state of maturity without rotting on the tree, if market conditions dictate that it is unwise to harvest. It's obvious to me, but probably not to everybody, that all berries, all types of stone fruit, all melon varieties, need to be harvested at optimum maturity, packed immediately and then shipped to market. All these fruits have only a very limited storage period.

So, what about the movement to market of the produce once it has been harvested? How do we move fresh fruit around the world on a daily basis? Who is involved and what actually happens?

Of course, there are companies that specialise in the transportation of produce. It's important to know that on arrival into port or airport in country of destination, that there will be customs, perhaps an inspection of the goods, possibly a duty tariff to be applied, depending on country of origin and type of produce. There will always be a freight forwarder, who will help you to customs-clear the merchandise and assist in onward transportation to desired point of delivery.

But way before we get to container arrivals in ports or to truck deliveries to depots, we need to get the produce from tree to ground and then from ground to pack house; from the soil and into appropriate receptacles in order to move that produce from field to production line and then on to market.

I will try to start from the beginning of the logistics process....

A farmer inspects his crop of apples. It is autumn in the northern hemisphere and the growing season is over. It's now time to harvest the crop. Inspections will have been made daily at this point. He's looking for external signs that the fruit is ready for harvest. Is this year's Royal Gala crop well coloured? What is the size range of the fruit on the tree – he'll be looking for a healthy percentage of fruits in a certain size range by diameter – say fifty percent of his crop falls into two size bands, 60/75mm and 65/70mm. Would that indicate that it's time for harvesting? No. We need to understand that the fruit is mature (not ripe) and that indication comes from an internal inspection. First indication would be that the pips are brown, but the main check here would be to test the sugar content of individual fruits to give an average level over the entire crop. Using an instrument called a refractometer, the method involves squeezing some juice from the apple onto the cleaned surface of the refractometer's inspection surface and then to point the closed instrument towards the light. We can see the level of sugar now, measured on a rising scale through the eyepiece of our special tool. We are looking at ten brix (ten percent) as a minimum level to commence harvest and this level is pretty much the standard across so many types of fruits, but it's not the only measure in all cases.

In the case of avocados, for example, one would not be checking for sugar levels. The two factors that are important in checking maturity of avocados before harvesting begins are firstly, a test of oil content per fruit. That is literally the level of 'fat' or natural oils within any number of tested fruits that can be computed to represent the whole crop. Acceptable oil content level in order to commence harvest would be between eleven to twelve percent. Similarly, there would be simultaneous tests on 'dry matter' content.

Dry matter is the solid content of the fruit minus the water. Thus, dry matter is all the carbohydrates, vitamins, proteins, fats, fibres and sugars found in the fruit. As the avocado grows, its dry matter content also increases. Studies have shown that dry matter has proven to be a reliable indicator of flavour, and by extension, consumer satisfaction as well.

Dry matter is, however, an indirect indicator of maturity in avocados. The development of the fruit can also be tracked by the increase in the oil content of the fruit.

A minimum of 11.2% oil content is considered necessary to declare a fruit mature. The higher the oil content, the better the fruit tastes. Leaving fruit on the tree longer allows more oil to develop. However, this leaves less time for transport and storage. The oil content of avocados at maturity will differ by variety and the region where the fruit is growing.

However, while oil content is a fantastic indicator of maturity, it is not an easy metric to calculate in avocados.

It has been found that as the oil content in avocados increases, water content decreases, because oil replaces water in the fruit. As dry matter is fruit content minus water, it did not long take long before the correlation between oil content and dry matter was established. As oil content increases, the dry matter content increases as well.

Methods to Estimate Dry Matter

Many ways have been used to estimate dry matter with the purpose of determining if avocados are mature enough to be harvested. There are simple conventional - and a few new - methods to measure dry matter content.

Conventional Methods

Here, a sample of fresh fruit is taken. The sample is weighed to obtain the 'wet weight'. Fruit is then dried in either an oven or microwave until all moisture has evaporated. It is then weighed again to obtain the dry weight. Dry matter content is calculated using the following relationship:

(Dry weight / wet weight) x 100 = % Dry Matter

The disadvantage of this method is that it is destructive, and incredibly time and labour intensive.

New Methods

Among alternative methods, near infrared (NIR) spectroscopy is one of the most popular. It is non-destructive and gives an accurate dry matter assessment (within 1 dry matter unit) and has been integrated into small handheld instruments. Measurements and results can be obtained instantly in the field and in packing warehouses, while the devices themselves are affordable and allow for organization of thousands of readings.

Best Practices with Dry Matter

To estimate dry matter accurately, some precautions must be taken:

Test fruits from shady parts of the tree and select the least ripe-looking fruits.

Many trees in an orchard should be tested; a single test is not enough.

Conduct dry matter estimation in the morning with NIR tools. Similarly, for conventional DM estimation, harvest fruit in the morning since fruit is most hydrated at this time of the day.

For conventional methods of DM estimation, wrap the fruit in plastic to prevent moisture loss, and conduct the analysis as soon as possible.

The distribution of dry matter in the avocado is not even from top to bottom, as Figure 1 shows. As a result, dry matter should be measured at the mid-point (widest diameter). Measurements should be taken from the same place on all fruit.

One more method of checking maturity in some fruits would be to take average pressure readings. In stone fruits for example, say peaches and nectarines, alongside a thorough check of average sugar levels for the variety that is going to be harvested, an additional check on average fruit pressures would also be essential. This combination of sugar levels averaging over ten brix and an ideal pressure average of between five and seven kilos per fruit, conducted using another specialised industry instrument called a penetrometer and measured against an industry-standard scale of acceptable pressures, would give the best possible signal that the fruit is ready for harvest.

I have digressed again, I know. But I wouldn't be doing my job properly if I haven't described the full logistical process, beginning with the essential-to-get-right decision to harvest.

Mr. Apple Farmer then. He's got his information, he has done his maturity and sugar level checks and it is time to get his picking teams into the orchards right away. The first thing that happens is the placement in the orchards of sufficient wooden or plastic bulk bins, placed strategically along the rows of trees, so that pickers can move freely. The same kind of container would be used in the harvest of other crops, by the way. Including citrus and stone fruit. Each bulk bin can hold approximately 300-400 kilos of fresh fruit and in the case of apples, each picker would pick from the tree and into a picking bucket hanging from a strap around his neck and with the bucket placed comfortably somewhere in between stomach and chest area. Once the bucket is full, the picker will move to the nearest bin and then gently release the apples into the bulk bin by releasing the clip that holds the liner of the picking bucket in place, allowing the apples to cascade slowly, with no drop involved.

Once full, the bins are collected using specialist trailers and tractors and taken directly to the packing station for the next stage of processing the fruit. Let´s be clear at this point that bulk bins are not always the best receptacle for tree harvested fruit. Often, the fruit is too sensitive to be placed in heavy weight conditions. Cherries, most peaches, avocados, mangos, and all soft fruit are harvested into smaller plastic containers usually weighing somewhere in the region of eighteen to twenty kilos each. (In fact, many berry types are picked directly into the plastic punnet that will go onto retail shelves, although these will also go straight from point of harvest to a packing station for check weighing, quality control and punnet labelling, before being boxed and then stacked into a full pallet that would then be strapped for rigidity and then placed into cold store, ready for despatch to the client). It´s the same process however: harvest from field into container, move the containers to the packing plant.

One thing that´s crucial at this point, is the beginning of what is known as traceability. Every commercial orchard, field, plot or area of land that is professionally cultivated in fruit or vegetable production is completely mapped. It will have accurate records of annual soil analysis for fertility, acidity and percentage of organic material. In some cases, studies of the ground used to produce our fruit and veggies will even include numbers of earthworms per cubic metre. This would be essential knowledge used in calculating drainage, erosion problems caused by compaction, or by wind or flooding. Each plot of land will also have comprehensive records of precisely what has been applied to the land, to the trees, to the crop itself. Each completed application record will detail exactly what percentage and quantity of "active ingredient" has been sprayed or used in crop protection, whether that is a fertiliser, a nutrient or perhaps a fungicide, possibly an insecticide if required. Way before any crop comes to be harvested, highly detailed application records are submitted to clients that will either be fruit importers or handlers - essentially the 'middle men' between the growers and the retailers – the guys that buy fruit in very large quantities and the guys that then manage a supermarket chain's daily orders and deliver to order to the supermarket's handling centres, or depots, that are strategically located in any country. Supermarkets these days have taken things one step further in their never-ending quest to reduce costs and to analyse every single part of the supply chain, and that step is to work directly with fruit growers around the world, negotiating their volume requirements and the prices they will pay for fruit to be delivered to their appointed service provider who will then take care of stock holding, appropriate cold storage and daily deliveries to the chains' stores and depots.

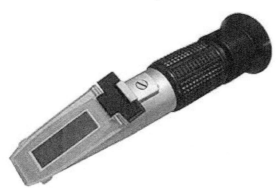

M IS FOR MOTHER NATURE

"If you think adventure is dangerous, try routine, it's lethal."
Paul Coelho

Mankind's relationship with Mother Nature is my number one passion in everything I do in my work in global agriculture. Public perception of the use of pesticides, fungicides and herbicides is often - not always, but often - misguided or even plain wrong. Apple production here in the south of France has revitalized my love for natural controls of pests and the essential nature of working with a correctly functioning, balanced food chain. We can demonstrate meaningful reductions in chemical usage using the biodiversity all around us, whilst complying with ever stricter laws over chemical residue limits. My belief is that we will never be able to feed the world's population without using conventional farming methods. Conventional farming involves the controlled use of approved pesticides at recorded and internationally agreed levels. It also involves the promotion of environmentally friendly practices such as IPM (Integrated Pest Management), where, for example, the use of predatory insects can be a solution against pests rather than using a chemical to resolve the problem. Organic (the non-use of all chemicals in production) production is 'cool' but it will not cut the mustard when it comes to good yielding crops, produced in sustainable ways across the world.

Here are some examples of brilliant but simple farming techniques that give us the best of both: Sustainable agriculture producing healthy and nutritious crops that are profitable but which work in harmony with the environment and nature, therefore protecting our biodiversity and conserving and encouraging a healthy and robust food chain.

Hedge and border planting to encourage natural species to live and multiply.

Beetle banks to provide havens for beneficial insects.

Bat population growth by providing bat-houses - any apple grower will tell you about Codling Moth damage and one Pipistrelle bat can eat several hundred moth larvae in a single night!

Owls, tits and other bird species that eat damaging insects and rodents. Even snakes that help us to control the damaging behaviour of rats and mice that destroy tree roots. Detailed analysis of soils to determine not just acidity levels and fertility, but importantly how we can understand the work of earthworms and other invertebrate species. Correct levels of irrigation and use of fertilizer, the list goes on...

We are moving towards a system known as 'precision agriculture' where even the smallest detail is examined and improved, and I am so proud to be a part of this process.

One final thought for those struggling with invasions of large spiders in their homes - did you know that their presence means that your local ecosystem is working correctly and that your biodiversity and food chains are in good shape?

M IS FOR THE MOON

Agriculture on the Moon. Not a dream. Reality. Fact.
Science wins.

It's my honour and privilege to be on this mission today to study sustainable food production on the Moon - courtesy of one of Earth´s most important space and aeronautical administrations.

Supply of food to space stations and other long duration missions is heavy and staggeringly expensive. One astronaut on the International Space Station requires approximately 1.8 kilograms of food and packaging per day. You can imagine the numbers required for a four-man long-term mission!

Due to the cost of resupply and the impracticality of resupplying interplanetary missions the prospect of growing food inflight and off-Earth is of major importance. The existence of a space farm would aid the creation of a sustainable environment, as plants can be used to recycle wastewater, generate oxygen, continuously purify the air and recycle faeces on the space station or spaceship. Just 10m² of crops produces 25% of the daily oxygen requirements of 1 person. This essentially allows the space farm to turn the spaceship into an artificial ecosystem with a hydrological cycle and nutrient recycling. In addition to maintaining a shelf-life and reducing total mass, the ability to grow food in space would help reduce the vitamin gap in astronaut's diets and provide fresh food with improved taste and texture. Currently, much of the food supplied to astronauts is heat treated or freeze dried. Both methods, for the most part, retain the properties of the food pre-treatment. However, vitamin degradation during storage can occur.

Supply of foodstuffs to others is likely to be a major part of early off-Earth settlements. Food production is a non-trivial task and is likely to be one of the most labour-intensive and vital tasks of early colonists.

However, this is not as easy as it sounds... there are many disadvantages. A variety of technical challenges will face colonists attempting off-Earth agriculture. These include the effect of reduced gravity, lighting, and pressure as well as increased radiation. Though greenhouses may solve many of the problems presented in space, their construction would come with their own set of technical challenges.

Plants grown inflight experience a microgravity environment, and plants grown on the surface of the Moon experience approximately 1/6 the gravity that earth plants do. However, so long as plants are provided with directional light, those grown in low gravity environments still experience normal growth. Normal growth is classified as opposite root and shoot growth direction.

The long lunar night (a lunar day lasts for two weeks and a lunar night also for two weeks) would impede reliance on solar power and require a colony to be designed that could withstand large temperature extremes. Two exceptions to this restriction are the so-called "peaks of eternal light" located at the lunar north pole that are constantly bathed in sunlight. The rim of Shackleton Crater, where I am today, towards the lunar south pole, also, has a near-constant solar illumination. The Moon lacks light elements (volatiles), such as carbon and nitrogen. Additionally, oxygen, though one of the most common elements in the regolith (the primary constituent of the Moon's surface) is only found bound up in minerals that would require complex industrial infrastructure using very high energy levels to isolate. Some or all of these volatiles are needed to generate breathable air, water, food, and rocket fuel, all of which would need to be imported from Earth until other cheaper sources are developed. This would limit the colony's rate of growth and keep it dependent on Earth. The cost of volatiles, however, could be reduced by constructing the upper stage of supply ships using materials high in volatiles, such as carbon fibre and other plastics, although converting these into forms useful for life would involve substantial difficulty.

Enough already I hear you say! I agree, this is mind-blowing stuff and there is so much for me to take in. I only hope that I am able to provide some usefulness here amongst some of the world's best in their fields. For professional reasons, I cannot name names, but this has been the greatest mission of my life!

Over and out from the light side of the Moon!

M IS FOR MOROCCO

Taroudant is known as the Grandmother of Marrakech, because it is a similar walled city, albeit smaller and with all the city inside the ramparts. It had its golden age in the sixteenth century under the Saadi dynasty. The city walls, the great mosque and its minaret were constructed in 1528 by Mohammed Ash-Sheikh and it was the capital for a short time under this dynasty before they moved it to Marrakech, and it was used as a base to attack the Portuguese in Agadir. The city was prosperous through the riches of the Sous Plain, marketing products such as sugar cane, rice, cotton and indigo. To this day it is a thriving market town.

Here in the Sous, we farm some of the earliest peaches and nectarines in the northern hemisphere. Even I find it hard to comprehend that Mother Nature can provide us with sweet and juicy fruit from the middle of March from deciduous trees that remain dormant all winter, from trees that need to spring into spring with new leaf, new flower, to be pollinated and with sufficient time for the pregnant flowers to mature and deliver mature fruit!

How can this be you ask? A combination of key factors: A micro-climate giving us enough winter to provide the trees with sufficient 'cold units' so that the trees can defoliate and sleep (one cold unit = one hour at less than seven centigrade). Fertile, well-tended soils and then the first warmth of spring here in the northern hemisphere aid us greatly. Additionally, we plant specially developed varieties known as 'Low-chill' that require fewer cold units than others (150+ cold units is good for these beauties as opposed to over 300 for later fruiting varieties). This is a range of early varieties developed by the University of Florida, specialist breeders of low-chill peaches and nectarines, bred to be the first to arrive on the international marketplace. Of course, we must not forget the very smart people that plant and nurture these juicy stone fruits that are pure nectar to the taste buds.

I cannot name names for professional reasons but my grower here is a consummate fruit producer and I salute you. These are not just any old run-of-the-mill peaches and nectarines, these are YOUR Moroccan peaches and nectarines! A privilege and an honour to be at your service.

N IS FOR NEAR DEATH EXPERIENCES

Double engine failure on a Boeing 747 one hundred miles from landing. Giant crocodile attack in Brazil, heavy-calibre groundfire on my helicopter transport in the jungle, close to murder in a South African shebeen, 'Gangster agriculture' in South America and the production of terrorist weapons to change a decision. All of these and more, punctuated my "normal" working life.

It is ten in the morning on a hot day in northern Israel. We are in the triangle of land where Israel meets The Lebanon and Syria. The disputed territory of The Golan Heights are above us and to the east, Lebanon is just to the north of us as we make our way deep into a field of fresh celery, our job is to inspect the crop, to judge the harvesting intervals between crops, sowed at different times to provide a seasonal offer, and to compute this availability into a commercially viable supply. We are focused on the task in hand, conscious of the hot sun and of the brooding presence of the mountains overlooking us. We know that we are close to a zone of conflict but we are professionals in the field and we proceed with the visit, learning and teaching all the while, as we move further east into the shadow of the mountains and away from our vehicles and means of escape to safety.

We hear a WOOMPH above us and to the right and our Israeli contact and farm guide immediately shouts, "Down!" and drops to the almost-zero-cover of the field between the rows of planted celery. It's a common misconception that artillery shells whistle in flight before impact. They don't! That was an idea conceived by war film makers to provide suspense in between the round's launch from its weapon to alert audiences that something is about to happen. The mortar battery is close enough for us to hear the launch – the reality is that the sound of launch would almost never be heard and that the trajectory of the missile would be silent. In other words, most times, you would be dead before you ever heard a launch take place. Our man knew what this was and he took cover as soon as he heard the unmistakeable noise. BOOM! The first shell landed seventy yards from our position but we were still shocked by the sound of the explosion and, not least, the shower of peaty earth that covered us as we lay prone in the dirt. WOOMPH, WOOMPH! Two more on their way and we are up and running for our lives towards the relative safety of our convoy of vehicles some two hundred and fifty yards away. BOOM, BOOM! The rounds come in. Closer, even though we are running as fast as is possible towards safety. The shock wave of the rounds is real, hitting us from behind but not strong enough to bring us down, dust all over us and chunks of fresh sod and celery crashing down all around us as we begin to reach the edge of the field. Suddenly, the firing stops and an earie silence reigns now that we have reached our transport. "Out of range now…." Our guide states matter-of-factly. This is a daily experience in this part of the world, danger is all around, but in these people, a sixth sense of knowledge and survival instinct burns strongly.

Up in The Heights, He had been waiting for three nights and two days. Holed up in a high rocky gully, his target was finally in sight. Survival and prosperity in these types of situations was now printed into his DNA. Cold rations only, defecate in a bag, no fires, no lights, keep warm, keep cool, hydrate and feed, hydrate and feed, be patient…

He was armed with the Barrett M82 rifle, chambered for a .50 calibre round with light charge and muzzle brake to reduce recoil. His weapon was designed primarily for material impact; to take out stored ordnance, parked aircraft, radar units, trucks or other important assets. In this case, he knew that his target's location would be fortified with solid concrete walls, so his choice of armament was a good one. With night-scope, detachable carrying handles and bi-pod fitted, he was prepared for all eventualities. The Mark appeared through the heat haze of a hot afternoon. Range at 1550 yards, wind easterly at three miles per hours, elevation of four hundred yards and the curvature of the earth to calculate, he quickly made his decisions and adjusted his weapon accordingly. A head shot at this distance was a possibility but a miss would be unacceptable so he adjusted for his shot, aiming for the upper torso. Breathing controlled and ultimate focus on the task in hand, he squeezed off his one shot. A loud crack, hard but controlled recoil to the shoulder, his round barrels toward the target. Six seconds in flight and a puff of smoke in the distance confirms a hit. Sometime later it would be noted that the .50 calibre round went straight through a three-foot thick concrete wall, took out the Mark through the upper left chest and went on to take out two other hostile personnel standing directly behind the objective.

N IS FOR NOT JUDGING

"Great things never came from comfort zones." ~ Anonymous

The flight did not begin well. Late to the airport and harassed and stressed from a tough trip, four weeks in remote north-east Brazil can do that to a man. I just about made last check-in and then through customs and passport control to the gate for boarding. I was one of the last to board the bird out of San Paolo bound for London Heathrow. This was a night flight and would not make terra firma in the UK until sometime the following afternoon. I make my way down the fuselage of the aircraft, seat 46F, window on the port side, I know my way to there. I am one of the last to find my place and the other two seats are already occupied; a young couple, Brazilian looking, are in seats D and E and as I stow my hand luggage in the locker above, I turn to the couple, expecting the normal courtesy of stepping out of the row to the aisle, or at least standing to allow me room to squeeze by them to my window seat. The girl makes a cursory attempt to move, giving me the smallest margin to get by, but I wait for the young man to at least make a move so that I can pass. Instead, I am met with a gaze of pure malevolence, jet black eyes bore into mine and it is clear that he is not moving anywhere for me. I am always reluctant to involve airline crew in on board squabbles, I think they have enough to do, so I make my only choice and I indicate to the couple that I am coming through. I squeeze past the young woman and then have no option but to step / climb over the young man and into my spot by the window. I can feel the fury emanating from the boy and a last glance at him as the crew prepare us for take-off confirms that he does indeed want me dead and cast into eternal damnation. I am sensitive soul, so this first episode in what was going to be a long flight through the night does bother me, but I settle into my usual long journey routine and I settle quickly.

Even the most seasoned travellers can only cross their legs for so long, and so sometime later in the night, I know that I need to get out to relieve myself and I prepare to evacuate my seat. Seat up, belt unclipped, blanket stowed, I touch the forearm of my angry young neighbour, not really expecting him to move for me, but still going through the motions of proper travel etiquette. Sure enough, I feel him tense and our eyes meet in the darkness of the sleeping cabin. There is enough animosity there to feed a war, so I again I have no alternative but to clamber over him and his partner to the aisle and to the cabin toilets there behind me to the right. I reverse my journey back to my seat, slight annoyance on my part but no big deal other than the confusion in my head as to exactly what I have done to upset this young traveller so much.

Hours later, we land smoothly at LHR and as always, having travelled lightly, I am eager to get up and get going as soon as the giant aircraft has taxied to our gate and the engines have been silenced. I know what's coming now and of course I am right as I politely request that the couple move and let me up and out of my cramped space. It is a straight refusal and another terrible, silent glare follows. Angry now, I protest, but to no avail as passengers in all parts of the cabin begin to exit. So, once again, I find myself clambering over the boy to escape then seat row and to reach up to the overhead locker and retrieve my bag. Now, I am riled and I turn to speak to the couple, to express my disappointment in their appalling behaviour, to give them a piece of my mind. Then and only then, do I make a terrible realisation… the boy has clearly - and recently - been through something truly awful. His trousers look normal, covering his upper legs as they should, but where his knees should be and below, his lower legs and feet, there is nothing there! He couldn´t move even if he wanted to, and I understand completely and immediately his hatred for me. All I want to happen is the earth to open and swallow me. How could I have missed this? I apologise profusely, wishing my Portuguese were better, I apologise in Spanish, French and English, deeply ashamed of my own actions and behaviour, and I am met with the same hate-filled, silent and black-eyed stare. My humbling is complete and a very painful lesson, as only the best ones can be, is over. Never judge others before you judge yourself. Look carefully at all sides of the situation and give everyone the benefit of the doubt.

N IS FOR NAIROBI

In Eastern Kenya, avocados do well in the Mua Hills, some two hundred kilometres north-east of the capital and it is this destination that is our objective for the following day. My mission here was to inspect, identify and coordinate groups of growers of Kenyan avocados for export and development in the European marketplace My host on this trip is the CEO of Sunshine vegetables, Virat Ashwin and we start our mission early, heading out of town in a mode of transport very typical for a Kenyan businessman, a solid and powerful Toyota Landcruiser. Not too new, not too flashy, but robust enough to cope with the terrible state of the roads – I am talking about the main roads here, the highways and major thoroughfares of the country. Off the national road network, if you didn´t drive a similarly capable vehicle, things get difficult very quickly. Immediately after leaving the city suburbs, we are stopped at a Police / Army checkpoint manned by a small group of heavily armed Kenyan soldiers. A short and quite aggressive conversation in Swahili follows and I have no idea what is going on, until my host, in the driver´s seat, fishes out a wad of banknotes, counts out fat sheaf and proceeds to hand them over to the leader of the patrol. We are released from our purgatory and we continue on our way. I ask Mr. A. what that was all about and he simply turns to me and shrugs his shoulders, "Day to day life in Kenya."

The countryside around us changes as we drive farther north. Lush, green, tea plantations on both sides, rising hills, clumps of small forests and simple villages dot the landscape. My brief here is to make a speech to a grower group in Mau and I am impressed to learn there could be as many as fifty producers awaiting my arrival and eager to hear from me about the European market potential and my company's plans to help them achieve success. I study my notes, eagerly anticipating a good reaction and the securing of a substantial tonnage of fresh supply for our client base. My mind wanders to a similar scenario in Chile that I experienced some years before. There, I had witnessed the amazing site of the biggest single avocado orchard ever seen in one place. There were 700 hectares planted on the slopes of a mountain range. Three-year old trees on the brink of bursting into full production, each hectare averaging more than 600 evenly spaced and individually irrigated trees. A total crop potential in a good year of more than three-quarters of a million boxes of fresh fruit. A volume to give an importer truly something to dream about.

We arrive at our destination and we alight from our transport, I have time to make a smoke and I survey the scene around me. It is a village of some ten or twelve basic wooden houses, large trees provide shade from the burning sun and there is a white-painted church dominating the dirt square around which the houses are situated. I note the dark green canopy of the avocado orchard, just a hundred yards or so away and I see immediately that these trees are tall, fully grown specimens, mature and with considerable girth to their trunks. I estimate that the age of this plantation must be upwards of 30 years and I ask myself if they are still in full production at this age. Conveniently, our grower group is emerging from the bush to the east of the avocado grove, and so we stride on down the baked earth track to meet them.

On entering the grove and beginning the meet and greet formalities with the leaders of the group, my thoughts on the age and condition of the trees are confirmed. They are well over 30 years old, they have not been grafted onto vigour-limiting rootstocks before planting, thereby enabling the farmer to produce a full crop but with trees of a limited size, allowing a much easier harvest. This orchard of trees has reached its full natural height I think, as I survey the canopy above me and I calculate at least 30 feet to the fruit-bearing branches. I look at the size of the trunks and try to calculate how many trees there are in this grove – an automatic process for me on trips such as this one, but impossible in this case as my view is curtailed by the sheer size of the trees stretching out in the shade before us. It is time to gather the crowd and to begin my presentation and I state my name and business here, realising that I need to be clear and succinct.

I ask how many hectares they have in production and I am informed that there are 60. My mind going into automatic calculating mode, "Sixty. Full production from mature trees, probably less than two hundred trees of this size per hectare though, so that would be in the region of a quarter of a million boxes of Cat 1 fruit in a good year," I muse. "And how many growers are in this cooperative?" I enquire politely, trying to get a feel for the potential volume of export quality fruit from this plot.

"We are sixty producers here," states the group's leader proudly, a huge smile beaming at me, his co-workers and grower partners behind him all bearing huge smiles too and seemingly swaying from side to side and bobbing their heads up and down with pride. The high number of growers in a producer group such as this does not surprise me. In Africa, it is common to work together in a cooperative in order that the work is shared, as would be the benefits of a good harvest. I am at the point of continuing my speech, encouraged by the possible volume on offer here when the group leader again interjects: "Yes Mr. Steve, yes. We all have one tree each."

I should have been a gambler; you never what the dealer is going to deal to you and it is essential that you can disguise ecstasy as well as you can disappointment.

O IS FOR OPERATION

Everything seemed "normal" high above East Africa, if normal was really a thing on an assignment such as this. The lights changed colour down towards the cargo ramp at the rear of the Lockheed C-130 Hercules and things started to happen. Cruising at 23,000 feet, the engines' note changed slightly, and shadowy figures began moving rearwards, lugging impossibly huge amounts of kit and weapons. Personal oxygen supply now connected, night vision goggles on and navigation boards strapped onto their chests, the ramp light turned from amber to green and the ten-man group of elite warriors, independently, but seemingly as one, dive from the ramp and into the pitch black, freezing night.

In freefall, skydiving head-first, and using his body to change direction according to his nav board, he quickly reached terminal velocity of 120 miles per hour. In twenty seconds, he would reach his target altitude of 4,000 feet, time to deploy his lightweight parachute and then descend safely and make quick time to the rendezvous in readiness for the joint mission of US and British forces to take out a nearby Al Shabaab stronghold. Ten, nine, eight, seven, SIX, FIVE, FOUR, THREE seconds...

His gloved hand reached and found the ripcord and he felt a slight pull as his 'chute began to unfurl above him. **CRASH!** Disaster! A massive mid-air collision with what can only be a clearly disorientated comrade, his upper torso taking the brunt of the huge impact and the breath knocked out of him, the two warriors now together and hopelessly entangled in their lines, gossamer parachutes only partially inflated and spiralling downwards at high speed. Out of control, the two men executed their emergency landing, hitting the ground hard and He knew immediately that he had suffered serious lower limb and back injuries. Unclipping himself from his 'chute's harness, grimacing from the pain, he reached for and found his stricken comrade, a US Navy SEAL, clearly in similar trouble; his legs buckled unnaturally beneath him. In horrendous pain, they knew that the mission was now over for them, that survival and escape were now their priorities; to be captured was not an option for they carried too much special equipment and held far too much knowledge to fall into enemy hands. There were no thoughts of the cyanide pills he carried to end things here if capture was likely. No, his survival instinct and training kicked in automatically and he made himself and his comrade as comfortable as possible, finding his Medi-Kit and injecting them both with a morphine jab, he located his field radio and made the call-in.

Within minutes, dozens of heavily armed SAS and SEAL troops scrambled onto CH-47 Chinook helicopters from a secret base nearby. They flew to the crash site and sprinted across rocky ground to form a protective circle around the injured men, the elite British and US soldiers training their weapons on the surrounding dark hillsides for any movement by Al Shabaab gunmen. Needing oxygen and lifesaving treatment on the chopper ride back to base, they nevertheless made it to fight another day.

Later, and without a doubt, in recovery, He knew that the year spent in training with 'M' had undoubtedly helped to save his life and that of his comrade. Some missions don't work out the way we plan; calmness under pressure and the will to block out pain and duress are sometimes the tools we need to get through this life.

Shot up, broken and messed up, he knew he needed help. Two days and three nights on the ward, and now in a satisfactory enough condition that would possibly enable him to get through what was to come, they came for him at five in the morning and to be fair, he had been waiting several hours for their arrival. Sometimes in life you find exactly the right people in the right job. Two muscular, shaven-headed hospital orderlies, now with the main lights on in his room, full one-hundred-watt light on his body, contrasting against the pitch black of pre-dawn outside. Bedside and calmly peeling back his sheets. Pyjamas off and his torso exposed, they shaved him carefully. He knew what was happening, and, save for the single sheet covering his now naked body, he prepared for the next journey in his life, a life frequently punctuated by danger and conflict. He knew he needed this; his body had been ravaged by decades of missions and the time had more than come for this renovation, this renewal of his body and his spirit. The fear came again, in a sudden wave as the orderlies silently wheeled his bed through the ward, past the public entrance up on the fifth floor and to the double set of elevator doors at the far end of the ward, the place where only those that were to head down go, down to the bowels of the hospital, to the operating theatres, two storeys below ground.

Into the dark, to the place where some never came back. There were no words to say on the journey, his two helpers now pushing him into the room where is life would be decided. Now lifting, naked and alone, cold, they placed him gently on the operating table, rubber coated, cold and short for his large frame, it was designed so that the body over-hanged each end of the table and so that his upward-facing belly would be stretched, easier for the surgeon's knife to cut through fat, muscle and tissue, deep inside him, through his guts and to his spine. It was to be a live evisceration and the fear came again in a giant wave crashing against his spirit and his consciousness as his eyes locked on to the multi-lamp overhead light just above his sweat drenched but freezing and goose-pimpled upper body. He had been trained in surviving torture, in sustained deprivation and starvation. He had withstood beatings, been shot more than once and he recognised the fear and he drew it inside himself. He had stared death in the face more than once but this time was different. His life was now in the hands of others and he felt helpless as he lay in the cold room, lit strongly directly above him, but otherwise silent and dark. After an interminable time, they came. There were no words, only masked faces and before he knew it, they had prepared him for the anaesthetic, a sharp jab to the arm and a vision of a mask coming down to cover his face, and he went away into the dark.

A day, a night, a lifetime later, he woke surrounded by Angels. It was dark and his eyes would not fully accustom themselves to his surroundings, but he felt them and he saw them, busying themselves around his prone body, wiping the sweat from his brow, adjusting his sheets, smoothing his sodden hair, all beautiful and all angels. Several times over the next two days and nights, he woke to experience the same vision and he found deep comfort in their continuous and meticulous care.

Later, back on the ward, he would learn that the operation had indeed saved his life. A seven-hour ordeal to remove shrapnel and spent bullets, a double femoral by-pass to repair his nerve-damaged legs. All his intestines, stomach and other vital lower body organs had been removed and placed carefully aside for access purposes whilst undergoing the repairs to his damaged body and later over 100 ten-millimetre staples to button up the gaping wounds inflicted by the surgeon's scalpel. They told him that he had had a fifty-fifty chance of meeting with Death on the table and that even now, it remained to be seen if the incisions that they had made into his flesh had damaged his nerves, potentially leaving him paralysed and unable to walk.

The accepted recuperation period for this operation would normally be three weeks in hospital. Ten days later, he was discharged and he returned to his day job to make a full recovery, changed and humbled by the experience, but ready to fight another day.

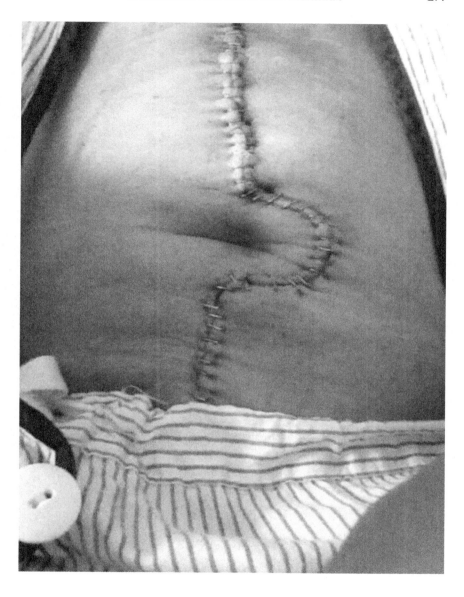

P IS FOR PERU

"If you are always trying to be normal, you will never know how amazing you can be." ~ Maya Angelou

Ancient Peru was the seat of several prominent Andean civilizations, most notably that of the Incas whose empire was captured by Spanish conquistadors in 1533. Peruvian independence was declared in 1821, and remaining Spanish forces were defeated in 1824.

After the arrival of Spanish soldiers in Peru, local people began dying in great numbers from Eurasian infectious diseases that were chronic among the invaders. These spread by contact across the New World by indigenous people along trading routes, often years ahead of direct contact with the invaders. As the natives had no natural immunity, they suffered high fatalities in epidemics of the new diseases. Later more people died because of the harsh treatment of the conquerors: they were killed in battle, forced from their lands, or died from the ill-treatment of forced labour. Many indigenous people refused to be enslaved, retreating into the backlands or, if captured, committing suicide.

Almost half of all Peruvians are Amerindian, or 45 percent of the total population. The two major indigenous ethnic groups are the Quechuas, followed closely by the Aymaras, as well as several dozen small Amerindian ethnic tribes scattered throughout the country beyond the Andes Mountains and in the Amazon basin. Mestizos, a term that denotes people of mixed European and Amerindian ancestry, constitute around 37% of the people. Peruvians of European descent make up about 15% of the population. The remaining 3% is constituted by Afro-Peruvians.

From the earliest years, Spanish soldiers and colonists intermarried with the indigenous women. The Spanish officers and elite married into the Inca elite, and other matches were made among other classes. A sizeable portion of the Peruvian population is Mixto, of indigenous and European ancestry, speaking Spanish, generally Roman Catholic, and assimilated as the majority culture. Here endeth the lesson... the long and complicated history of a major civilization and a melting pot of people of the world, settling into the 20th largest country in the world, in what is a staggeringly diverse and constantly fascinating continent. Suffice to say that I have rarely encountered such inherently open and friendly people in all my travels. Genuinely interested in the modern world whilst being fiercely proud of their roots, heritage and culture. I feel honoured and privileged to meet lifetime friends in this marvellous country.

My most common reason for visiting Peru is for avocado and mango. I love Peru. The diversity, the colours, the people.

I am on a mission. It is mango time and I have a dozen farms to look at in two quite different parts of the country. I have been a week already in Piura, north of Peru. I have travelled fifteen hours overnight on a sleeper bus and I have finished a farm walk and an assessment of growing conditions and the fruit that is being harvested for us. I like this farm, even though they are using traditional (basic) irrigation methods. Normally, in fruit production one would expect to see good water resource management; not just the quality of the water, its origin and care of that water, but also the quantity of water used. It was the Israelis that pioneered the modern method of tree irrigation by recycling all household water used in cities as many as two or three times before it could then be made available for agriculture. Plastic pipelines are run under and against the lines of trees that make up an orchard. At every tree there is a drip or sprinkler system and necessary nutrients and fertilisers are added in a mixing station or pump house, somewhere else on the farm. In this way, each tree gets only what it requires. Water is conserved and not wasted. Expensive fertiliser costs are kept sensible. In this case, they dig channels throughout the orchard and using little gates, they allow a quantity of water into the channels from nearby brooks and streams. I have seen this method hundreds of times before and it works well. If water is available and there is no adverse effect on the environment or on local flora and fauna, I can work with them for now, I think, as long as everything is safe, they have good controls in place and the fruit is up to the very exacting standard that I need. So I signal that I'm ready to go back to the farm offices to check paperwork, to ask my questions and begin to fill in the gaps in what is a very strict audit. I am thinking I like this farm as we sit down in an open farmyard. It is enclosed on all sides by a high wall. There are machines, tractors, stacks of fertiliser sacks, various tools and implements all neatly organised around the yard. Tidy farmyard, well maintained machinery, good chemical management, all of these I am mentally ticking off as I begin my report, preparing my questions and start to look at supporting documentation to the processes I have seen in the field. I am struck by the background noise around us. It is the unmistakable sound of cockerels and although it's not particularly loud, I know that there are a lot of birds nearby. My curiosity manifests itself into a question. I think my facial expression is enough and the grower gets my drift. We stand and he motions for me to follow him and we pass into another part of the yard that I had not noticed before. It is a shock. There in a large courtyard with a grassy centre and what is clearly some sort of training ring in the middle are literally hundreds of small cages, stacked in rows on every side and with two to three cages in every stack. We walk silently around the courtyard, I am peering into the cages, I see what they are and I am correct. One cockerel per cage, over two hundred birds. The farmer is proud, I like pride in farmers, it gets me good fruit and good systems, but this farmer is proud of his birds. Every single one of them is under two years old, he tells me, they only have the best possible conditions, feed etc. and they are pure bred from famous parents. I look him in the eye from time to time as stroll, I am a good listener, I always get the best from my hosts when they're talking and I know what's coming. They are all fighting cocks! It turns out later, after I have done my research, that not only is cockfighting legal in Peru, but that my farmer himself is the biggest owner of fighting birds in the country and also the President of the National Association for Cockfighting. This is a 'sport' that was banned in England and all overseas territory back in 1835 under the Cruelty to Animals Act. Yet here I am feeling like I have travelled back in time and I am perturbed.

That night, I finish my paperwork, the audit is complete and I know that this farm will pass and will thereafter have access and permission to supply probably the best food retailer in the world. I am rational and I reason that the cock breeding and fighting have no significance at all to the growing, harvesting and packing of high-quality fresh mangos for my client. However, morally I feel I have a duty to call this in. I want to pass it up the line. I want someone to know what is going here and I want responsibility, accountability and decision making on this issue to be made by somebody else. So, I write up my audit, I upload it onto the system for independent analysis and verification and I write a separate report about the birds. I am objective, factually accurate and non-judgemental. Two months later, I am told that there is to be no action taken, that this a legal and acceptable local practice and that it does not have an impact on mango supply from this farm. Just saying, be straight, tell the truth, do not judge.

One of my more recent trips to Peru was around the time that Formula 1 was going though big change. Liberty Group had bought out the erstwhile owner, a certain Bernie Ecclestone, and I recall there being quite a lot of media comment and speculation about what Mr. Ecclestone was going to do now that he was washed up with F1.

I am happy to report that he is in fact alive and well and is happily working away on a mango farm in northern Peru!

P IS FOR PASSION FRUIT

I am in Ghana, West Africa. It is my first of many visits to this beautiful country. Michael is my host and he is a passion fruit farmer on the banks of the huge and immensely important artery of Ghana, the Volta River. Passion fruit is grown in many tropical countries of the world. It is gaining in importance, not just because it is a wonderful fruit in itself, but also because of the huge rise in popularity of fruit-based drinks and it's increasingly common use as a very tasty ingredient. In terms of fresh consumption, it is a common sight on most good retailers' shelves.

The reason we take expensively air-freighted passion fruit from Ghana is twofold: Firstly, for freshness. We can harvest pack and ship on day one and we can have fruit on shelves on day three. Sea-freighted fruit can take three to four weeks to arrive and be put on sale. The second reason is that we farm a special variety here called Esther – I love some of the varietal names for fruit out here. Did you know that the Galia melon is named after the seed breeder's daughter, Galia? What about a juicy Williams Bon Chretien pear or a Doyenne de Comice? Perhaps an Angeleno plum or a Star Ruby grapefruit? I think I will create a chapter now: V IS FOR VARIETIES OF FRUITS…

And passion fruit yields are lower and it is not conducive to long freight times if we want it to deliver its unique combination of powerful flavour and juiciness. You want the best you say? I know where to get it!

This is quite a large farm and it is well run with lots of investment, some of which is impressive. I had never seen such a professional soil-analysis and management set up us the one in place here. Sensors deep in the earth strategically positioned around the farm monitor soil temperature and humidity and tell us when it is time to irrigate. Weather stations too are dotted around the farm, and all the land is specifically inspected and divided into individual parcels, planted and in production, recently harvested, fallow to allow recovery and prepared in readiness for new plantings. Passion fruit plants will produce fruit throughout a season, so it's a question of continuous harvesting over a nine-month period. Once that season is done however, the old plants must be taken down and new production initiated in the next, carefully prepared area. It grows much like a kiwifruit does; on a vine, held by trellises, about five feet off the ground.

I love this farm. I love their enthusiasm and their commitment. This is the first year of certification to supply a big chain and there is a lot to do. I move from the farm to the packing station and my problems begin. There are no worker toilets in the packhouse. Workers are walking two hundred yards to a semi-open shed with holes in the ground and a bag of lime for cover. The packhouse is open on two sides – anything or anyone can enter freely. I don't like the hand washing facilities and I note that there is an unofficial creche inside for the workers' children. I am mentally judging the number of issues and the order in which I am approaching them according to their seriousness. At this point I am striding purposefully around the exterior of the shed, camera in hand, notebook at the ready. I am looking for a well-maintained exterior, no weeds or rubbish and only one entry / exit for staff. I am looking for evidence of an established and well-managed pest control system – usually this would be designed to keep out rats and mice, birds and other undesirable potential contaminants. I see movement out of the corner of my eye and as I turn, I can see an enormous Iguana hastily making its retreat from my advance. I realise, this the main pest to be controlled here – Iguanas eat rats, birds and mice, so they're off my list of problems, but lizards are major problems in fresh produce. Whilst they are unlikely to attack humans (See S IS FOR SWAZILAND), they are curious, and they will enter buildings in search of food and shelter. We have maybe sixty workers in the packing shed, we have a creche of perhaps a dozen children and I know that the problem is serious. You see, reptiles can carry an abnormally high level of salmonella in their faeces and salmonella is bacteria that you definitely don't want in your food production process. So, whilst I am frequently to be found looking for evidence of a rodent presence, this time I am inside an almost open packing station looking for Iguana shit!

Two days later and we have a closed packing station, aside from just one, clearly designated worker entrance. Traps specifically designed for the lizards have been commissioned from a local supplier and an urgent construction plan is under way to provide adequate facilities for safe packing and good housekeeping processes. Two years later, this farm passes its audit and a year later they attain the second highest standard possible in this particular certification process. This is an example of the best part of my job: to identify the problems and to see growers all over the world overcome them and to improve beyond their expectations.

P IS ALSO FOR PEARS

"Make you laugh, make you cry." That is a very old fruit trade phrase used when discussing pears. It´s because when you trade in volume of pears, you can win big… but you can lose big also.

I was a young buyer / seller, in charge of apple and pear sales and procurement for a fast-growing import company. I found apples to be easy to trade and develop, especially at this time as there were lots of new varieties coming to market. I was involved in the successful development of Gala, Royal Gala, Fuji, Pink Lady - even in the rejuvenation of old and traditional English varieties such as Egremont Russet, the great Worcester Pearmain and others. At that time, the British retail sector was very keen on resuscitating old-fashioned fruits from the past, as well as launching all the new stuff. They also started selecting ranges of the better tasting varieties and then putting them under their own generic 'brands of excellence', such as Finest, or Taste the Difference.

But pears were a different story. It seemed to me at the time that nobody in the industry had really looked at pears properly. Sure, there was always a pear offer in whichever supermarket chain you chose to look at, but the offer was terrible. It was always a total jumble of just about every variety that was available, and I realised that the consumer was confused. By identifying just four or five varieties that were available year-round, using the northern and southern hemisphere sources that I knew well, I was able to take a fresh look at the pear category and I launched an easier to understand range of pears soon afterwards.

Some pears are better eaten crunchy, some not. If you like tinned pears, I can tell you that the variety used for canning is Williams Bon Chretien and it is a fabulous piece of fruit; to me the perfect pear. But I used other well-known commercial varieties as well, so let's see if you know them. Doyenne Du Comice – a gorgeous pear that is best eaten soft. In fact, it was the Comice pear that was the first to be used year-round in my new pack of four 'ready-to-eat' pears and it was a major success. I used to source these from a little Dutch guy called Jan Timmermans and it was a fun time when I made my once-a-week call to Jannie to confirm my volume needs for the second week and to confirm an ongoing price that would work in my four-pack costing. Just saying that, in my experience, the Dutch people are one of the top two trading races on Earth – the other one is the Israelis. God help us if they ever created a hybrid trader of the two races!

Eventually, the order got so big, I had to involve other partners and so began my long-term relationship with the Dutch boys – Joop Van Doorn (I used to call him Joopen Verstappen, after the F1 racing driver) and his partner in crime, Edwin de Witt (Lucky Eddie!). They are a chapter on their own, so I'll leave them for another day.

The Conference. Typically English and a good eat when crunchy. Iconically-shaped and typical when it is both green and russet. Forelle, a blushed pear, originally discovered and grown in South Africa. Packham's Triumph, a wonderfully versatile pear, typically large and very robust. Juicy, with white, melting flesh. To complete my range, I also used the Buerre Bosc, a fully russeted pear that is crisp and woody with a honey sweetness and best eaten firm. I also introduced some "speciality" pears from time to time to use as a promotional tool or to help to add focus to my now shortened but easier to understand range. It is fair to say that I made my first name in the business from putting all my focus into one fruit – the humble pear!

P IS FOR PESTS AND PESTICIDES

It is a common misconception amongst consumers of fresh produce that pesticides are used as a total solution to kill pests that destroy trees, plants and crops.

In fact, farmers of the world are united in fighting these problems by using natural predators around them and with environmentally friendly resources, only using authorised chemical solutions as a last resort and even then, using correct doses and observing strict intervals between application and crop harvest, all the while adhering to rigorous testing programs to ensure safe limits are met every time.

My favourite part of my work is seeing these solutions in action, often brilliantly thought out and controlled.

Can you match the pest / damage caused with the
cause or the solution?

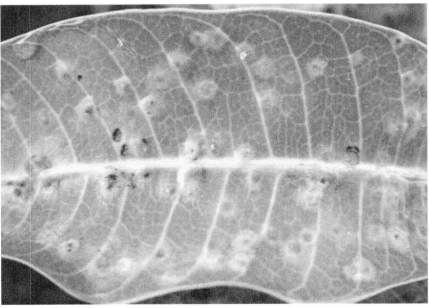

P IS FOR PINEAPPLES

"Fear is only temporary. Regrets last forever."

In 2016, the global pineapple market was worth some $15 billion. Don't skip that – just think a moment. Just pineapples. Fifteen Billion US Dollars in annual consumption! In volume terms, that would be something like thirty million tonnes of fresh pineapples.

The word pineapple in English was first recorded in 1398, when it was originally used to describe the reproductive organs of conifer trees. In the mid-seventeenth century, European explorers discovered a prickly tropical fruit that they began to also call pineapples because of their resemblance to what is now known as the pine cone (originally called pineapples). The term pine cone was first recorded in 1694 and was used to replace the original meaning of pineapple.

A pineapple is not a pine or an apple. In fact, technically, a pineapple is a *berry*! Actually, a mass of individual berries fused to a central stalk. More than two hundred flowers are produced by a single pineapple plant. These flowers have their individual fruits which look like scales. These individual fruits join together to form a single pineapple.

Once harvested, pineapples don't continue to ripen. That means that every single pineapple in the grocery store is as ripe as it will ever be so don't buy one and save it for a week, thinking it will ripen. The difference in colours would be based on where the pineapples were grown and which variety the fruit is, so a green pineapple can be just as sweet and delicious as a golden brown one.

Fascinating day in eastern Ghana looking at pineapple production. Queen Victoria, Smooth Cayenne, MD2 and Sugarloaf to name a few varieties. And no, they don't grow on trees; one plant equals one pineapple and you can plant up to 70,000 plants per hectare. That's a lot of Piña Colada! It takes thirteen months from planting to harvest and then nine months after harvest to get the suckers that produce a new plant and then a further six months in fallow before planting afresh. Three years for a one-fruit plant, but a single plant can continue providing fruit for up to fifty years!

Thanks to my teacher today Mr. Koumbou for your tuition and knowledge, what an honour. And if you've never eaten field-fresh pineapple at air temperature, hand-cut with a giant razor-sharp panga by a man with just seven and a half fingers, well you haven't lived.

The call came in just after dawn. A suspected pirate boarding has been reported on a cargo vessel in the Gulf of Guinea. The incident reportedly occurred in the early morning approximately one hundred nautical miles from Accra, Ghana. The condition of the crew is unclear; however, reports indicate that they are mustered in the vessel's citadel, following a twenty-minute firefight during which one of the vessel's security personnel was shot and killed.

The Gulf of Guinea's coastal waters constitute a central shipping lane and experience a high piracy threat. Pirates regularly target commercial ships, bulk carriers, cargo ships and their crews. There was nothing unusual about this call but for one thing: One of the ship's officers had identified the leader of the pirate boarding party during the crew's retreat to the 'safe' area of the ship and from there, a radio connection to the outside world made good communication possible. The pirate leader was one of the most sought after of all terrorists, the Commander of the Movement for the Emancipation of the Niger Delta, a particularly nasty ex-militant group that specialised in stealing crude oil from tankers in the Gulf and then selling it on to buyers in the black market.

The call came directly to Him, primarily because He was on assignment in the area at that time, but also because He was attached to a squadron of the Special Boat Squadron (SBS) who were on exercise in the Gulf of Guinea aboard one of Her Majesty's newest attack vessels.

Within hours of the call, two Royal Navy Merlin HC3's and a pair of Wildcat AH1 helicopters took off from their carrier; the Wildcats acting as top cover for the insertion and each carrying a 43 Commando Sniper team. Purpose-built for siege situations at sea like this, the Merlin was the perfect tool for the job. With a capacity for twenty-four fully laden troops, two helicopters with eight troopers in each provided back up and allowed the SBS to land in separate parts of the ship to surround the suspects. Two Chinooks with twelve more troopers and a pair of armoured Rigid inflatable Boats (RIBs), followed closely behind, highly capable of a water born insertion onto the target vessel after being dropped into the sea from the Chinooks. On board the first Merlin, alongside seven other elite troopers, now was the time to gather as much information as possible on the pirates and their locations, to fine tune their strategy and to prepare their kit for battle, principal weapons in this case being the C8 SFW Carbine fitted with laser sight, torch and grenade launcher and chambered for the 5.56mm NATO round. Sidearm was the Sig P228 pistol, 9mm rounds and extended 20-round magazine.

It is 19:45 and night had fallen as the choppers closed in on their objective. The ship's master was clearly acting under instructions and had turned the tanker into a westerly heading into the wind to assist the helicopters in the hover, the deck floodlighting suddenly extinguished as the four helicopters arrived over the ship. The noise, downdraft and blinding searchlights disorientating the adversary as the sixteen SBS men quickly descended by rope onto the deck, the snipers in the Wildcats providing cover, should it be needed.

Caught in a pincer movement by the small SBS team in a single group on the central part of the upper deck, resistance was short lived. Massively outgunned and under-trained, they were no match for the Special Forces, taking four fatal casualties, including the dangerous leader who took a laser guided round between the eyes. The battle for the ship was over in less than five minutes. On the Heli-ride home, the radio message came through on the crew's open channel: "Terrorists 0, Shakies 4 - Good job guys!"

Q IS FOR QUICK, NIGEL QUICK

My dear friend and fellow fruit trade worker is holed up in Singapore, en route to Australia for business. It is monsoon time and it is impossible to be outside. His flights are cancelled and he is effectively quarantined in his hotel until further notice. Things could be worse however, as his billet is in one of the best hotels in the world: The Hilton Centennial.

Despite his luxurious surroundings, Mr. Quick eventually becomes bored with the amenities on offer in his hotel. He decides to explore fully the services on offer and he discovers that indeed, this hotel has more to offer than first appreciated. He finds his way down to the basement, to the world-renowned Spa and Wellness Centre, ensconced two floors below ground level and lavishly equipped with pool, spa, jacuzzi, Turkish baths and innumerable treatments and massages on offer. It is quiet and the attentive and professional staff make it clear that this guest can indeed enjoy ALL or just some of the treats on offer, all in for the price of his accommodation and every day for as long as he stays in the Hilton's care.

A long and relaxing day follows, Mr. Q has been thoroughly pampered from head to toe, he has explored every treatment available and now in the early evening, he his positioned face-down on the massage table, naked barring a small towel strategically placed over his buttocks. The masseuse has been wonderful and although he has been rather obviously aroused by proceedings, he didn't do too much to hide the fact, because he was rather hoping the subject of 'extras' might come up.

After a teasingly long time in which the subject frustratingly refuses to come up, the words he was waiting for finally arrived. She leans into towards him, whispering confidentially in his ear, her silver Hilton name badge pinned to the top pocket of her crisp, white medical coat gleaming as she says softly, "Mr. Quick, would you like a wank?" He nods dreamily, half asleep and now flexing slightly in readiness for this unexpected treat. His beautiful treat-giver smiles and nods knowingly and she silently exits the room.

Twenty, twenty-five minutes pass slowly. Eventually, he hears the unmistakable sound of the automatic sliding door hiss and click as she re-enters the salon, padding softly across the tiled floor to the still-prone guest on the massage table. Their eyes meet for a second time and she whispers once more into his ear, "Have you finished, Mr. Quick?"

Q IS FOR QUIZ TIME!

Fruity quiz time...

Can you name the fruits that come from these flowers? Fruit names against the pictures please. Some are easy and some are more difficult. Clue: They don't all grow on trees!

And the answers are : Pineapple, Strawberry, Tamarillo, Guava, Kiwi, Banana, Lychee, Passion Fruit, Pomegranate, Papaya, Chirimoya or Custard Apple, Avocado, Sweet Cheery, Mango, Tomato

R IS FOR RETAILERS

I guess that, fundamentally, everything that I am writing about in this book is going to come back to retailers. After all, everything I did out there and for all those years, was almost exclusively for the benefit of one supermarket chain or another. After all, in Europe, the percentage of fresh fruit and vegetables sold by the supermarkets is upwards of 80% of the whole. Perhaps, I should write S is for Supermarkets then, but I prefer the word retailer and by that I do mean a business that operates across multiple retail sites, hence the term in our industry, indeed the terms used in the whole grocery industry, 'multiples', 'multiple sector' or the retail sector.

In my career, I have had direct supply relationships with many of these businesses. I have supplied fresh produce and had business relationships with supermarket chains in the UK and all over Europe, in South Africa, in Australia and in Chile. I have been their focal point of contact; I have been in charge of sourcing and supply - procurement is the word we often use - I have fronted accounts in a sales role and I have directed departments and businesses that exclusively handle fresh fruit supply to one retailer or another. In the UK of course, I am familiar with all the players in this most tightly contested arena. From chains that have thousands of stores across the land, down to smaller groups that are regionally based and with much fewer store numbers. All of them operate to a similar business plan and there is certainly a similarity in the way that their business plans function. Most of the big ones also have a tagline; a little saying or expression that they use for their 'public face'. In the case of Marks and Spencer, possibly the first chain to use a tagline, theirs remains consistent to this day and probably sums them up in a truer way than most: "Quality, Value, Service," was theirs, if I'm not mistaken, for decades. It wasn't until 2009 that they changed their slogan to "Quality worth every penny" and yet this still stands up for them as truly representing two of their pillar brand principles - Quality and Value.

You will have heard some of the others a thousand times ASDA, "Pocket the difference" or "ASDA be ASDA" and more recently, "Save Money, Live Better." You know the ones, adverts with the obligatory satisfied shopper and the 'tap, tap' on the back pocket! The obvious message to the main pitch of ASDA's marketing campaigns: lower prices.

Tesco's: "Every Little Helps". A clever slogan because it's rooted in folk wisdom – a saying that's been passed down through generations. Exactly the kind of thing your grandma used to say. So it carries the everyday authority of a proverb. It's tonally appropriate – conversational and impossible to misunderstand. It's strategically spot-on, because it taps into the customer's mindset, and also works as a brilliant internal motivator. It's about the tiny things that add up to a big difference – the penny cheaper on the baked beans, or the penny off the price you get from a supplier. Multiply tiny differences by an organisation as big as this one and you have world domination.

Morrison's: "Eat Fresh, Pay Less". "More Reasons to Shop at Morrison's". "Our Brand, Lower Prices". None of these are staggeringly original or interesting but all forgettable and super-cheap. Thrifty shoppers should feel reassured! Sainsbury's again, "Try Something New Today", or "Live Well for Less", both trying to deliver a message of quality and value.

You get the picture. But slogans and taglines are just one way that retailers operate similarly to each other. All have centralised buying, so that's one office, usually the headquarters of the company. One buyer for each of the 'categories' that they would sell. In terms of fresh produce, and depending on the size of the business, there could easily be a couple of hundred personnel in the fruit buying department. So, if you're a fruit supplier and you are in business with a supermarket chain, depending on the types of produce that you are supplying and, of course, the number of lines that they rely on you to consistently supply, you will need to match their resources across all areas. This is from senior management downwards and throughout your whole business: account managers completely in tune with their opposite number in the supermarket HQ; procurement personnel working to agreed objectives, price parameters and product specifications; technical personnel charged with the huge responsibility of ensuring that the produce is safe and that the source has been certified as such, across dozens of measured factors.

A point of interest here. If I were auditing a farming business for Marks and Spencer, the audit for the farm(s) and packhouse(s), would be broken down into ten different categories, starting with a key but basic requirement to check that the business has in place a full Risk Assessment that covers every aspect of that farm's operation from planting to departure of finished product. We would need to ensure that the business has done a full HACCP (Hazard Analysis and Critical Control Point), which is an industry-recognised food safety system that examines in detail all the operational aspects of the business. We would need to be convinced that the farm has an acceptable team of trained personnel in place and that staff training is ongoing, verified and recorded. We would certainly need to see that a documented and effective hygiene policy and system is in place and that personnel record their checks, including the implementation and monitoring of a robust cleaning schedule, appropriately designed and maintained facilities, and that field and packhouse workers receive good personal hygiene training and acceptable washing facilities. This would be before we looked at the other parameters of the audit, such as 'Site Selection' or, 'Why would you plant what you're going to plant here?' This would involve an extremely thorough investigation into the history of the land and the risks involved in planting in that area, what the land has been used for in the past, is there a risk from neighbouring sites, are there issues with contamination from manure, wild animals or domestic pets, for example?

Next issue would be, 'Water supply, usage, water treatment and irrigation', which is a huge sector and probably the most important of all the range of checks that a farming business must pass in order to achieve certification and permission to supply or to continue to supply. Bacterial or chemical contamination is a supermarket's worst nightmare and dirty or contaminated water is up there with the potentially most dangerous issues that one can face in fresh food supply. The other? Bad personal hygiene, especially poor hand-washing procedures.

All produce farming businesses on this planet require one essential element: Water, and the majority of them would have as their primary water source, a river or a canal system ultimately fed by a river. There are many farming businesses that are blessed with a clean water supply. By clean, I mean "Potable" water, which means safe for human consumption without treatment. This could be water already in existence on the farm from possibly a well or a borehole and not requiring treatment at all. However, rivers, lakes, canals, streams, even 'contained water', as in a reservoir or a pond, are all potentially dangerous because the condition of that water can change and, in the case of moving water, its condition can change every second as the water flows because it is influenced by what is happening upstream. So, what are we looking for? One particular strain of E. coli (Escherichia coli), despite it being found in the intestines of healthy people and animals, is one of the most common and dangerous bacteria, that is not to diminish the significance of other bacteria and viruses such as Salmonella, Listeria, Novovirus, Covid 19 and many more.

Imagine growing lettuce or spinach, or fresh herbs. Or anything that grows in soil, that does not require cooking in order to eat it or does not have a skin that is removed before eating. These are the products that carry the highest risk of contamination and pose the most danger to humans for the reasons just mentioned. Let's say that the farm's main source of water for irrigation directly onto the crop is from a river and that samples of said river water have proved to be negative for E coli or at least below a very low level of internationally accepted tolerance (less than 200 coliforms per 100 ml of water). This does not mean that the water is safe. Paint a picture of a major E coli outbreak in your town; the product is fresh spinach; the cause is discovered to be water contamination and that further investigation has revealed that the farmer draws his irrigation water directly from a river. It turns out that five miles upstream, a large cattle herd has grazed in a particular pasture next to the river and a storm comes and washes all that fresh manure into the river. Twenty minutes later, our farmer is extracting a high volume of river water by pump and he is directly applying this water to his crop. Problem identified. The weakness is poor risk assessment in that the risk of this should have been foreseen and quantified, even though it is fifteen miles upstream! Solutions could include removing the problem, implement a more frequent sampling and testing program or possibly to treat the water before it is applied to the crop. But it could easily have been a chemical contamination, perhaps heavy industry upstream emptying tanks or another form of water contamination. The message is the same: Clean water in the right places, please, and excellent personal hygiene thereafter.

Next would be a really good look at harvesting. Are there scissors or secateurs or are there sharp knives or blades involved? Are there toilets in the field and are they cleaned daily and fully equipped with potable water, soap and paper towels? Is there a risk of cross contamination from machinery or equipment that is shared between crops? Is the workforce trained sufficiently in good working practices and in food safety and can you prove it?

Up next would be control and usage of chemicals and pesticides. Clearly a topic close to the hearts of many consumers. Is my fruit and veg safe to eat? I can tell you that despite a groundswell of opinion against the use of pesticides in food production and a misinformed idea that conventionally farmed fresh produce is automatically covered in chemicals, this is incorrect. Firstly, I can inform you that the use of these products is very strictly controlled. Way before a season's supply to a retailer can commence, a mandatory declaration is required of what products and in what quantities are proposed. This declaration must include full details of the crops involved, the application rates and timings and the harvest interval - the minimum legal time in days that a crop is allowed to be harvested after the last application of the designated phytosanitary product. Once this list is checked and approved, first harvesting can begin, but supply to the client cannot until certified laboratory test results are received and verified as within the agreed limits of the destination. These limits or MRL's (Maximum Residue Levels) are set by governments globally and although they can vary slightly depending on country, they are basically the same. It is also possible that a particular retailer (I can think of one in Germany and one in Holland) will insist on working to MRL's that are at lower levels than their government have set, harder to achieve levels of compliance that the grower, supplier, importer and distributor will have to attain. The next check on MRL would be done by the receivers of the fresh goods, either in the same country of production or in an international destination. Only then can daily supply to the supermarket chain begin. Checks on the use of chemicals and pesticides are in place at this point. They are necessarily tough and that's not just on the fruit or veg itself. Operators of spraying machinery or equipment must be qualified and certified. Machinery must be regularly calibrated and serviced and chemical stores must be properly constructed and rigidly maintained.

I'm not going to go into a debate about organic production other than to say that I believe that it has its place in any society, but in my opinion, it has a limited usefulness. I believe that it is uneconomical – a retailer will not pay what a farmer needs for his organic production to make it worth his effort. It will not produce the yield in kilos that means a profit after deduction of all the production costs, and it will be difficult to comply to a physical specification for appearance and uniformity that a supermarket will require. We will not be able to feed the world's growing population using organic farming methods - fact - so I am an advocate of safe, sustainable, but conventional farming, provided that we continue to invest in learning and understanding best farming practices and of course in checking that we actually follow these principles. I honestly believe that we are in great hands.

Anyway, you get the picture regarding auditing and monitoring a live fresh produce farming operation. To conclude my summary of how to overview whilst still being hyper-critical of a farm in two days, next I would be giving the packing station a thorough going over and probably following the flow of production, from raw material coming in, to finished product ready to leave the door. Water source and subsequent treatment would, of course, be at the top of my list as these are the likeliest sources of contamination. Ideally, water used in post-harvest processes needs to be potable water (from the mains, drinkable), and if it's not and therefore needs to be treated in order to make it safe, well that would lead me down another avenue of investigation. I would be looking for cold stores, anything loose on the floors, are the walls sealed, what sort of refrigeration equipment and method they use, is there a presence of listeria anywhere here? The packing lines and machinery - well-maintained and frequently cleaned? The toilets and hand washing facilities: Are they sufficient; are the taps elbow, foot or knee operated only; are cleaning records accurate and up to date?

Workers: Are they trained in food safety on initiation; are there frequent refresher courses and are these recorded; do they conduct internal audits and if so, are there notes that are signed off by management?

I would probably finish my physical audit in the despatch area. I want to see not just good out-loading facilities and procedures, I want to see that only contracted hauliers are loading our goods and that they are compliant with strict protocols too, regarding vehicle suitability, temperature and cleanliness. I may also take a second look at traceability of the product. I want to do a check on the barcoded labels on each end of every one of the cases, cartons or bins. Are they all on pallets ready for despatch? As well as stating obvious information about the producer, the variety of the product and its calibre or size, its barcode or series of digits will also convert right back to the day of harvest, specific lot or area of harvest and amount harvested and by whom. I can check from this what has been applied to the crop in that season or from planting, when the last application was, how much was applied and in what dosage, what it was and even what the weather conditions were that day. Same thing applies with matching this data to the water usage, supply volumes and timings and test results as to the quality of the water used at that time.

Finishing my assessment of any business, I would be remiss if I didn't look into the welfare of the worker and the conditions that they work in. It's important to look at wages to see that people are being paid properly and on time, and that the working week is fair. Is there sick pay and how are workers cleared to return to their posts after sickness, especially if there isn't a sick pay policy in place, often meaning that workers will try to return to work whilst still sick Is protective clothing issued and how is it laundered?

So, it might take two full days to audit a large farming operation with just one packing facility. It may take a couple of days to fully write it up, and please bear in mind that an auditor doing a full assessment would ask over four hundred different questions across ten defining parameters. Each question requires a full answer or comment and nearly all must be supported with photographic or documentary evidence. In the protocol I have described above, there are also thirty-two essential CCP's (Critical Control Points). A failure to pass any of these critical measurements, would result in a failure and therefore a probable immediate halt in supply to the retailer, until the issue has been rectified. I once shut down a strawberry business somewhere in the Middle East. The strawberries were in high demand and not just for us. This grower was quite unusual in that he was focussed on the airline business, specifically passenger airlines and the obvious in-flight catering that goes with it. He would supply the retail sector, but only when he had peaks in production. So, I'm in the field on a hot day and it's busy. Maybe a couple of hundred field workers in clear sight and all around, pickers, loaders and tractor operators. New packaging deliveries arrive from time to time because they work fast and they are picking the fruit directly into punnets and then into cases that will stack onto pallets and will then be taken to a packing station for weighing, final selection and labelling, before despatch to the client. I always go to the production sites first, before looking at receipt, handling and distribution, more often than not in a warehouse not far away. After all, it's impossible to turn crappy fruit into good fruit, even in a twenty million-dollar packhouse. All good merchandise starts in the field or on the tree. After that, it's up to us to not make it worse because it sure ain't getting any better!

We've not had much history with this grower and there hasn't been a recent technical visit, so I am quite focused on the task in hand as I take in the modus operandi of this little open air fruit factory beavering away all around. It looks good, I like the orderliness and the rhythm of the men and women working away. They are dressed appropriately for field work; I can see that the field crates are clean and have been washed; there's no sign of dirty packaging, it's clearly new or has been covered. I see nothing serious that worries me regarding nasties. There are no piles of manure in sight, no empty chemical containers. I've been assured that their pesticide usage and spraying records comply with protocol and that MRL scan test results reveal no pesticide exceedance, so this is not an audit, this is a first mission to quickly assess a new zone of production that has been identified as useful in the demanding berry category, where spikes in demand and quick changes in supply can make it challenging to work in. Harder than bananas anyway.

Normally, looking at fruit on any kind of evaluation mission would be low on my list of priorities. After all, if we were in business with them and that warranted my presence, then their fruit was usually good enough. I am not a quality controller and I don't spend time taking quality tests on an audit visit. This is different. I'm interested in the strawberries and I do spend some time making sure that standards are high and that the fruit is fresh and clean. I'm satisfied that all seems to be in order and that our new supplier is competent and has at least sufficient procedures in place to continue supply. I head towards the end of the field where I can see our transport waiting. There's an eating area in the field and a hand wash set up that I take advantage of. In these scenarios, field and orchards all over the world are the same. After months of care, nutrition and love, carried out by diligent and committed people, it is time to harvest the crop and so the teams of men and women arrive in numbers. Amongst other things, these workers will possibly need places to sleep, they will almost certainly need a place to take their breaks and to eat. They will need hand washing facilities and they will definitely need the use of a toilet from time to time. So, in remoter production sites, where the construction of permanent facilities is perhaps uneconomic or there is no availability of water, portable field toilets are a good solution. Often contracted to a third party that will clean and service them according to the requirements of the client, they do a very good, basic job in providing a toilet, soap, clean water and paper towels. Normally it's a formality when inspecting field toilets. Really it's more about making sure they've not just been made pristine for your visit, which is an evidence check and a paper trail. I'm just going to open the door and take a quick look inside. Is the water to wash inside or outside? Does it work? Is there appropriate and sufficient paper stock? Is there soap? I'm moving towards the row of Portaloos and I can see straight away that there is an issue and it gets worse. The positioning of one of the units is what's brought it to my attention. I'm guessing that it's been hit by a tractor or possibly was just badly sited in the first place, but it is leaning at an unnatural angle towards the field and I can see the door is ajar. On approaching, it's clear that something has happened; there is raw sewage in a large enough quantity to make me gag and it is coming from the corner of the mobile field toilet. I can see that it's a serious situation, we have a substantial pool of raw sewage in the field and I can see that tractors have already passed over this area and have spread the problem up the track that is bordering the strawberry field, and that workers have walked it into the crop from there. I have to call it in, and I don't have long to wait until I get confirmation that it's an obvious and immediate stop on production and a quarantine of everything that's been produced today. All this fruit will be destroyed. Sometime later, I get the call to confirm that the next step is a full product recall for every single punnet of fruit that is on the shelf for sale back in Blighty. These recalls are incredibly expensive for the supplier, but in cases of a severe safety issue, they are essential practice.

I've done these farm assessments all over the world and it's extremely rare to have to put a stop on a live business, but you can't be afraid to make a tough call if the situation demands it. Aside from occasional safety issues - and I've seen quite a few of varying degrees of danger - most of the time I'm extremely proud in that I believe that I have helped push on and take forwards the growing, farming and packing standards of so many products and so many farming businesses. If you need a guy for your pub quiz team, my speciality subject would definitely be 'Fruit and Veg', but if that's too strict a category, put me down for 'Food and Drink'. I reckon I'm pretty good!

Anyway, if you've now returned from your snooze, I was talking about matching up to the retailers and it's true that big suppliers need big infrastructures, and these things cost. Above all, what the supermarkets are excellent at - and they are excellent at a lot of things - is cost examination.

Raising farming standards and ensuring that our fruit and vegetables are safely and sustainably produced are things that the retailers are clearly very good at. They are also clever in the way they will take a large proportion of the crop and then sell it across a range of value-targeted offers, for example, offering the best of the crop as the best of their range. Smaller or sometimes 'uglier' fruits or veggies, scarred or miss shaped veg, or sometimes a Class II product may find its way into a keenly priced selling format. Perhaps a punnet of plums, where the biggest and best fruits of that variety are sold as loose fruit or perhaps put into a 'Ready to Eat' offer of four or six fruits packed together. In times past, you could have accused the supermarkets of cherry-picking (hence the expression…!) only the best product but I'm not sure that is so true these days. They've finally got around to selling vegetables and fruits that, in the past, would have had no market and I think that's a good thing.

Since the rise of the multiple sector, from around the 1970s, clearly the polarising of the retail sector and therefore the creation of a much easier way to shop in one place, raises the question. Does this mean that consumption of fruit and vegetables has risen with the growth of the supermarkets, or is it just that it's purchased in fewer places? Well, some things are less popular today than they were thirty years ago. Take apple consumption and development of new varieties as an example. Consumption of "traditional" varieties such as Granny Smith and Golden Delicious has been falling inexorably for years. It doesn't mean that sales of apples are falling, in fact the opposite is happening. Because of the supermarkets ability to generate new sales and the fact that these sales are much more concentrated in a more sparsely populated selling arena, it is easier to collate consumer trends, market information, and movement towards new products. This in turn drives the fruit growing industry to constantly innovate and to research and develop new varieties. As a result, apple sales globally are much higher now than ever before, it's just that we now eat more bi-coloured or 'stripy' apples than we did in the past!

Supermarkets are also almost single-handedly responsible for creating sales of products on a year-round basis. No longer must we wait for the new potato season to commence or lament that we can't have fresh strawberries at Christmas or make a cheesecake or trifle in January because there are no raspberries on the shelves in mid-winter. A lot of people bemoan this and call it out as a "'ack of seasonality'. I don't buy this as I have been involved in the global hunt for complimentary supplies of fruit to match our own production or indeed to fill holes in supply over a calendar year. If I can find these products, then clearly, they are in season or they wouldn't be growing there. Fresh Braeburn apples from New Zealand in April? Why not? There would be very few apples for sale in our spring and summer if we didn't look at supplies from the southern hemisphere. New potatoes from Israel, Cyprus or Majorca? Absolutely, yes!

Another activity at which retailers have been highly successful is the identification of public eating habits. Using data from loyalty cards and purchase information, they are able to look closely at people's preferences for a fresh peach or a fresh nectarine and then to drill deeper into the data to establish if said person would choose between the two but given another choice, they could choose between a white fleshed variety or a yellow fleshed one. Dovetailing with their supply base and then being able to partner with like-minded and forward-thinking growers around the world, it was a triumph to be able to put together a whole range of peach and nectarines using white fleshed varieties that could now be sold head-to-head against more traditional yellow fleshed ones. The result? A clear distinction in consumer preferences, increased sales in peaches and nectarines overall, a revitalised global stone fruit industry and varietal innovation and development that will last for years.

Let's say that I am a major year-round supplier of fresh avocados to the European supermarket sector. I am their 'Category Manager', in that I manage their category of avocados. I have their trust and their order, and I am responsible, not just for supply to predicted sales quantities, but I am also tasked with price competitiveness and product innovation. Let's say that I'm looking at supply of avocados from the southern hemisphere and I am holding an order for between thirty and forty sea containers of fruit per week for a six-month period. I would be looking at my best growers in Peru, Chile, Colombia and South Africa. I might give a little of the order to Brazil and possibly keep a little bit of supply coming out of the Caribbean, probably from the Dominican Republic. So, I'm giving provisional weekly orders of very significant quantities of fresh fruit to quite a small group of large-scale producers (I would not be discounting small growers either, especially if they had a 'Story'; something different to offer across a wide range of deciding factors). They now have a provisional order for their goods for their whole season, still depending on technical certification (see audits), quality of the fruit and of course, price. This is called a 'Programme' and it is one of the best things that the supermarket sector has brought to the fresh produce industry – the knowledge in the numbers, the power to go to a shipping line with the numbers and to strike a deal on freight costs, to plan your workforce for crop husbandry, for harvesting and for packing and to make a plan for the future of your farm.

You'll note that I am giving the supermarkets credit here and I think that is correct. For sure, they do a good job generally in providing a one-stop shop for a tremendous range of goods. I believe that, in terms of fresh produce, they have done and continue to do a tremendous job in raising farming and quality standards across the globe, as well as continuously searching for improvement, whether that is in the product itself or what goes around it, and there are so many ways that they have achieved that. No, I'm talking about the incessant push for improvement. It could be in packaging, although I think that the overuse of plastic in selling fruit and veg has been going on for far too many years. It's not all bad on packaging though. I've seen excellent developments designed to lose the plastic in packaging where one very well-known retailer directly partnered with a small punnet supplying company and together, they came up with a very eco-friendly solution. For the last fifteen years, any fresh fruit or veg that you may have purchased from their stores would have been in packages made from corn starch that will degrade with no environmental impact whatsoever within one month. They've also done a good job with recycled materials and have been major supporters of so-called MA or Modified Atmosphere packaging, made from materials that actually maintain atmospheric conditions inside a pack or bag of whatever – fresh cherries would be a good example - allowing the fruits to breath slowly, semi-dormant if you like, in cold conditions, but NOT frozen, for as long as takes the container ship from say, Valparaiso, far away on the coast of Chile, to steam up the west coast of South America, pass through the Panama Canal and across The Atlantic Ocean and into Europe. That would be around 21 days sailing. Take delivery of your cherries, picked freshly in an orchard somewhere around Santiago. Because it has been a continuous cold chain, for the following two or three weeks after the sea container's arrival you can open the bags, collate your daily orders and be confident in sending out beautiful crunchy, sweet cherries, as good as they day that they were picked. That is with a zero use of preservatives or any chemicals – no fungicide, no insecticide, no pesticide whatsoever.

I've talked already about the safety and security protocols that the supermarkets pioneered, and I remain certain that the vast majority of fresh produce production in the world is safe, sustainably grown and in harmony with its local eco-systems. Yes, I would still wash my apples and berries and really anything that is grown in the ground that you don't have to cook in order to eat it, but if it's got a skin that I can't eat or I'm going to cook it, I'm not worried – I hear so many myths about fruit and veg, I had to say that!

So, are the supermarkets bad at anything?

I can say that there have been moments in my life of working with them when I have felt emotional about supermarkets!

I was twenty. Faversham in Kent, mid-apprenticeship with Saphir Produce and I had already done on year in production control; a lot of time in a raised glass office in the middle of a busy fruit sorting and packing warehouse, where I spent a great deal of my time on the lines with the ladies, chatting, handling and learning about the produce. I am now working in QC - Quality Control. It's a seven-days-a-week operation supplying the multiples, so I work a long week and my days are full of checks. I check on the fruit quality of course; lots of cutting and chopping and writing figures down on check sheets. I carry a clipboard, I wear a white lab coat, a hair net and I wash my hands a lot. I'm young, I have found something in my work, a passion actually, that would last forever, it is fun to go to work and life is good.

As a management trainee, I was permitted to eat in the management section of the canteen, which was a comfortably furnished room behind the works kitchen, the opposite side of which was the main canteen for the packhouse goods-handling workers. It is Friday, early afternoon and I have eaten lunch and I am contemplating returning to my post for the afternoon's tasks. I always felt privileged but nervous in that room. Here was I, management trainee, no qualifications, no knowledge, little experience mingling with the powerful and the mighty. Men and women who held down the big jobs on this site of maybe fifty acres of cold stores and warehouses, fruit packhouses and little food factories - Saphir was also a pioneer in those days. The creator of ready-to-eat dinners - another thing that the supermarkets were particularly good at!

Somebody answers the telephone on a wall across the room and I am called over. It's named, my boss from QC. I'm to return to the department immediately, there is a mission. Turns out that we've been threatened with being delisted as a supplier. That is the worst thing that could happen to a supplier. The customer was furious apparently. Our apples were rotting on the shelves and they wanted a company representative to their head office immediately to collect a sample (and receive a royal bollocking no doubt). Our account manager had taken the call, he's in London at our offices in the Fruit Exchange and I would imagine that he has passed on the fury of the buyer. He has made the call to us in quality control, and let rip at Phillip about a clear failure to select the right stock, to spot that a problem was growing and lots more. We were to delegate an individual from the QC department immediately, who would be despatched to said client's HQ in Leeds, West Yorkshire to collect the evidence. Phillip was to stay on site, to begin the investigation into what could have gone wrong and I can tell you that any number of things could have gone pear-shaped, including our sales boss's allegation that our team had picked the wrong stock from store. It may also have been an error in the client's stock rotation in their warehouse, so it was important to work backwards with the information that we had been given.

So there's Phillip, the boss. He's off the 'phone and we can see that he is shaken. Phillip was an absolute gent. Very posh, with beautiful manners and a wicked sense of humour. Phillip loved all sport, especially hockey. He ended up working for the very best of the 'other side', as a supermarket fruit technologist, and at the highest level. I loved being in his department. Sue the fruit chopper was there. She was a white coat member and would fetch samples of fruits from the lines and chop, chop, chop all day, looking for problems. Bryan Flint was there, another MT and a friend but a rival. We were competitive and Bryan had been in QC a year longer than me. We both wanted the next move first. He was good at his job, although I think he went on to sell wine. I volunteer to take the mission and I take command of Phillip's Vauxhall Cavalier company car keys. Faversham to Leeds then, that's got to be 250 miles. On a Friday afternoon.

Lots of time to think on a five-hour journey with no distractions. No mobile phones then, just the radio and the task of physically driving there. Like heading downhill to the edge of the crater and to the lava boiling there below, going into the bear's den, like walking into battle. It was a build-up of feelings. What could we have we done wrong? What will be the consequences be? Is there a possibility that they are wrong? What should my response be?

I arrive in Leeds. I am driving in the city centre. It is just dark. I don't have an appointment as such, but I know the boss is waiting for me and that their office won't close for a couple of hours yet, which is lucky because I can't find the bloody great edifice that is their HQ.

One and a half hour later and I am visitor-badged and registered and still sat in reception, in what is obviously a giant, steel-tube framed greenhouse. Two huge, gleaming chrome travellators whine quietly in one corner; one for up and one for down. They are clearly designed for dynamic office workers as well as more sedentary types, the breadth of the things and angles at which they are attached to the next floor allows foot traffic to pass on either journey. Having not much else to look at, it quickly became clear that this retailer is a very dynamic organisation to work for!

The receptionist motions for me to go up and I cross the foyer to join the bees travelling upwards. Everyone seems busy, briefcase or bag carrying and unperturbed. Some even semi-jog past me, with an eager-to-tear-into- some- -poor-supplier-somewhere look about them. I haven't got a briefcase and I don't even walk up the machine. My 'meeting' is in the first glass office in front of me and to the right as I exit the travellator, and as I approach the unappealing end of a short-carpeted glass walkway, open to the rest of the building, I can see that our meeting room is the worst office there is. From the travellator to the glass wall with a door in front of me - this shed - there is nothing. Behind and beyond this office, there is nothing. This is the end of the world, this is where suppliers go to die, to be executed in the name of the Grand Lords of Putting Other People's Stuff on Their Shelves and Calling It Theirs. This is the Shamed Supplier room, until now only a rumour, a sanctum that only the weak, the poor and the failed were ever likely to enter. I wonder if anybody leaves as I tentatively pull the door open and enter the room. I am alone. I breathe out. The room is empty save for various open cases of fruit on tables around the room and a few open sacks of potatoes and onions leaning against a wall. I walk to the tables and there are two big cardboard displays against the wall, in the middle of two tables. These are the Shamed Supplier lists. One is this week and the other is cumulative. There we are, bottom supplier this week, at the top of the list, and a commentary is there describing exactly what our misdemeanour is. "Saphir Produce. Total failure to deliver quality to agreed specification. Failure to adhere to KPI in supply contract. Action pending."

"Great," I think. "They actually do have a room where naughty suppliers are called to, where their names are displayed in shame and where we are called to account for our shameful ways."

My eyes are drawn to the two open twelve-kilogram cartons of loose apples on the table, to my left. These are ours, I assume, as I lean in to check the labels on the end of the boxes, noticing that not all of the apples looking up at me are sound. There is a cidery smell and the unmistakable waft of rotting - my confirmation that the issue is a genuine one. As I see proof on the box-end labels that this is indeed a sample of a delivery of fruit supplied by us, I am about to read the code that tells me on what day this fruit would have been despatched from our warehouse, when I hear the door swish open and I turn to see the main man directly in front of me and clearly bristling. Jonathan Sager, Buying Director, Fresh Produce. A very powerful man. probably reporting directly to the board and undoubtedly master of his own domain here. Immaculate in a good suit, an expensive shirt and tie, cufflinks gleaming, his Italian shoes spotless and his Mont Blanc fountain pen clenched in his tight little fist, he shook my hand and then proceeded to kill me with his words. I don´t remember the words exactly but I can recall that he was even-tempered throughout, angry and forceful but not impolite. My dressing down was so severe that there was not one opportunity for a defence, so I took the rollicking for the full fifteen minutes. It was made clear that not only were we to report the results of our investigation immediately and that if we had not done so in the next twenty-four hours our contract would be cancelled and the ramifications would spread to other areas of our business. Meanwhile, I am expected to carry the two cartons to my vehicle and home to our depot. On and on it goes. I have, however, been studying the codes on the box-end labels and I can tell that in fact these cases of apples have come from a delivery into one of their distribution centres some eight weeks beforehand. The only logical explanation is that the depot has 'lost' some or all of this delivery in their warehouse and that at some time between then and now, the stock had been relocated and then picked for store orders.

My interrogator stops his rant for a moment, and I seize my chance. As humbly as I can, I explain what the codes mean on the box-end labels and that, therefore, there is a zero possibility that my company can be at fault and that the blame lies firmly at the door of the distribution centre staff. I am highly trained in hiding my emotions - however compromising my situation might be - but I did struggle that day as I watched the buying director's power drain away and his face turn a lovely shade of pink. He was still silently fiddling with his fountain pen as I loaded up the evidence, forklift truck-style in my arms, and I left him there to stew.

Some years later, Jonathan 'joined our side' and our paths crossed again. I was even tempered and not impolite throughout our short meeting, but I had no hesitation in reminding him of our previous encounter!

Another time, I am called immediately to Tasbury's head office in Stamford Street in south London. Three hours' driving later and I have to wait in reception for an hour before I am given the signal to take the lift up to the fourth floor. I am met from the lift by the Alex Pierce-Dory - Produce Department Director. We have an issue with our potatoes in stores across the country and I must collect a sample. It is one thing, carrying a 25kg sack of rotting spuds from their produce department, down to reception and out, across the road to my car in the multi-storey car park. Getting the telling-off of my life is another. Pierce-Dory was known for his treatment of mis-demeaning suppliers and I was no exception, but aside from a verbal assault, various threats to our business and a long-lasting sense of self-pity, I am unharmed. Life goes on and business will return to normal eventually.

Guy McCorken, Main Board Director, Marks and Spencer, was another industry captain who gave me the shake-down treatment. Rhone Valley, south of France, beautiful country hotel. A very posh lunch. Peaches and nectarines are in short supply that year. Early spring frost had taken out much of the fruit. Demand is high and supply is terribly short. Prices are too low, and we struggle to keep supply when our growers are clamouring for a higher price than our current supply allows us to give them. Pierre Deranger and Lilian Hostier, the business owners, are natural diplomats and they start the ball rolling as dessert arrives - that's approximately half-way through a French lunch. As they end their preliminary pleas, they turn to me, the English side of the business equation before us.

I begin my pitch. "Prices for stone fruit across Europe are rising, Mr. McCorken. Take a look at the current state of the stone fruit sector, supply is so tight that to maintain consistent supply, we really must see an immediate price increase."

I've had this guy flown first class down to Lyons. I have hired a helicopter to bring him from Lyon to the hotel and I have collected him in a hired limousine. I know that he's far too important to be here on a buying mission, he won't have any knowledge of current pricing structures and he is here in an ambassadorial capacity only. Really, we couldn't have had a more high-profile figure here, other than the chairman of Marks and Spencer himself. Nevertheless, we are obliged to confront him regarding the under-supply, under-price crisis that is threatening both of our businesses. It is a beautiful summer's day and the surroundings are perfect for a business lunch with our VIP visitor from the north. Powerful people always have an aura, regardless of appearance and Mr. McC. is no exception. Turning to meet my gaze, as I utter the final words of my first and only sentence so far, his steel-grey eyes meet mine and without so much as a pause, he kills me.

"I am not here to talk about the market, I am here to talk about Marks and Spencer."

It's not what you say, it's how you say it and I take the lesson. We did not get a price increase!

These demonstrations of power from industry high-flyers are small beer in the scheme of things and you could hardly call them megalomania, especially when we are talking about supply deals worth tens of millions of pounds for just one product area, and the fact that this type of behaviour would be common in any other business situation. It's just that I felt that in many cases and for too many years, the balance of power was unfair and that a lot of supermarket personnel took advantage of that. What I'm saying is that the private face - the supplier-fronting face - of the retailers is a quite different prospect from the consumer-facing one. Remember Dudley Moore rattling along in a tuk-tuk through a dusty field of Italian grapes back in the eighties? "Tesco grapes..." this, "Our grapes..." that, "Our farms... blah, blah." They're not your grapes, they're ours! We took all the risks in preparing the land and planting. We provided all the husbandry skills, the nurture and care for five years and we provided ALL of the funds needed to be in a position to get to a harvest of good quality table grapes. Lack of recognition for farmers all over the world is something that the retailers have done too little to address over the decades. And the claim of ownership of the produce, reinforced by labelling all items with their branded labels, is boastful and wrong, in my opinion. The often-used implication that they also own the farms, just because of a purchase of the fresh final product, remains scandalous.

You'll notice also that nearly all supermarket stores have their fresh produce departments right at the front of the store, as you enter. Often, these produce departments will be themed, perhaps dressed up to look like a local market. It is essential for them to give the consumer the impression of freshness as soon as the shopping experience begins, but they don't tell you that fresh fruit and veg is also the most profitable for their businesses. Mark-up and margin are the key terms here.

A supermarket may pay a supplier fifty pence for a one kilo bag of apples, delivered to his depot, anywhere in the country. Almost certainly, that bag of apples will then go into store, for sale at ninety-nine pence. If you take the difference in the two amounts and then divide that into the higher one, that will give you the supermarket margin. In this case, that is over forty-nine percent gross margin. Of course, they will argue that they have distribution costs to add, potential waste of particularly perishable produce in store to predict and discount from profit. They will tell you that these costs plus the expenses of running their businesses justify the margins they put on fresh produce. They are not justified. And they are not comparable with any other product that is supplied to the retailers for them to then sell-on at a profit.

Mark-up is even worse. If you take the price paid for the goods from the supplier and then divide that into the retail price, the mark-up here is just under one hundred percent. Take the retail price of ninety-nine pence and then deduct all the costs involved in putting a bag of fruit on a supermarket shelf, and you will probably come up with around ten pence a bag for a kilo of fruit, going back to the grower, who also has his overheads and business costs to deduct. And that grower would have invested at least four years in his orchards, from planning stages, through planting and husbandry, care, nutrition and a lot of labour and money, before that produce could even come to harvest. And they then mark it up by one hundred percent? What's that called then? That is right and I am going to say it. IT IS GREED!

The retailers are also not shy about taking a look at their suppliers' financials either, if they feel that there are costs to be saved or if a business gives the impression of being too successful. My friend had a supply contract with a major chain. A year-round deal to supply all of their 'exotic fruit' that encompassed total procurement and daily supply of volumes of avocados, mangos, pineapples, kiwifruit and all of the other tropical fruits that fell into this category. The supply of these fruits was worth over one hundred million pounds in sale value every year.

I say a deal, but really these supply contracts are totally without legal caveats in that they are really handshake agreements that can be terminated instantly. One day, unannounced, a team of auditors arrived from Deloitte and Touche, the retailer's appointed accounting firm. Over the next couple of weeks, they conducted a full audit of my pal's business and they identified several areas in the business that would have to change. Employee's company cars were sent back or downgraded, client entertainment budgets were butchered, and staff salary reviews were suspended for two years. Six months later, the retailer gave the one-hundred-million-pound supply deal to a competitor, with no recourse or appeal.

Oh, and by the way, there will also almost certainly be a rebate to the retailers due on that bag of apples. A what? A rebate or a kickback and it will probably be at a level of two or three percent of the cost of the fruit. So, let's say that you supply one million pounds worth of these apples to a supermarket chain. Yeah, those apples that they are marking up by one hundred percent; taking an almost fifty percent gross margin on. A million pounds of business with a two percent rebate applied would give them a cheque for twenty thousand pounds. That is not a discount of the price. A discount is deducted before a sale takes place. A rebate is a sum of money given back to the purchaser once a sale is made and in the case of fresh produce, is accumulated over a season and then paid back to the retailer in a one-off transaction. I once gave a major British retailer a rebate cheque for nine million pounds that represented a rebate tariff of five percent and that was for one seven-month season of citrus supply, during which we endured the worst prices in the marketplace, consistently appalling treatment from both their commercial and technical departments and a totally dominating relationship from retailer to supplier.

What the retailers do with these rebated funds is not subject to legislation either. They can choose to spend the money on visible marketing campaigns, maybe advertising on the sides of buses or bus shelters for example. Perhaps they may spend some cash on price or value related promotions in-store, maybe even organising some sampling and tasting sessions in some stores to promote consumption and repeat purchases. This is called 'Above the line marketing'.

But most of these funds are used for no such thing. They go directly into the coffers of the retailer and are simply used to inflate overall profit margins in fresh produce. This is called 'Below the line marketing'. This is so wrong but sadly these days, it is used as yet another tactic to introduce competition in the supply base to get the best deal possible. Tasbury´s even have a building that they use just for the purpose of bringing in suppliers to 'negotiate' even higher rebates. It´s called Discounter House.

One day soon, I may write some more about supermarket personnel and events and behaviour in the field and on supplier visits. I would love to detail some of the things that I have done 'for the good of the business'. Although I never did, they 'crossed the line' many times, but before I do that, I will need to escape libel proceedings for this one!

R IS ALSO FOR RIO
GRANDE DO NORTE

"Stop worrying about the potholes in the road and enjoy the journey" ~ Babs Hoffman

Río Grande do Norte. One of the States of Brazil and occupying the north easternmost tip of South America. Strategically important for that alone but also known for sea salt production and agriculture, if not more for its famous beaches and lagoons.

I stayed in Natal last night, the State capital, in Ponta Negra. (Note: one of the great undiscovered beach resorts of the world I reckon - go there!)

My journey from Mexico was twenty-six hours. Several taxi rides, three flights - a little one and two big ones - including overnight from Mexico City to São Paulo AND two different hotels just to get to a pickup point ready for an early start and a three-hour drive to a very isolated farm here in north-east Brazil. I knew that leg of my mission wasn't going to be a 'hop' but I still wasn't expecting as long a trek as that!

Should check my itinerary more carefully but it's easy to forget how big this continent is. For example, this marvellous little state is approximately 60,000 square kilometres or roughly the same size as Scotland!

Farming here is of course a big deal. From tiny plots to very large farms, banana and mango are the deals to be done here. This area used to be the home of Brazilian banana production, but climate change has affected that. Weather here is hot all year round and it is very dry. Deep, rich and fertile clay soils, excellent soil management, nutrient rich and with high percentages of organic material. All these factors contribute to an ideal environment for producing robust, healthy and happy trees and of course, therefore, healthy and happy offspring - not just any old mangos, but your mangos. My pleasure and honour to visit this team of professionals at the top of their game - tilling the land and reaping the rewards of their labours. You know who you are and I salute you.

Brazilian people? It doesn't matter what colour, creed, race or religion you are; we are all Brazilian.

I love the Latin world, South and Central America in particular. I find this world to be so much more respectful and kinder to each other than other cultures, including my own. Not everything is always rosy in the garden and corruption and crime are huge issues on this vast continent, but not at my level! I'm with the farmers and the people on the land. I love Latin America, I love Brazil, I love Río Grande do Norte and I love responsible and professional farming. This has been a wonderful mission and it's given me lots of food for thought, but now it is time to come home - a long ride, some waits, two birds and a pick-up and I'm done for now.

Cannot wait now to relax and see my family, friends and adored creatures back home.

S IS FOR SOIL

Soil. One of the cornerstones of crop production. Without good soil, light and water, it is impossible to produce crops economically and sustainably. Soil erosion, by wind, flood, poorly managed animal grazing, compaction or other means, is devastating. Planted agricultural areas can become deserts very quickly without good management.

But good soil management is not just about erosion issues. Fertility, composition, good nutrients, sufficient organic material content, active micro-organisms and beneficial insects living in the soil that control pests are also essential components, as is an acceptable pH level and good drainage. Most fruit producing trees get something like 95% of their nutrients from good root systems in the soil and with a drip irrigation system that allows us to apply both water and fertilizer to each tree, precisely to their needs, coupled with a robust program of soil analysis, we are able to maximise our use of precious water and produce good viable commercial crops. Note how last year's pruned branches are pulverised and mixed into the top layer of the earth. This gives us a mulch for moisture and heat retention and also helps keep the nutrients where they're meant to be. Earthworms are vital components too, allowing good drainage and enabling a robust root system to develop. Next time you look at the dirt before you, remember how precious it is. God isn't making any more land. It's up to us to protect and nurture what we've got!

S IS FOR SOUTH AFRICA

"Life begins at the end of your comfort zone."

I am privileged to have visited South Africa more than 40 times, over a 30-year period. I have been to hundreds of fruit farms, producing anything and everything, including strawberries, melons, apples, pears, nectarines, seedless grapes, pineapples, all kinds of citrus. I was even offered a job there. And I bought a farm.

My daughters were possibly two and three at the time, very young at any rate. I had a very good business relationship with Joop van Doorn, a Dutch trader I had got to know well over the previous five or six years. He helped me a great deal when I was on my pear development mission. Joop was the son of a highly successful fruit business owner, Henck was his name; an extremely flamboyant man who was driven everywhere in a huge, black S600 twelve-cylinder Mercedes coupe. His company had invested in a fruit growing and exporting business in South Africa and they wanted a new trading manager there and my friend, his son Joop, put me up for the role. I clearly recall making arrangements to leave my daughters with my brother for a long weekend so that we could make the journey to Cape

Town to meet the guys there and to take a snapshot look at the business and the country we were considering emigrating to. Although I did already have reservations about living in RSA, I also felt excited about the prospect of huge change in my life and what was undoubtedly a big step up in my career at that time.

I was travelling with my young wife and I wanted her to be impressed. After all, this move was very much for both of us and for our young girls. I made arrangements to have a limousine collect us from the airport and soon after landing, there we were in the back of our stretched motor, drinking champagne and laughing as we cruised along the highway into Cape Town; Table Mountain in front of us to our left, the Cape Flats and the huge slums on either side and an immediate sense of the paradoxes that come with this wonderful country. The sun is out but it begins to rain and before long, my wife puts it out there, "Do you get rainbows in the southern hemisphere?" I had to suppress some of my laughter as the brightest and biggest rainbow I had ever seen proceeded to appear, directly across our tarmacadam route to the fabled citadel.

On paper, this employment offer was a dream: Two million Rand a year, plus bonus, a fantastic house in the country with servants, a new five-series BMW, and a hugely challenging but highly achievable job to boot. We also had free flights home and a generous relocation allowance as a part of our offer, so when I say I had reservations about taking the position, you may say I'm crazy, but I'll tell you why.

It's Thursday. I've been in South Africa for ten days already. I am on business; my mission is to begin new relationships with large scale fruit growers across the Cape. It is the mid-nineties and the DFB (the Deciduous Fruit Board) has broken up. Until now, this body - a government regulated, single-channel marketing entity that controlled the whole country's exports of fresh produce - was responsible for the national coordinating and exporting of over two hundred million cartons of fresh fruit each year. The DFB was synonymous with two famous brands in the fruit industry, you'll recognise them, as every piece of fruit from RSA at that time had little blue stickers on them - Outspan for citrus fruits and Cape for all other deciduous fruits. Now that the DFB had gone, the future was an open market of private businesses which henceforth were permitted to forge new international relationships and to be allowed to grow, pack and export, independently of the former Government controlled channels.

I am in my hire car heading out of the Cape Town metropolis and into the network of highways that lead you into the Cape area generally and then onto the national grid of major thoroughfares that crisscross the country. I am headed for Paarl, specifically for Durbanville, supposedly a suburb of Cape Town, but in reality, a town located some twenty kilometres out of the City. I am due to have a meeting with a major fruit growing family and I am lost. As I make mistake after mistake (no Satnav in those days!), I cross the main highway again, separating Durbanville from Bellville, in my increasingly frustrating search for my destination. My nose takes me into an old industrial area that's clearly the wrong place and I have to stop and turn back.

I drive up a concrete ramp and onto a large, flat concrete yard, open to the elements and with a hangar-like structure at one end, clearly decrepit and in a bad state of repair. As I drive onto the yard, I can see an open fire in the awnings of the seemingly deserted building, there are some wrecked and burned-out cars and I can see a group of men gathered around the fire. I have one eye on my location; I know that I am in the wrong place and I can see that the yard perimeter ends some twenty yards ahead of me, giving way to a three- or four-foot drop to a paved road below. As I realise that I will have to stop and turn my car around to exit the yard, I can now see that the gathering of men is much larger than I originally thought and that the majority are drinking from unmarked bottles, brown paper bags or from the very common five-litre plastic wine containers that the locals were fond of purchasing.

As I manoeuvre my vehicle into a position where I can stop short of the drop to the road and begin a three-point turn, I now know that I am definitely in the wrong place. This is clearly a shabeen; a drinking den, and certainly not a place a white man in a hire car would need to be even on a Thursday afternoon in daylight. I am suddenly surrounded by the mob and am grateful immediately that the hire car has automatic locking doors. My mind is racing as my eyes take in a sea of angry faces all around my car. My briefcase is in plain sight on the rear seat and the attention of the mass of men all around me is divided between me at the wheel and my brief case sitting behind me. Short of driving through the throng at speed, probably causing death and injury to any man in my path and the other thought of "Well I'm fucked here. Goodnight Vienna!" I did feel that I had run out of options. I am almost totally surrounded, and faces are pressing against my windows, all the doors are being tested to their limits and now my car begins to rock. Initially it's a slight rocking sensation but it quickly becomes violent, as if the by now baying crowd are trying to turn over my vehicle. Hang on, that's exactly what they are trying to do. I must want to live; self-preservation kicks in in a big way and I take my other option. I slam the car into reverse gear and I roar backwards at speed and directly off the raised edge of the concrete yard and SMASH! into the road. It could have been my back but it's the rear suspension collapse as I crash onto the paved road and I know that the next few seconds will see me live or die, as I observe that I am now some ten yards or so away from the mob and that I must escape right now. I think the car is jiggered, it has stalled and the whole rear end is on the ground. She starts first time however, and I grind the lever into first gear, revving the crap out of the car and praying we will move. I slowly release the clutch, plenty of revs to make sure I don't stall it, I begin to swear and then finally, yell with relief, my heart crashing against my ribcage, as my beauty does indeed go forwards, crunching and groaning and scraping as I coax it into a limp and a then a screeching, weaving lurch up the road and we are away, away from the mortal danger behind me.

Two days later, some goons dropped a concrete slab off a motorway bridge and wiped out a whole family in their car below. No apparent motive, just random, casual death. It's not that I'm not used to trouble. I have spent a lot of time in places where trouble finds you if you don't pay attention or if you're disrespectful in any way. I absolutely love Central and South America. It's my Spanish side. I could happily find a place to settle and live a quiet and humble family life in Colombia, in Panama, Chile, Brazil, in Argentina or Peru. But of course, like everywhere, there's trouble there and yes, I would need my highly developed sense of alert, of personal safety and of imminent danger if I put myself in the wrong place or situation, but I don't think I would ever have to carry the constant worry of a random and possibly brutal death in the family at any moment if I were to live in South America. I think I would have carried that constant worry if I had taken that job offer in South Africa.

I'd say the opposite if I was considering just about any other characteristic of the country. I've had great times here, seen the whole country and made hundreds of lifetime friends. It's just that it is a dangerous place to live and I can't see that ever changing, but it's not just the people in RSA that scare you…

A couple of years later, I am here for business again. My base is in Strand in Somerset West, a beach resort to the east of Cape Town. My days are full and they're not on the beach. Each day is booked and the diary is filled with appointments in the field. We are building a portfolio of independent growers that will eventually form a powerful group of fruit suppliers to our hungry and demanding UK customers. Every day I am on the road to the key fruit producing areas; Ceres, Worcester, Franschoek, Villiersdorp, Wellington and more. Today, I am with a very well-known seedless grape grower, Edwina de Villiers. She is hugely successful. She has a winery, a horse stud, a renowned animal sanctuary and her pride and joy: A magnificent one-hundred-hectare table grape farm. I am here to 'bring her into the fold'. To do business. To make a deal to market a serious volume of high-class product to our customer base.

We have had a great morning on the De Villiers estate. It sounds very grand to say estate, but farms like this one, and you can find farms like this all over the world, can often be a kind of a hub covering a large area of sparsely populated land. They are centres for employment, for creches and schooling, for health care and vaccinations and for whole communities to have a source of income and respect for each other. Our negotiations have gone well, and we lunch informally on the terrace at the farmhouse. Presently, I find myself with a few minutes alone and I am able to answer a call or two, to read and answer an email, to be busy immediately. You know how it goes when you're in a busy job and you've left it for half a day!

I roll myself a cig, phone glued to my ear as I leave the table and wander towards the herb and vegetable garden over to my left. I am talking away and wandering along a track, small out-buildings on either side now, as I half engage with my surroundings. Long call, message, long call, email. I know I've got at least half an hour free so I'm content to stroll in the hot sun, kind of exploring but busy with my commercial life all the while.

I come to the end of the track, perhaps a couple of hundred yards from the farmhouse and I stop and stand a while, looking at my path to this spot. On all sides of my little dusty cul-de-sac are little wooden shed things and I think I can now detect a specific noise from farther away. Monkeys, I think. I'm curious so I step away from the track and take a look at one or two of the shacks. It's clear that these have not been use for some time, some are in a poor state of repair and I can see that the indigenous flora and fauna are reclaiming the land and buildings around me. I begin my wander downhill back towards the farm and I realise that I am in an old part of the animal reserve and that I am now in the region of the source of the noise I had heard earlier. I reason that I am in the old baboon sanctuary but now I'm in a bit of a tangle. Somehow, I've got myself to the other side of one of the old sheds and I have stepped down into a dip in the ground and I am in long grass and brambles. Although I've never been a fan of long grass and spiders in the tropics, I am not in the tropics and it doesn't panic me or worry me unduly. I'm wearing good trousers, boots and long socks, but my arms are bare.

I'm struggling to pull my feet through and out of the thick brambles, grass up to my chest, trying to reach the corner of the shed, where I can see shorter grass and a way back to the path and the farmhouse. I reach the corner and pull myself upwards and free, resting my arms and upper body on the side of the rickety building. Panting a little and beginning to perspire, I dust myself down, plucking sticky seeds and buds from my hair and clothing and making sure I didn't have any bastard scorpions or spiders on me. Satisfied, I step boldly around the corner, eyes on the ground, making sure my step was into a good place. Firm ground, relief, positivity, a minor irritant Steveo, let's move back to the lunch table...

AND BANG!!!!!

Three feet away from me and at least six feet five inches tall, a gigantic snake is staring into my eyes. I know what it is immediately. It is a Black Mamba, one of the World's deadliest snakes. Known for its aggression — the only serpent on earth that will physically chase you, hunt you down in anger - it can rear up to one third of its length, so if I am facing more than six feet in the vertical... this Mamba is twenty feet long then. My mind registers the length of the snake in its unique way of pigeonholing everything: it is fucking huge and it is very, very alive. I have an out-of-body experience just being stared at by this enormous reptile. If you can picture a well arched arrow slamming into a target and quivering, well, Mr. Mamba wasn't just quivering like a well arched arrow, he was also swaying hypnotically side to side, a move designed to mesmerise prey or enemy. I AM completely mesmerised. I am staring into two black unblinking eyes. I see scales everywhere, all in a beautiful and perfect sheen of uniformity. I can see an open, dry, totally black mouth, and I can see two inch-and-a-half long fangs, shining and dripping with venom. I am transfixed and I feel myself swaying to the rhythm of the giant serpent before me, undoubtedly the same serpent that is about to strike me dead.

As I am duly resigned to my fate, strangely accepting that I would pass at the hands of Nature in Her own back yard, there is a sudden huge swooooosh of air and noise and real turbulence in front of me as, in one powerful and liquid movement, the Mamba spins, twists, turns and flies, as if in slow motion, and back to earth and away in a dust cloud inducing blur of speed into the bush and gone.

I am saved by human noise from the lunch table search party, sent to find me and bring me home safely. Thank God for humans.

YES, S IS FOR SNAKES!

I am twenty. I'm in the main packing area for fresh fruit deliveries in the Eurocentre complex in Faversham in Kent and this is my first job as a Management Trainee with Hunter Saphir, major fresh produce suppliers to just about every retail chain in the UK at the time. I am an assistant production manager, which means that my team has the responsibility for planning and fulfilling orders to the chains across a wide range of products and different pack types of fruit. We are packing grapes from Israel, citrus from South Africa, apples from Europe, watermelons, Galia melons, anything and anyhow. If the fruit needs to be passed down a line, it is either for sorting quality, labelling, bagging or in the case of grapes today, the simple opening of each carton of 5kg of seedless grapes and the removal of the sulphur pad that is placed on top of the grapes at source. The purpose of the pads is to reduce water loss, to prevent decay of the grapes and to keep the stems fresh and green. They provide a slow release of sulphur dioxide during the often-long journey from source to table and the pads need to be removed before the cartons of grapes are sent off to depots to fulfil supermarket orders. It's a big job. If you understood penetration - measure of what sells best in supermarkets – you will remember that seedless grapes have a penetration level of around 66 percent. This means that two thirds of all shoppers pick up and buy a bag or a punnet of grapes on every shop. This is a high number when you consider that stone fruit only reaches around eleven percent, and that is only in summer.

Still not bad when you consider that a large supermarket or a hypermarket for example could stock upwards of 40,000 different lines for sale. Anything and everything from dog food to toothbrushes.

I digress. The packhouse is large and we have twenty different lines operating at any one time. Most of the line workers are women – bizarrely, this is the case all over the world and it's because the women are able to focus on a fruit packing task to a high level of quality and productivity, whilst being able to keep up a conversation with their co-workers. Men just aren't able to do that, so there is proof that only women can genuinely multi-task! The men in a fruit packing environment are generally at the beginning of these lines; they may be delivering and loading raw materials onto the lines. Alternatively, they could be at the end of the lines, stacking the finished cartons or crates, making them into full pallets and then using pallet cars of forklifts to move the pallets to cold store or a despatch area. The women are the brains, the men the brawn!

The lines in our case are staffed and managed by supervisors and they are all ladies. They are all no-nonsense characters and I have realised early on that if I am to succeed in my new position, then I must form strong relationships with all the line supervisors (I can picture them all now. Very strong ladies, big personalities and with so much fruit knowledge that I just have to tap into). I also decide that

I must spend at least an hour of each day packing fruit on the lines. This is a most unusual occurrence and I am pilloried hard and often by the male staff onsite. Bearing in mind that I am male, I am young and I am not from the small town where we are based and from where we draw ninety percent of our labour. It takes me six months to gain the respect of my male co-workers, but, on the other hand, my fruit knowledge is moving upwards exponentially every day.

Most fruit importing and packing companies have good relationships with local businesses – there's always a demand for fruit baskets for raffle prizes or for special orders. Often there is a close relationship with the nearest zoo or wildlife park. Apart from the supply of produce deemed unfit for human consumption to the zoos as animal food, there is a more important reason: The identification and capture of live creatures that have somehow found their way into cartons of fruit or into the container or truck in which the fruit is transported long distances. This is quite a common occurrence.

A couple of months before the event that I am about to describe, I was standing at the starting end of a citrus packing line. We were lifting the telescopic lids from boxes of oranges and we are tipping the oranges onto a moving conveyor, from which the female line workers are removing the protective paper wraps from each orange. The fruit is then repacked 'naked' into the original cartons. I am working alongside two male colleagues and it's heavy but easy work. One after the other, I reach for the pallet of fruit next to me. The lid of the box is off, the fruit is tipped onto the conveyor and I move for the next full box of oranges. Movement on the top of the pallet catches my eye and I pause to have a closer look. Ten inches from my eye and very much alive, stands a large scorpion, tail up, pincers waving aggressively at me, very clearly unhappy with its situation and seemingly looking to do something about it. I don't panic. I call for help. Everything stops and soon I am joined by staff from the quality control department. A glass jar is produced and Mr. Scorpion is contained and secured. We resume our line-loading task as if nothing has happened.

A couple of days later, over lunch in the staff canteen, we hear from the head of QC that the scorpion has been identified. All scorpions are venomous but despite the six-inch plus length of our specimen, this one is not a threat to humans. This one has been taken in and rehomed in London Zoo.

There are over 1,750 different scorpion species. In the UK, there is a large colony thriving in and around the harbour walls in Sheerness port in Kent. They have arrived on fruit boats from all over the world and they have established themselves as a colony of over 20,000. They are so adaptable that there are members of this species in all the continents of the world, except Antarctica.

A couple of months after the scorpion incident, I am working on the grape line. It's a simple job as I have begun to describe earlier. Full cartons of seedless grapes from Israel, contained in individual open bags of approximately 500g, are moving down the conveyors. The job is one of observation; are the grapes sound? Do they look right? If not a quick sort, some snipping with scissors and a repack into the carton. The sulphur pads are removed and the grape cartons move down to the end of the line for restacking and onward despatch.

A scream goes up. It's obvious from where and all eyes are trained immediately on a mid-section of the grape line. A female worker has the grape carton in front of her on a small packing bench directly off the conveyor. She has opened the split lid of the top of the carton to begin her checks and there, in the air, swaying from side to side and at perhaps two thirds of its full length, a foot high, is a small snake. I am close by and I can see it clearly. It is beautiful and mesmerising at the same time. My mind cannot help but identify the gorgeous markings on the body and head of the serpent as it continues to sway in front of the paralysed worker. I can see that it has a sky-blue underbelly. I try to move closer just as Hissing Sid decides that he can't stay where he is and in a blur of colourful movement, he's off. Down the steel supports of the conveyor belt, onto the packhouse floor and off like a flash towards the cold stores at the other end of the building.

I have a feeling about this guy, so I allow most of the male workers on duty to go snake-hunting. Eventually word gets out that Sid has been cornered and apprehended. The snake department from the zoo has been contacted and some hours later we discover that this little beastie evidently fancied a nice box of grapes to rest in and he has made the ten-day journey by boat from Israel to the UK. We are also informed that this particular snake is an Egyptian Asp (think Queen Cleopatra's suicide by Asp) and that it is highly venomous!

I have arrived in Swaziland. I've had a day's tour of a large citrus farm and it's time for dinner. We are sitting on the terrace, the back of our hosts' beautiful home. Gin and tonics are the aperitif of choice as we sit in plush garden chairs under the wooden roof that covers the terrace. I can't help but notice the movement in the wooden rafters of the roof and my eyes focus on an exceptionally large spider, busy doing what spiders do. I know it's not a threat to me there, so my gaze moves back to our hosts and the marvellous situation we find ourselves in. It's still daylight and the lush and verdant lawn of the property stretches away before us, moving down a gradual gradient to the treeline, fifty yards or so below us. It's heavenly, but I spot sudden movement down at the beginning of the lawned area. I can see immediately that there is a very large and fast-moving snake seemingly swimming up the lawn and on a direct path upwards to us. Fifty feet, forty feet, thirty feet and closing in fast. I am rigid with fear, too shocked to move. I sense movement next to me and my senses struggle to catch up with the reality. In one movement, a fluid action that must have been habit born from necessity, my host produces an automatic shotgun. A blast. One shot. The serpent is obliterated. It is a Hooded or King Cobra and a big one at maybe 15 feet in length. The servants are already in snake removal mode as my host turns to me. "One more G-and-T before dinner, Mr. Steve?"

Batlow, New South Wales, Australia. I am 35 years old.

It's 11.00 a.m., it is extremely hot and I am in a majestic place. Two hundred or so kilometres west of Canberra, with the Great Dividing Range to the east and standing on a plateau of never-ending rolling hills. I am where I want to be.

This is a newly planted orchard of Pink Lady apples and I'm liking what I am seeing. Australia is the home of this very popular apple and this orchard has been prepared and planted with care. I always talk to growers about uniformity on the farm; no amount of money spent on all-singing, all-dancing packing stations can change what happens in the field. You can't improve the quality of fresh produce once it has been harvested, so I am always keen to see evenness and equal care throughout crop production. In this case, I can see that the trees are uniform in height and density. I can see that there has been no use of herbicides to clear grass from between the evenly spaced trees. The apples are well-sized and with good colour as I walk from row to row, from tree to tree. This is my passion, and this is what I do.

I move to another row, the first tree. I like to get 'inside' the tree if it is mature enough for me to do this. From this perspective it is sometimes easier to look from the inside out. Upwards and outwards I peer. I can see that the fruit ready for harvest is well spaced on each branch. "They've done a good job with husbandry here, the pruning guys know their stuff," I muse, as I can't help but calculate mentally how many kilos per tree we can expect to harvest, how many trees we have here and what sort of size range I'm going to get from this orchard.

I am with a colleague, he knows me well, he knows how I like to work. No words are needed as I do my calculations. There is a touch on my arm from my companion. "Stop Steve. Be very still. Do not move," he whispers, whilst pointing down at a spot near to my booted feet. I don't see it for a second or two, but I've spent enough time in foreign parts. I know enough about the animal kingdom to stop what I am doing immediately. I am stationary, hot but shaded by the tree's foliage, my view through the dappled sunlight beginning to become focused as I peer downwards, towards my feet and the trunk of the tree. It's a large snake. Easily eight feet in length, even though I can see that it is coiled and still. We move carefully out from the tree and to a safe distance from the reptile that is basking there beneath.

My host informs me that this is a common species in this area. It is a Tiger Snake and it falls into the top ten most venomous snakes in the world.

On this trip I have already been to Tasmania. An island about the same size as the British Isles. Heavily forested and with relatively few roads, Tasmania is home to nine of the ten most deadly snakes on earth. These are the days before ABS braking was invented and I have been taught that in summer in Tasmania, it is common to see snakes basking on the hot tarmac. They are cold blooded, so summer warmth during the day is essential to them if they are to gain sufficient energy to hunt their prey at night. If you see a snake in the road, then the danger is that by just driving over it, the creature can sometimes be 'flicked up' by the car's wheels into the underside of the vehicle. On reaching the destination, many fatal snake bites have occurred as the driver or passenger dismount from the car only to encounter a very angry and often very poisonous snake right there and ready to strike, as their feet touch the ground.

The correct procedure at that time therefore, on encountering a snake on the highway, was to make sure that you locked your brakes as you cross over the snake. To ensure that it was staying where it belonged and not to be accidentally collected as an unwanted and extremely dangerous hitchhiker!

Throughout my career, I have encountered many creatures on my travels. Occasionally I am scared – the juvenile elephant charging at me from the bush in the Kruger will stay with me forever – but I always remember that the animals were here first. Nature has provided them with their habitat and in many cases, they are far better adapted to their environment than we humans are. For this reason, Mother Nature is my God and I have nothing but awe, respect and admiration for her.

T IS ALSO FOR TEAMWORK

"Travel doesn't become adventure until you leave yourself behind."

My favourite role in my long career was as a farm auditor for Marks and Spencer. I specialised in fruit, stone fruit, apples and pears, mangos, avocados; I travelled the world for eight years looking at farms and packhouses in this role. I visited some of these farms every year, and to see the improvements in their businesses was truly gratifying, although some were more difficult to motivate than others!

Doesn't matter if it's a 700-hectare avocado farm producing thousands of tonnes of fruit for export to all corners of the globe, or a one-hectare market garden, our job is to make sure that good practices are followed, that the environment is taken into account – sustainability is a word often used to describe many parts of good farming procedures. Many people have big concerns about the use of pesticides for example and I can tell you categorically that the 'police' are out there, that excellent checks are in place and that the laws are very strict and well controlled and that rigorous test are done every day to ensure that global supply of fresh produce is free from excessive pesticide use. I do not believe in organic production on a commercial scale. They say that by 2050, we will have a global population of nine billion people and that we will not be able to feed everyone. Try to remember that absolutely everything in life depends absolutely on agriculture, almost everything that you eat and most of the content of what you drink, is farmed in one way or another. Without conventional farming, using pesticides, but only when necessary and even then, making sure that reduction in usage year after year, is a priority, we will definitely not be able to feed the world. What about the bees, I hear you say? Believe me, I have an entomological passion and I have seen some quite remarkable efforts in using Nature to combat pests as opposed to using an insecticide (See P is for Pests and Pesticides).

I am on a very well-known French apricot farm of upwards of two hundred hectares of production. My technical contact for my audit is Polish and he's been in this apricot business for 20 years. His job is production of fruit in the orchards and over the next two days he demonstrates that the farm, whilst not quite organic - that is, completely free of any chemical usage - has some progressive solutions in place to ensure that the natural habitat is functioning well and that all native species are present, correct and prosperous. What I'm looking for, he gives me. And then some. Good places and locations for bats to roost (bats eat certain insects that are not conducive to fruit production), check. Bird houses for a particular species of tit that feed on earwigs, check. Grease around the base of each tree trunks that will deter climbing ants from manoeuvring upwards into the fruit producing part of the tree, check. Beetle banks or cultivated banks of earth that are planted with selected species of wildflowers to provide a home for these strange creatures that will move from their home each day, into the orchards to feed on aphids, check. An analysis across the whole farm of samples of a cubic metre of soil in order to gauge accurately the numbers of earthworms present that will ensure the soil is aerated and well drained, check. Erosion by compaction, by wind, by flood. All covered. I gave him a Gold Standard audit result. I think there are maybe six fruit farms in the world operating to this level.

So, by working with teams in the world of fresh fruit production, I have been fortunate to see big changes in farming practices, all for the good of the planet and for the safety and well-being of the workers and of course, in order to be able to deliver a well grown, fresh product for the consumers.

April 2020 and I am on lockdown in my Spanish home, along with every other member of the whole population, excepting key workers, frontline health workers, truck and van drivers and of course, all emergency services personnel.

Netflix is a life saver in these trying times and I, like everyone else, I'm sure, am binge watching all the things I never had time for. I have just finished watching the third set of *Narcos*, which is El Chapo, mainly set in Mexico. I started with the first series, which is about the rise and the fall of Pablo Escobar, which of course is filmed in Colombia. What you see a lot of in this extraordinary series, are the farms and the countryside – the ranches of the drug Lords, their tierra, their campo, the fincas, growing fields and the rugged landscapes, greenery, jungle and unmade roads throughout. The isolated towns and poor villagers and the vastness of the countries and the rural areas. If you can imagine my working life visiting these countries to meet farmers and workers, the terrain is exactly as you see it in Narcos!

T IS FOR TASMANIA

"Climb the mountain so you can see the world, not so the world can see you. ~ David McCullough

I am 29-years-old. I have already visited Australia a lot of times for work. I've been accosted by a Tiger Snake in a peach orchard, I've seen the Murray River, been to Perth, Sidney, Adelaide. I had given a speech two years previously in Melbourne.

I am asked to go immediately to Tasmania to inspect and assess farms and to plan imminent fresh supply of fruit from a new area of production still relatively unknown in terms of import to Europe and the UK. Of course, I accept the mission. It is a long journey however you look at it. Flight to Bangkok from Heathrow, change for flight to Melbourne, change again for flight to Hobart. I am a very experienced air-traveller however, and these long-haul flights never bothered me even though I have always liked a hand-rolled cigarette here and there. I know that it's not possible to smoke a fag so I never allow the feeling of craving to enter my psyche. I am actually always relieved to get on a flight, to turn off my cell phone, in the knowledge that nobody can get me whilst I am in the air. This is a guilt-free experience for me, as

I believe that in this trade, certain things are obligatory. Things such as always answering the call when it comes; indeed, never turning off the mobile. Things such as never leaving emails unanswered. Integrity, honesty, availability, these are my dogmas, my principles that have shaped my career.

We arrive. It's a tiny airport and I wait by the luggage carousel for my small bag. Customs officers suddenly appear, perhaps five or six of Hobart's finest girls and boys, fully uniformed up and each with their own sniffer dog. I realise that anybody carrying any type of drugs, be it some hash, some weed or maybe some Charlie, is very soon going to end up in the historic Hobart jail. After all, I muse, this is the first place that English convicts would have arrived throughout the late eighteenth and the nineteenth centuries. What happens next is remains firmly imprinted on my mind as a reminder of the importance of safe food production and the essential controls that must be in place to prevent spread of disease in the fruit world. The officers perform a canine search of all passengers' luggage, only they are not looking for drugs at all. They are trained to detect pieces of fruit in luggage – a forgotten apple or maybe a satsuma, perhaps a banana stowed in your bag for later consumption. I marvel at the dogs' intelligence and diligence. These are not drug sniffer dogs, these are FRUIT sniffer dogs!

This is staggeringly beautiful country. Around the banks of the River Huon, some of the world's best apricots and fresh cherries are grown. I am looking at fruit growing of the highest calibre and even I am amazed to see cherries of 32mm diameter and above. That's like looking at small plums and we want these, of that there is no doubt. I spend a day or two assessing farms and working out my programs for fruit supply to come and then it's time to head to the airport to begin my journey home.

However, although I am going home, there is a twist in the plot. Due to a miscommunication about my trip and the sudden but definite interest in our newly discovered cherry and apricot supply zone, I'm told that on arrival at Heathrow, I am pretty much to turn around and head straight back to Hobart. My client from the UK, Mr. Simon the Pieman is heading out and he wants to see what I have seen on the ground. Another 24 hours in the air sees me back in the tiny arrival's hall. I know what's coming and I stand and admire the working dogs as they discover and unearth various fruits here and there from unsuspecting passengers, watching them get the tug from customs as they are led unceremoniously away for a severe ticking off about the dangers of crossing certain international boundaries with a fruity snack. Of course, I knew this, which is why the Belgian customs man could go stick it as I went through security with my prize of a box of fresh cherries, many years later.

Mr. Simon is mightily impressed with the new potential suppliers, their cultivation techniques, processes and of course, with the fabulous size and quality of the fruits. We are in business and as the day draws to close, Mr. S. wants to plan the evening's activities. Do I know the best restaurant in Hobart, what are the local delicacies and have I researched the location of the best club? We dine handsomely and I pay. I always pay. We head to a recommended establishment, in fact it's called the Gentlemen's Balcony and it's 'up my street' in the sense that, yes it's a strip club, so Simon can do his usual thing. It is also a pool club, American pool, like billiards, so the venue is a long room basically divide by a bar that has two sides. One side is facing the pool hall of four or five table and the other side is facing the strip joint. I get the drinks in and I make sure my guest is where he wants to be, doing what he wants to do. I am very used to his demands and vices, so I easily get him established.

I walk to the pool side of the bar and I soon get a game going with a local guy. It turns out that he's a dick however, too drunk to play and bloody annoying with his constant stream of nonsense of how he knows all the girls in the bar intimately; their habits, best and worst characteristics and their quirks. Simon re-joins me and I am happy to leave this sucker and to sit at the bar with two generous gin and tonics, as we begin to chat and to contemplate what has been a highly successful day indeed. It's funny that these guys are the best in the world during the day; so knowledgeable, so professional, but at night a completely different animal. I do what I am told in these situations and I am already an expert in client care, so I am relaxed as we order a second drink, just as local boy decides to join us at the bar. He's telling us all about our delightful barmaid that is serving us now.

"Never wears drawers, that one," he begins. "Commando one hundred percent of the time," he says, proceeding to drone on and on and on.

I'm thinking, "How I can get rid of this guy?" but insults and pointed comments in the general sense of "Why don't you just clear off?" have no effect. His skin is like that of a rhinoceros and I need Plan B. I jump up, I go around to the other side of the bar, to the strip club side.

Our girl is attentive to me immediately, and she cups her hand to her ear as I explain my predicament. "Is she commando? Would she consider being non-commando for a few minutes?" And I explain my plan to get rid of unwanted boy-next-door.

She smiles, she nods, she is in. So I wander the ten yards back to my spot in the other bar to re-join Simon. I say to the guy who is still there annoying the hell out of my guest, that he's making it up, there's no way this girl is underwear-less, he's just trying to impress us and ingratiate himself with us. I bet him that she's clothed downstairs, so to speak, and he takes the hook. He produces his wad and he places it there on the bar counter, grinning like a fool. It was over 250 Australian dollars. I am overseas, I am on business and I have an important client. Of course, I can match his stake in cash, so I do. There is close to 500 dollars there as he gleefully calls our hostess over and declares that she must now perform her party-trick and flash us to show that she is indeed "going commando." She winks, she smiles and she duly flashes and she is very clearly non-commando! The look on your man's face tells it. He's gone, ruined and he's shown the door. I am a wolf in a dog's world. As I split my winnings with one very happy hostess, Simon and I chink glasses. Cheers. Nothing more is said. It is an unwritten rule that the supplier deals with these things and that he always pays!

U IS FOR UNITED STATES OF AMERICA

Washington State. Rattlesnakes, pool halls, wooden packhouses, my first set of golf clubs.

I am search of the famous Washington Reds. No not the football team, but the spectacularly bright red coloured and uniquely shaped Washington Red apples – you know the ones, shiny, bright skin and crispy, juicy white flesh when you bite into them. I am in an orchard, the sun is shining brightly, and I cannot help but let my mind´s eye wander as I gaze at the topology of the land that surrounds me. Rolling but craggy, green looking hills. A fine and massive land. I can see swathes of native American Indians on horseback, arriving and stopping on the crests and rises of the grassy hills all around me. They are dressed and armed for war. I feel the menace and I feel like the evil white man invader just for a few seconds.

We are pulling into the orchard in my host´s pick up. The grass is green, and it comes up to my calves as I leap down from the truck. I am eager to pursue my goal and it´s there in front of me as I skip through the grass towards the trees. I feel immediately in sync with nature. I can see the shining apples on the tree, ready for harvest and I'm liking the style of this farm; no herbicide usage, certainly not to keep the grass down. Nice. My host calls to me, almost to bring me back from my daydreams and almost puppy-like passion to get to the trees and inspect my prize. By the way, these apples were already sold to me and then already booked to be on a large UK retailer's shelf in a month. I needed them to be great, I wanted them to be majestic, I knew they would be.

My host, Bob called again, "Stevie, be careful where you step!" He was holding and shaking a boiled sweet tin.

"I don't want a boiled sweet," I thought, watching him open the tin to persuade me otherwise. Inside, perhaps a dozen or more two to three-inch, dry looking objects that were immediately apparent to me, to be what they were. Rattlesnake tails!!

I think I was about 30 when this occurred and it's possible that I have calmed down a little bit since. I have always had, however, from the beginning to the end, a natural passion for the fruit. How and where it's grown and very importantly, how I was going to get it to the person that was going to it, in the best possible way. I needed to become a master of every aspect of the supply chain, including the nemesis of several unnecessary aspects. My career has lasted forty years and I am a master.

V IS FOR VOLTA RIVER

"Jobs fill your pocket but adventures fill your soul."
Jamie Lyn Beatty

Fresh water. The most important resource we have on Earth. Here in West Africa, the Volta River is the powerhouse for all agriculture, indeed for life itself. All crops and human and animal life are fed from this giant liquid artery, originating in Burkina Faso, north of where I am now. Dammed in 1965 in Akosombo and then again in Senchi to form two lakes - The Volta Lake (the largest man-made lake in the world at 8,502 square kilometres or 148 cubic kilometres of water, 114 metres deep, shoreline of 7,250 kms!) and Kpong Lake. Everything south of these points depends on this precious commodity. I am humbled yet again by how rich life is and how mankind must live correctly and in harmony with nature. I am falling in love with this land.

Ever wondered why it's called Passion Fruit?

When early missionaries to South America saw the flower, the stigma reminded them of the cross on which Christ was crucified. What's more, they decided the corona (the purple prickly part around the yellow stigma) resembled the crown of thorns on Jesus's head. In other words, elements from the passion of Christ, were replicated by nature in this flower. No wonder they named the fruit from the flower the Passion Fruit. It is not because it possesses aphrodisiacal qualities - it doesn't - although it is hugely rich in nutritional and medicinal properties.

This is the Upper Volta River in east Ghana in Sogakope. Unique production of a special variety gives us extra-large and extra sweet fruit, not found elsewhere in the World. Hand pollination ensures good fruit set and a high yield. Labour intensive and only air freighted, it is available in the UK high street. This is not just any Passion Fruit, this is YOUR Passion Fruit.

V IS FOR VENEZUELA

The call comes in. There is word of an imminent military coup in Venezuela, a particularly sensitive country in the eyes of Britain and her allies at this time. It is considered essential to maintain democracy there and a plan is confirmed – the coup leaders must be neutralised at the earliest opportunity and an agent who is capable of executing the mission without detection is quickly located. The problem is that all land borders have been closed; worse, coastal entry points are being constantly monitored and patrolled, and the likelihood of detection and capture is high.

He takes his first briefing on a papaya farm in Montego Bay in northern Jamaica. He is the nearest operative to Venezuela and He is soon informed, en route to Norman Manley international airport in Kingston, that the only way into the target zone is by air, but a conventional drop is quickly ruled out: the high-ranking military personnel behind the coup have also taken over the country's air force and its bases; the skies are now also off limits for conventional intervention. There is a way in however...

Plugged into the oxygen supply of his transport aircraft, He prepared to change to his independent supply in readiness for the jump. The aircraft droned on, at over five miles above the Earth's surface. Inside sits a very special cargo: A problem solver. Radio chatter crackles inside and people begin to stand. The door at the back of the aircraft slowly lowers down. A sharp, cold air almost devoid of oxygen fills the space. In the glow of the minimal interior light, shape begins to take form: Helmet, oxygen mask, goggles, endless gear and weapons. Hand signals flurry and a light changes colour. In an instant, the oddly clad ghost disappears into the night sky as He steps off the lowered door. Another HALO (High-Altitude Low-Opening) insertion has begun.

He is not a daredevil nor a ghost, He is a painstakingly well-trained special operations operative, using one of his more hair-raising skills: Free-fall (HALO) parachuting. This is where a parachutist will leave an aircraft at altitudes at or above 25,000 feet, free-fall for most of the distance and then open their parachute at lower altitudes. The technique is popular because the extreme speed reduces the amount of time a parachute can be seen. It can also defeat radar, which in turn provides a stealthy insertion.

There can be a temperature swing of over one hundred degrees Fahrenheit from the time you leave an aircraft to the time you hit the ground. A lack of sufficient oxygen at altitude required him to carry his own air, in the form of a portable system and mask. It is hard to dress for these extremes, not to mention trying to put your weapon into operation upon landing when you have no feeling in your hands. While a parachute, warm clothes and oxygen will help the operator get to the ground, it is the reason for his jump that now needs to be factored in. This technique is designed to put warriors into harm's way and to execute an important mission. With that comes the need for weapons, radios, ammunition, maps and everything else this modern warrior needs. This can turn into an unbelievable load. It begins with a parachute system coming in at approximately 40 pounds. Add to that an average Bergen pack of 80 pounds (sometimes more). Now we add a weapon, body armour, ammunition, first aid and other miscellaneous gear onto his 210-pound frame and the exit weight can average 400 pounds. This type of jump is not for the faint of heart and so now is not the time to be afraid, now is the time to fall back on his knowledge gained from eight jumps a day in training and more than fifty hours spent in a wind tunnel.

Down and fast unpacking his kit in readiness for a night march to his objective, high up on the sea cliffs above him, the oil installations beckoned and there would be his mark.

This was an assignment to take out a high-ranking army officer, even now planning and preparing his troops for a government coup, a move that in the eyes of the free world will plunge this already stricken country into chaos and civil war. His gear now separated into combat gear for his immediate assignment and gear for his extraction in 24 hours' time, he now established his precise position using his GPS / CNS (Celestial Navigation System). He moved silently and inexorably upwards and onwards to the objective. To the east he could see the sun beginning to rise, now was the time to locate the target and to find cover for the day ahead.

Dawn had broken and the sun was heading up into the sky as He settled into his rocky nook, high above the barracks and parade grounds stretching out before him, Light rations, personal relief and a weapons check were the order of the day for him. His weapon of choice for this mission was the FN SCAR-L; the L being for 'light' in that it was chambered for the lighter 5.56mm NATO cartridge as opposed to the heavier 7.62mm 'heavy' round. Although both rifles were available in long or short barrelled versions, he had chosen the longer barrel for accuracy versus the versatility of the shorter weapon, really designed for close quarters combat. Both guns had single shot or rapid-fire capability.

Down below, things were taking shape. He had patiently waited all day and now, as the sun was beginning to fall towards the far horizon, His mark appeared. A full parade ground before him, the General was exhorting his troops to action, his voice carrying clearly up to the rocky crag where He waited for the shot.

Four successive repeats, so close together they could have been one, the Mark was eliminated, and so were a full colonel and two other ranking officers. Now, under the cover of darkness was the moment to leave his hide and to get out the only way that was possible, via the sea. He left a half-hour-timed charge that would destroy his mission kit and any other evidence of his presence and, within minutes, he was on the beach and sending contact and proposed location to his pick-up. Already wearing his neoprene wetsuit, his battle vest stripped off, main weapon stowed and side arms safe, he unhesitatingly entered the cold dark surf. A two-kilometre night swim to the east, on a heading of his guiding star followed, ten minutes to tread water, three-hundred-and-sixty-degree observation through the waves and the chop, and THERE! He saw the scope first, rising from the waves, the conning tower immediately following and with a WHOOOOSH of suction and sea water flowing at speed from its dark fuselage, the gigantic British submarine emerged from the depths. He would soon be back on station, safe and warm, with another mission completed.

W IS FOR WOMBATS

The night is long and dark. The grey and unlit highway snakes away in front of us, driving through the gum tree forests of Victoria State, three hours north of Melbourne and following the course of the Murray River, northwest towards Adelaide. We have stopped once for coffee and a refuel in the last five hours and we are tired. We are restricted by Australia's strict speeding laws – you cannot believe that in the middle of nowhere, hours even from the nearest town, that a state trooper can appear and stop and fine you for exceeding the 55mph speed limit. I say town, but that could mean a hamlet of just a few houses, perhaps a school, but with two things absolutely guaranteed in this part of the world, the town will have a pub and it will have a bowling club!

I feel myself nodding in the front passenger seat of my host's 4x4, fighting off the desire to sleep as we plough on and on into the starless night, our headlights illuminating the way ahead of us. Conversation has dried up; it is a question of keeping going on the twisting and forever rising and falling tarmacadam forest road; an endless journey into a fantasy world of towering trunks and snaking road. My eyes are fixed on the carriageway when I see a big but blurred shape in the road ahead. My driver swerves violently to avoid the object and for a brief moment, I believe that we will overturn and die in a flaming wreck on the verge of our own personal road to nowhere. We right the ship and come to a smoking, juddering halt fifty yards or so from the unidentified night creature. We step out of our vehicle and with torches in hand, we slowly retrace our steps back towards the dark shape that had so nearly caused our end.

Australia is known for its strange and deadly wildlife, with plenty of attention given to venomous snakes and bird-eating spiders. But it seems one terrifying aspect of outback fauna has been thoroughly ignored: the wombat's deadly bum.

The rump of the wombat is hard as rock, used for defence, burrowing, bonding, mating and also for violently crushing the skulls of its fox and dingo enemies against the roof of its burrow.

The marsupials' posteriors are made up of four plates fused together and surrounded by cartilage, fat, skin and fur. Some experts in wombat bottoms, from the University of Adelaide, says wombats will use their backside to "plug" up their burrows, stopping predators entering and protecting softer areas of their anatomy.

A bite from a dingo could cause harm but it wouldn't kill it. These are pretty hardy rumps. They are big, and they back it up with a fair old kick. I have heard that a wombat kick can lift other wombats off the ground. They are a force, and for a lot of predators it simply isn't worth going up against a wombat for what they will get out of it. And so it is that adult wombats are not necessarily on the menu for foxes and even larger `potential predators, their powerful defence mechanisms making them 'more effort than it's worth'.

Our class in Antipodean zoology is over, our newly discovered marsupial is unharmed and she continues to forage away in the undergrowth that borders the highway. We board our vehicle with renewed energy and a new line of conversation to follow that will take us to our destination, far ahead in the new dawn rising.

W IS FOR WASPS!

Hands up from all of you that thought wasps were nothing but a nuisance! Not only are they excellent fruit tree pollinators, they are also brilliant, expert predators of other harmful species.

Here in Piura, northern Peru, I have discovered a mango business that actually breed wasps to aid in controlling a very particular problem. In each of the boxes in the image below is a new colony of micro wasps. It's effectively a nursery situation. These babies are predators of harmful scale insects, Proto Pulvinaria, that live underneath and eat the leaves of the mango tree (and citrus, avocado and other tropical fruits), eventually causing failure of photosynthesis; the process a plant uses to use sunlight to convert carbon dioxide into sugar (its food) and oxygen as a biproduct. Eventually the trees will die if the pest scale insects are not controlled.

Rather than use pesticides, a much more environmentally friendly way is to introduce a new colony of adult predatory micro wasps to the affected areas in a fruit orchard. The wasps will lay their eggs inside the escamas and in a short period of time, out emerges a new wasp from the now dead scale that the juvenile wasp has feasted on to survive and to grow. Brilliant, eh??

X IS FOR X-RAYS

I have passed through airport and port security thousands of times and in hundreds of places around the world. I have lost count of the number of stops, searches and x-rays that I have been through and as I am a firm believer in safe travel and robust anti-terrorism measures, I never had a problem with any of it, anywhere.

To this day, one airport in particular makes me laugh out loud every time I pass through its security section. That airport is London Stansted and that's an odd name for starters as anyone will tell you that Stansted is nowhere near London! No, there's a reason why Stansted always makes me chuckle, and it's quite ironic really because it is one of the world's most crowded and frustrating checkpoints that I have ever passed through. I am all for strong measures and I will do exactly as I am asked, staying patient whilst removing my belt or shoes or whatever it is on that day that the security personnel order me to do. I respect these guys and gals properly because after all, they have a vital job to do. We all know there are dark forces out there planning every day to bring our culture down, literally, physically and metaphorically. So, when I am in a queue, or maybe a part of half a dozen queues, of perhaps a thousand people or more, patiently moving and observing all the myriad rules and regulations in order to pass as quickly and efficiently as possible through the checkpoint, I tend to kill time by observing the staff working the lines.

"Laptop out please sir, phone in the separate tray, take your belt off, move forward sir!" All now recognised as normal expressions and perfectly reasonable requests in these dangerous times, but then I watch for longer; you can often see the shift changes taking place even as one queues, there are new staff arriving for duty and others leaving their posts for a break perhaps or end of their shift. Everyone seems to know each other well, they call out to each other in greeting or even to chat whilst all the while performing their essential duty to find, stop or detain anything or anybody that could be suspected of infringing security regulations or endangering safe travel for the majority.

"Alright, Dave!"

"Alright, Trace!"

"Did you watch Eastenders last night?"

"Nah, was too busy de-flea-ing the cat."

"Oi, you, STOP! Take those boots off!"

"Jewellery and watch off, Madam, and move forward!"

"Watcha Trev, you alright? Did ya see West Ham Saturday? Utter shite we are."

"Yeah, manager has to go soon, don't he, Dave?"

"BELT OFF, Sir! And move here quickly so that I can x-ray your balls. Take your boots and socks off, so that I check your feet in this foot machine."

Check my feet for what??

Is it me or is there something deeply paradoxical about the quality of the staff employed here? Either these guards are total experts in their field, so highly trained and super-bright, that they are able to carry out these essential checks like automatons, whilst simultaneously checking in and carrying on mind-numbingly dull and inane conversations with all their mates? Or is it that the contracted security firm that covers the whole airport only offers its employees a zero-hours contract on the lowest permissible pay bracket in the country, therefore guaranteeing that they will attract only Essex's finest to perform one of the most important life-preserving tasks that exist?

I am in Los Angeles, mission completed and now heading home for a deserved bit of R&R. LAX is one of the worlds' biggest airline hubs; hundreds of thousands of passengers pass through here every day. It is a huge airport and if you're not capable of walking at least five miles unassisted, you could be in trouble here. It is time to head airside, so I get my carry-on luggage and gear together and I begin the long walk towards my boarding gate, having to pass through international security in order to get there. There is a long queue, unsurprisingly, but I have plenty of time and I am patient as always as I gradually reach the X-ray point through which all passengers must pass. Without warning, the burly guard at the checkpoint stabs me in the chest with his index finger, "Sir, you have been selected for a random search, please step from the queue and come with me."

Nothing unusual in this for me, it's happened hundreds of times in the past and I only have slight qualms about accompanying the agent literally three yards to my right and to a screened off part of the corridor that is almost next to the queue of passengers waiting to pass through the X-Ray. I say slight qualms, because I was in the habit of carrying a small lump of quality hashish on my travels, something that I found I needed to ease the aching of my body, ravaged by injury and endless missions. In this case, my stash was in my leather tobacco pouch. I had been in the habit of smoking hand-rolling tobacco for years now and at that time, I liked to take a new fifty-gram packet of Drum and then "decant" it into my leather pouch, taking time to remove the lumps and bumps and stray strands of plant and leaf in order that when I wanted a smoke, my baccy would be smooth and rollable without problems. My 'lump' is small and is well hidden, deep inside the full pouch, but it's there nevertheless and I believe that I am for the high jump, as my guard looks me up and down before resting his eyes on my leather pouch in the pocket of my business shirt, along with my disposable lighter. He reaches towards me and seizes my cache of tobacco, immediately opening the pouch and having a good suck in through his nostrils, deep into my freshly decanted Drum half-shag. Meeting his gaze directly, I smile inside, but say and do nothing as I watch him close and place the pouch and lighter on the desk table beside us. I am then forced to strip for a thorough search, just a few feet from the endless line of passengers that pass me by to my left. The search reveals nothing of course, and I am instructed to dress, to collect my belongings, including my stash, and I join the exodus of travellers, now safely airside and heading for their respective gates. I am a very naughty boy but I am not a terrorist or a drug smuggler and I always totally respect airport security personnel.

Y IS FOR YORKSHIRE AND THE RHUBARB TRIANGLE

"There is nothing safer than flying, it's the crashing that's dangerous." ~ Theo Cowa

The Rhubarb Triangle (or Tusky Triangle, after an old Yorkshire name for rhubarb) is a nine square mile area in West Yorkshire between Wakefield, Morley and Rothwell famous for producing early forced rhubarb.

Rhubarb is native to Siberia and thrives in the cold, wet winters in Yorkshire. West Yorkshire once produced ninety per cent of the world's winter forced rhubarb from the long, dark sheds that were common across the fields there. At its height in the mid-nineteenth century, there were more than two hundred growers in an area of more than 30 square miles. Trains known as Rhubarb Expresses would leave each night from Ardleigh Station, loaded with up to two hundred tonnes on each, all destined for the markets of London and overseas. In use since at least 2700 BC as a medicine to cure ailments of the gut, lungs and liver, it was worth more than three times the price of opium in 17th century Britain.

Amusingly, the trade nicknames for rhubarb, and I can recall these being shouted across the early-morning trading floors of Covent Garden and Spitalfields London markets, include 'Physic' and 'Squirt', both in recognition of the amazing laxative and human digestion-assisting properties of this unique species. Bizarrely, this plant is actually a root vegetable, the leaves of which are poisonous and only the fleshy stalks are eaten. The first rhubarb of the year is, to this day, harvested by candlelight; exposure to light would initiate photosynthesis thereby robbing the stalks of their colour and sweetness. It is called 'forced' rhubarb because of the process of exposing immature plants to frost and then forcing it to grow in the coal-fired boiler-heated sheds in the dark. People say that plant growth under these circumstances is so astonishingly rapid that if you're quiet, you can hear it growing! It is also said that cultivating rhubarb is harder than working in the mines, a theory supported by scores of ex-coal miners working in this industry who swear that the work is more backbreaking than digging for coal – every single task involved in forced rhubarb production is performed by hand, because of the delicate nature of the work. The word rhubarb is also used in everyday English to describe speech that is undecipherable to the listener because it is in a language that he or she does not understand. Is it mumbo jumbo or is it rhubarb?

This actually originates in a tradition of stage actors, who would repeat the word rhubarb over and over when simulating background conversation. This isn't just one of those odd theatrical traditions like calling *Macbeth* 'The Scottish Play'. There is in fact, a pretty solid logic to it.

The word has no sharp or instantly recognisable phonemes (the smallest units of sound in a language). It's a very soft word, with nothing that stands out at you. *Carrot* wouldn't work, with its hard T. Nor would *cucumber,* or *courgette,* or *beetroot.* All of those would stand out too much, and you'd recognise the words, or at least the repeated hard consonant or long vowel sounds. Rhubarb works just fine. When you hear it from a distance, it just sounds like a vague murmur.

The skyline of metropolitan Leeds is easily visible on a clear day, but these are the foothills of the Pennines, a notorious 'frost pocket' that mimics Siberian conditions. The soil is perfect, and moisture levels just right. Rhubarb has been cultivated here for generations, grown first in open fields, and then removed to long, low sheds. There, heat is applied, tricking the plants into thinking it is spring. After three weeks, the first shoots appear and a gentle popping sound can be heard. That is the first buds coming out. In the dark, the plant's carbohydrate is turned into glucose and the absence of photosynthesis softens the stems, producing sweet, tender, brilliant crimson stalks.

What was once a staple feature of the local diet – cooked in pies and even eaten raw by kids, dipped in sugar (as I did many a time) – is these days a delicacy prepared for the tables of the well-off by celebrity chefs. Do any of those diners realise how it gets to their plate? Lifting the roots from the open fields for replanting in the sheds is back-breaking work. Some of the roots are so massive they require three men to load on to trailers.

I am here in the Tusky Triangle for Sainsbury's, the British retail sector now taking a belated long look at the magical properties of this unique product. Of course, they had been selling it for years, but focused only on the outdoor variety, grown in volume in Holland and Poland and without the sweetness / tartness combination of the forced type, unique to the Yorkshire triangle. Our host is the renowned local grower, Nigel Duffy. At home in his farmhouse kitchen, Nigel explains to us the intricacies and idiosyncrasies of growing forced rhubarb, the fact that he is a proud fifth generation grower and that his children and now his grandchildren are deeply involved in this ancient industry. His farm produces a range of varieties to give a season: names such as Stockbridge Arrow, Harbinger, Timperley, Dawes, Canada Red, Strawberry, Cawood Delight, Red Champagne, and Victoria and Albert, begin to sound familiar as we immerse ourselves in this strange culture.

Does Nigel eat it? Oh yes. "It's a very good metabolic stimulant. I cook it in pure orange juice, a big panful every morning. That is how I like it. In London, they do it in meringues and panna cotta. And they serve it in glasses, so the diners can see its sharply defined colours: bright red outside and pure white inside. Not for us Tykes. My wife cooks it in pies, served with custard and it's just as nice – if not better – cold."

Earlier we had spent time in the biggest of the Duffy family forcing sheds. It was a Friday morning and we entered through a dark, cavernous doorway into what Nigel calls his 'unearthly world' – a hangar-sized shed alive with the sound of several types of rhubarb in varying stages of accelerated growth.

You could easily disappear in the wintry mist outdoors, or in the Stygian darkness of the growing sheds. It's like something out of a Charles Dickens novel. Workmen, hooded against the cold, move silently through the rows of rhubarb, pulling up juicy stems by candlelight.

They have only one candle each, because too much light would spoil the delicate process of producing artificial life in the dark. It's eerie. Slow-motion cameras have even caught the plants turning towards any scintilla of light, like Triffids. At first there was a pop, then a mesmerising sound that drifted through the air like crackling wildfire. An unfamiliar snap and fizz echoed from the inky blackness, followed by another wonderfully alien noise and a phantom whisper of gently rustling leaves.

"Listen," our host and High Priest of Rhubarb murmurs excitedly. "This is the moment of reckoning." The vegetable was growing so fast, the air seemed to ripple with applause as it matured. The green-leaved, pink-stalked plant was familiar to me, but the situation was not. Every detail inside the out-of-time barn carried hidden meaning. There were flickering candles elevated on spikes, all thinly spread out to help workers navigate the blackness without fear of treading on the prized crop. There were shadowy hoes propped against the brick walls to help mulch the earth. There was the outline of gas propane heaters, and a sprinkler system to intensify the heat and humidity in the dark. There were around half a million buds – all cultivated in rows and all making groaning sounds as they germinated at unnatural speed. It was a riveting exhibition of Mother Nature at work, yet a display teetering on the edge of the surreal. And one all-the-more glorious for rarely being seen by outsiders.

It has been my pleasure to introduce you to the literally Dark Art of forcing rhubarb. I will wager money that in the days to come you will join the ranks of the knowledgeable in purchasing and creating wizardry from this remarkable plant!

Z IS FOR ZIMBABWE

"Jet Lag is for Amateurs." ~ Dick Clark

I am on the northern banks of the mighty Limpopo River in Zimbabwe and I am here on the famous farming lands of Paul Kroos, stone fruit grower extraordinaire – our search for innovation and development is never ending, and here, on Sand River Farm, we have something that is world-beating. Paul is a pioneer of plum growing in some of the most arduous agricultural conditions you could imagine. He is first in the southern hemisphere to reach the European winter market, due to his geographic location and his skills as a grower, it is certainly a gamble worth taking to hit the lucrative sales period when the northern hemisphere season is over and the world is waiting for fresh supplies. Most agronomists, however, would take one look at the earth and the terrain here and say, "No, you can´t grow deciduous fruit trees here, the land is barren," and that is true. Craggy kopjes dominant the horizon and the soil is dark and rocky. A multitude of difficulties face this farmer and yet with careful use of the life-giving properties of this liquid artery, he has created an oasis of outstanding brilliance in this forbidding land.

We move on foot through the different plantings on the farm. Thorny scrub bordering one orchard gives way to lush grass, waving gently in the light breeze and now leading us down a hard-baked earthy trail to a new trial plot, on the edge of a large watering hole and in sight of the vast and glistening surface of the Limpopo before us.

I heard him before I saw him and I just knew. At this time of the year, the beginning of the rainy season, small herds of hippos leave the safety of the river to graze and to mate. We had stumbled into one such herd and now the Alpha male had scented us and boy, was he angry. Considered to be the most dangerous land animal on the planet, I could well believe it as I stopped dead in my tracks, the massive beast up ahead of me on the trail, already booming at me with a volume of noise at about the same level as the speakers at a rock concert, jaws gaped and his massive teeth dripping with crushed grass and saliva.

All my knowledge of Africa and of these creatures flashed into my mind in a rush as I realised that the beast was about to charge. To turn and run would be fatal, the hippo can reach top speed quicker than humans and it can reach a top speed that is faster than humans. To jump into a nearby water source would also be a very bad idea.

Some years before, I had been in the bush, near the Kruger Park, involved in avocado production with a business that also produced significant volumes of timber for the paper industry. Dotted throughout this farm, a mixture of avocado groves and vast gum tree forests, were numerous small man-made ponds, created specifically for irrigation purposes. Known as dams, they were often frequented by herds of hippos. The creatures could spend as long as sixteen hours per day in the water, mostly submerged to keep their skin cool and moist. I heard stories on that trip of farm workers crossing between dams, only to be confronted and charged by aggressive hippos, the outcome frequently being a hideous and pretty instant death. I recalled the advice I was given, should I ever find myself in this situation.

If the hippo is close to you, then you are dead. You cannot outrun it. At some twenty yards ahead of me, I knew I had one chance to save myself. I turned to stare at the terrifying monster, I knew that male hippos could reach ten thousand pounds in weight and I knew that one bite from those massive jaws would see me meet my maker. This seasoned old male was at least that big and as he bellowed again, literally stamping and ripping at the ground at his feet, my fear was overtaken by adrenalin and instinct based on knowledge, as I prepared for the charge.

I backed up a few yards, keeping my eyes locked on my nemesis ahead. He charges, dust and earth and the most horrendous cacophony of grunts, wheezes and bellows filling the air as the gap between us rapidly closed, twenty yards, fifteen yards, ten yards, five yards, stand still, let him come, he's on me NOW and MOVE! Hippos have evolved to swim against strong currents and for this reason, they have almost no neck. They cannot turn at speed unless they're under water, and so the only possible way to escape a hippo charge is to stand and face it, until it is almost upon you. Wait, wait, wait and then dive, bolt, duck, whatever you have to do, just go either way, either left or right, dodge it and then run as fast as you can to higher ground.

He is on me now and left is not an option as the reeds on that side of the path tell me that we are at the edge of the watering hole and to take that route would be suicide. At the very last moment, I dive hard right and the thundering bull passes me in an earth-shuddering blur. He brakes hard in the dust, blinking and screaming and turning to face me again, in the sunlight, preparing another charge, but I AM GONE, up the grassy slope, heart in my mouth. and away slipping, sliding and scraping for my life and safe into the brush above the grassy field.

If you had asked me before this event, if I had the balls to do what I did, I would have said to you, "NO." But then again, it´s not every day that you need to face down a very angry hippopotamus!

I am an emotional person. I always have been. Recently, however, I have started to come to terms with mortality - to be fair, I've had more than one warning and some serious scrapes and bumps along the way and some pretty brutal encounters and adventures. Life is not a trial run; we are here but once and it is essential that we live our lives in a fulfilling way - that we may be decent to each other, cherish and care for each other and that we may listen and not judge. Enjoy the joys of this earthly paradise but leave something for those in more need than us or those less well travelled or those who are much less fortunate. I have been an out and out capitalist for almost all of my career – now a full forty years in the fresh produce industry - the world's second oldest business. I sincerely hope that you´ve enjoyed my book about the oldest business in the world ... and my travels within them.

But now, nearing the end of my time on this mortal coil and coming towards the end of my amazing journey, a sense of humbleness and humility has finally enveloped me - a realisation that I will be eternally grateful for, for I have been an arrogant f ** k for too of much of my life. Thank you, Lord, for the enormous privileges you have seen fit to give me. Thank you for the lifetime friendships I have made and am continuing to make. Thanks for the most amazing trip, a trip that I could never have imagined at the beginning. I have one message: be nice to people. give them the benefit of the doubt. Listen and have patience. Don't waste your time on this Earth and leave something behind for those who follow.

News coming in....

I've had the call and there's a new mission offered: Commercial manager of a $100 million-dollar vegetable and flower export company in Kenya. A two-year contract to live and work in Nairobi is an adventure that I cannot turn down. So, it's over and out from me for now. Hoping to catch you again soon for more tales from my fruity world.

Printed in Great Britain
by Amazon